STUDY GUIDE

Operations Management

CONCEPTS IN MANUFACTURING AND SERVICES

2nd Edition

Robert E. Markland
  University of South Carolina
Shawnee K. Vickery
  Michigan State University
Robert A. Davis
  Texas A & M University

Prepared by
Gail M. Zank
  Eastern Connecticut State University
and
Robert J. Vokurka
  Texas A & M University

SOUTH-WESTERN College Publishing

An International Thomson Publishing Company

Sponsoring Editor: John R. Szilagyi
Developmental Editor: Alice C. Denny
Production Editor: Deanna Quinn
Marketing Manager: Steve Scoble

Copyright © 1998
By SOUTH-WESTERN COLLEGE PUBLISHING
An International Thomson Publishing Company

ALL RIGHTS RESERVED
The text of this publication, or any part thereof, may not be reproduced or transmitted in any form or by any means, electronic or mechanical, including photocopying, recording, storage in any information retrieval system, or otherwise, without the prior written permission of the publisher.

ISBN: 0-538-87834-7

1 2 3 4 5 6 7 8 9 PN 6 5 4 3 2 1 0 9 8

I(T)P®
International Thomson Publishing
The ITP trademark is used under license.

STUDY GUIDE CONTENTS

1. Manufacturing Operations 1
2. Service Operations 13
3. Operations Strategy 25
4. Forecasting Demand for Products and Services 37
5. Product Planning and Process Design 55
6. Long-Range Capacity Planning and Facility Location 69
7. Managing Quality 87
8. Technological Developments in Operations Management 101
9. Organization and Human Resources 113
10. Global Supply Chain Management 129
11. Aggregate Production Planning 143
12. Independent Demand Inventory Management 159
13. Dependent Demand Inventory Management: Material Requirements Planning 181
14. Medium- and Short-Range Capacity Planning 199
15. Shop-Floor Control 213
16. Just-in-Time Production 229
17. Design and Scheduling of Service Systems. 241
18. Project Management. 257
19. Quality Analysis, Measurement, and Improvement. 271
20. Building Competitive Advantage Through World-Class Manufacturing: Allen-Bradley's World Contactor Facility 285

CHAPTER SOLUTIONS 295

CHAPTER 1
MANUFACTURING OPERATIONS

INTRODUCTION

THE TRANSFORMATION PROCESS
Productivity and the Transformation Process
Managing the Transformation Process: The Operations Manager
OPERATIONS MANAGEMENT IN PRACTICE 1.1: Portrait of a Quality Manager at an Award-Winning Manufacturing Company
Ecologically Sound Manufacturing
OPERATIONS MANAGEMENT IN PRACTICE 1.2: Green Manufacturing at AT&T

TYPES OF MANUFACTURING OPERATIONS
Project Manufacturing
The Job Shop
Line-Flow Production
Batch Production
Hybrid Processes
The Product-Process Matrix

COMPANY ACTIVITIES AND STRATEGIC ADVANTAGE: THE VALUE CHAIN

THE HISTORY OF OPERATIONS MANAGEMENT
Eli Whitney
Frederick Winslow Taylor
Henry Ford
Alfred P. Sloan, Jr.
The Field of Operations Management

RECENT TRENDS IN OPERATIONS MANAGEMENT
Just-in-Time Production
Total Quality Management
Computers and Computer-Related Operations Technologies
Time-Based Competition
Business Process Reengineering
OPERATIONS MANAGEMENT IN PRACTICE 1.3: Reengineering at Ford Motor Company
The Service Factory

CHAPTER SUMMARY

1. This chapter focuses on manufacturing operations rather than service operations, which are covered in the next chapter. Manufacturing operations is concerned with the concepts, systems, and methods that relate to effective management of the production of physical goods. The study of this subject is important to the long-run competitiveness of a firm.

2. Manufacturing and service operations transform a set of inputs into a set of outputs of greater value. Inputs are resources, such as human resources, capital, raw materials, land, energy, and information. Outputs include products, services, and services auxiliary to products.

3. Productivity is the total value of all outputs produced by the transformation process divided by the total cost of the inputs. Three ways to increase productivity are (a) more output from same inputs, (b) same output from lower inputs, and (c) more output from lower inputs. In general, workers in the U.S. are more productive than workers in Germany or Japan. U.S. productivity continues to grow at rates roughly equal to those of Europe, but below that of Japan. A study by MIT found weakness in several important U.S. industries, and blamed these problems on American managers' attitudes, capabilities, and strategies.

4. The operations manager is responsible for the success of the manufacturing unit. This person needs a solid knowledge base (technology of products and processes) and human relations skills (decision-making, communication, motivation). An area where operations managers can affect their companies in positive ways while having a positive effect on current and future generations is ecologically sound manufacturing or green manufacturing.

5. Types of organizations. One way to classify organizations is by the amount of processing work done after an order is received from a customer.

   a. A make-to-order (MTO) firm does not begin processing the material and component inputs to the product until it has received a customer order for the product.

   b. A make-to-stock (MTS) firm manufactures products that are completed and placed in inventory prior to the receipt of the customer's order.

   c. An assemble-to-order (ATO) firm manufactures standardized, option modules according to forecast and then assembles a specific combination or package of modules after the customer order is received.

6. Another way to classify organizations is by their product flexibility. Product flexibility is the ability of the operation to efficiently produce highly customized and unique outputs as opposed to highly standardized outputs. Flexibility is strongly related to machine or department sequencing, or layout. The items below begin with the most flexible, and end with the least flexible.

   a. In project manufacturing, all inputs are brought to the manufacturing site in the production of large, costly and highly customized items.

   b. A job shop is a process-focused grouping of resources producing highly customized products.

   c. Batch production is similar to the job shop but usually has a set mix of products that it produces in standard lot sizes.

   d. Hybrid processes exhibit characteristics of both line flow production systems and job shops.

   e. Line-flow production is the product-focused manufacture of discrete units.

f. Continuous production is the product-focused manufacture of bulk products, not discrete units.

7. The value chain is a conceptual model that can help a firm (1) recognize strategically important activities, (2) examine the behavior of its costs, and (3) identify existing and potential sources of differentiation.

   a. The value chain is comprised of value activities (physically distinct activities) and margin (difference between value and cost). Value activities are divided into primary activities and support activities. Primary activities relate to the creation and disposition of the firm's product. Support activities are less direct, and relate closely other company wide functions.

   b. Primary activities are:

      (1) Inbound logistics

      (2) Operations

      (3) Outbound logistics

      (4) Marketing and sales

      (5) Service

   c. Support activities are

      (1) Procurement

      (2) Technology development

      (3) Human resource management

      (4) Firm infrastructure

   d. Linkages interrelate value chain activities, and show how the way one value activity is performed affects the cost or performance of another. Different sets of activities are critical to different industries.

8. Some important people in manufacturing operations

   a. Eli Whitney pioneered work in the manufacturing concept of interchangeable parts around the beginning of the 19th century. The methods developed allowed a less skilled class of workers to produce a higher quality product more efficiently. This was very important in Colonial times when skilled labor was scarce.

   b. Frederick Winslow Taylor began the scientific management movement as the 20th century was beginning. While Taylor's detailed work on time and motion studies is little used, his systems approach to manufacturing retains its value: Every aspect of a manufacturing operation is part of an integrated system; changing any of the parts has consequences for the system."

    c. Henry Ford achieved large productivity gains applying the assembly line to automobile manufacturing. He is credited with applying assembly line technology to automobile manufacturing thus realizing dramatic gains in productivity. Some say his efforts provided the inspiration for what we know of today as just-in-time production. He is also known for his use of vertical integration - internalizing sources of supply.

    d. Alfred P. Sloan, Jr., practiced management by exception, espoused centralized firm planning with decentralized control.

9. The academic field of operations management has its origins in the discipline of industrial management of the '30s and '40s. Powered by the influences of computers and mathematical models, the areas of operations research and management science overshadowed industrial engineering through the '50s and '60s. Operations management, a blending of both mathematical and managerial tools, emerged as an academic discipline in the '70s. A key development in this emergence was the concept of material requirements planning (MRP), that provided a way for companies to keep track of customer orders and due dates. This has since evolved into manufacturing resource planing (MRPII), providing a comprehensive approach to the effective planning of resources for a manufacturing organization.

10. Current trends in operations management

    a. Just-in-time production seeks responsiveness to consumer demand by eliminating waste and increasing productivity. Lot sizes are small, inventory is small, machine setups are dramatically reduced. JIT systems require high levels of coordination because there is so little inventory to provide slack.

    b. Total quality management is based on the principles that (1) quality is built in, not inspected in, (2) quality improvements save money rather than cost money, and (3) continuous improvement (kaizen).

    c. Computers and related operations technologies have revolutionized the manufacturing workplace and its supporting areas. One impact is that workers and managers in this new environment need increased knowledge and technical skills.

        (1) Many of the newest products and process related technologies are computer-based. Examples include computer-aided design (CAD) and computer-aided manufacturing (CAM).

        (2) Many managerial tools require computer support. Examples include decision support systems (DSS) and planning and control systems such as material requirements planning (MRP).

        (3) The areas that support manufacturing are increasingly computerized and integrated into manufacturing through computers. Examples include electronic data interchange and computer-aided design.

d. Time-based competition is the extension of just-in-time principles into every facet of the product delivery cycle, from research and development through procurement and manufacturing and on to marketing and distribution. Reduced lead times, reduced development times, and higher levels of customer satisfaction result. Technologies such as electronic data interchange (EDI), and methodologies such as concurrent engineering are important to this strategy. In concurrent engineering, the development of products and of processes are concurrent, not serial in nature.

e. Business process reengineering is the fundamental rethinking and radical redesign of business processes to achieve improvements. Whereas TQM works within an existing framework, reengineering discards current processes and starts with new ones.

f. The service factory competes not only on the basis of its products but also on the basis of its services. The inclusion of product-related services, often information-intensive or time-related, are increasingly of strategic importance. In keeping with value chain logic, firms should emphasize those services that provide the most value to customers.

KEY TERMS

a. assemble-to-order (ATO)
b. batch production
c. business process reengineering
d. concurrent engineering
e. continuous flow production
f. continuous improvement
g. cross functional team
h. ecologically sound manufacturing
i. green manufacturing
j. hybrid production process
k. job shop
l. just-in-time production
m. line flow production
n. make-to-order (MTO)
o. make-to-stock (MTS)
p. management science
q. manufacturing operation
r. manufacturing resource planning (MRP II)
s. material requirements planning (MRP)
t. operations manager
u. product flexibility
v. productivity
w. product-process matrix
x. project manufacturing
y. scientific management
z. service factory
aa. time-based competition (TBC)
bb. total quality management (TQM)
cc. value chain

DEFINITIONS

Directions: Select from the key terms list, the word or phrase being defined below.

_____ 1. is concerned with the concepts, systems, and methods that relate to effective management of the production of physical goods.

_____ 2. is the total value of all outputs produced by the transformation process divided by the total cost of the inputs.

_____ 3. is managing the transformation process in an environmentally responsible way.

_____ 4. is when processing the material and component inputs to the product does not begin until a customer order has been received.

_____ 5. products are completed and placed in inventory prior to the receipt of the customer's order.

_____ 6. standardized, option modules are manufactured according to forecast; a specific combination or package of modules is assembled after an order is received.

_____ 7. is the ability of the operation to efficiently produce highly customized and unique outputs as opposed to highly standardized outputs.

_____ 8. is a conceptual model that can help a firm (1) recognize strategically important activities, (2) examine the behavior of its costs, and (3) identify existing and potential sources of differentiation.

_____ 9. provides a comprehensive approach for effective resource planning in a manufacturing environment.

_____ 10. is the extension of just-in-time principles into every facet of the product delivery cycle.

_____ 11. is a radical approach to achieving improvements, which discards current processes and starts with new ones.

_____ 12. competes not only on the basis of its products but also on the basis of its services.

_____ 13. performs the management activities of planning, organizing, staffing, directing and controlling of the manufacturing unit.

_____ 14. is the term used to describe large, costly and highly customized physical goods.

_____ 15. is the term used to describe process-focused, jumbled flow, intermittent production manufacturing.

_____ 16. is the term used to describe product-focused, fixed sequence, high volume manufacturing.

MULTIPLE CHOICE QUESTIONS

Directions: Indicate your choice of the best answer to each question.

1. Which of the following statements about production operations is TRUE?
   a. Project manufacturing is usually associated with standardized products.
   b. Job shop production is the most flexible type of manufacturing.
   c. Hybrid systems always exhibit characteristics of line flow systems and job shops.
   d. Continuous flow production is the product-focused manufacture of bulk products, not discrete units.
   e. Assembly line production is the process-focused manufacture of discrete units.

2. You want to pursue a career as an operations manager. Which of the following statements about successful operations managers is (are) TRUE?
   a. Operations managers need people skills.
   b. Operations managers don't need a technical knowledge base.
   c. Operations managers' primary concern is the planning function.
   d. Operations managers don't influence the strategic direction of the firm.
   e. Operations managers don't impact ethical issues within the firm.

3. Outputs of the transportation process may include
   a. physical goods.
   b. rapid delivery.
   c. productivity.
   d. all of the above.
   e. only a and b.

4. The ability of an operation to efficiently produce highly customized and unique outputs as opposed to highly standardized outputs is
   a. time-based competition.
   b. productivity.
   c. product flexibility.
   d. green manufacturing.
   e. a job shop.

5. The term concurrent engineering is most closely associated with which of the following trends in operations management?
   a. just-in-time production
   b. service factory
   c. computer-related production technologies
   d. time-based competition
   e. business process reengineering

6. "Products are completed and placed in inventory prior to the receipt of the customer's order" describes
   a. operations strategy.
   b. make-to-stock.
   c. make-to-order.
   d. manufacturing operations.
   e. service factory.

7. Which of the following statements is TRUE?
   a. The origins of management by exception are generally credited to Frederick Winslow Taylor.
   b. The origins of the scientific management movement are generally credited to Henry Ford.
   c. Mass production is closely identified with Frederick Winslow Taylor.
   d. The person most responsible for initiating use of interchangeable parts in manufacturing was Eli Whitney.
   e. The scientific management movement started in the mid 1900s.

8   *Chapter 1 - Manufacturing Operations*

8. The total value of all outputs produced by the transformation process divided by the total cost of the inputs is
   a. utilization.
   b. effectiveness.
   c. efficiency.
   d. productivity.
   e. return on investment.

9. The oldest term in this group is
   a. operations management.
   b. production operations management.
   c. scientific management.
   d. strategic operations management.
   e. total quality management.

10. The person who espoused views very much like modern JIT philosophies was
    a. Eli Whitney.
    b. Frederick Winslow Taylor.
    c. Henry Ford.
    d. Alfred P. Sloan, Jr.
    e. Lillian Gilbreth.

11. The person most responsible for initiating the scientific management movement was
    a. Eli Whitney.
    b. Frederick Winslow Taylor.
    c. Henry Ford.
    d. Alfred P. Sloan, Jr.
    e. Lillian Gilbreth.

12. Current trends in manufacturing operations include ALL BUT which of the following?
    a. just-in-time production
    b. total quality management
    c. time-based competition
    d. business process reengineering
    e. all of the above are current trends

13. Which of the following is a current trend in manufacturing operations?
    a. just-in-time production
    b. intermittent production
    c. scientific management
    d. time and motion studies
    e. all of the above are current trends

14. The fullest version of MRP, with links to capacity planning and to financial terms, is
    a. closed-loop MRP.
    b. manufacturing resource planning (MRP II).
    c. capacity requirements planning (CRP).
    d. aggregate production planning.
    e. none of the above.

15. Leading edge manufacturers such as Allen-Bradley, Hewlett-Packard and Tektronic are singled out by the authors as trend-setters in
    a. just-in-time production.
    b. service factory.
    c. computer-related production technologies.
    d. time-based competition.
    e. business process reengineering.

16. Which of the following statements concerning trends in manufacturing operations is TRUE?
    a. Time-based competition is the extension of just-in-time principles into selected facets of the product delivery cycle.
    b. Business process reengineering is a conservative approach to achieving improvements.
    c. Business process reengineering discards current processes and starts with new ones.
    d. All of the above statements are true.
    e. None of the statements above is true.

17. Which of the following statements is FALSE?
    a. Alfred P. Sloan, Jr. practiced management by exception.
    b. The origins of the scientific management movement are generally credited to Frederick Winslow Taylor.
    c. Henry Ford is credited with concepts very similar to just-in-time concepts.
    d. The person most responsible for initiating use of interchangeable parts in manufacturing was Eli Whitney.
    e. All of the above statements are true.

18. Which of the following statements about modern operations management is TRUE?
    a. It is due entirely to the work of Alfred P. Sloan, Jr.
    b. It was spurred by the development of MRP.
    c. Modern operations management emerged shortly before World War II.
    d. Operations management was the precursor to management science.
    e. All of the above are true.

19. A cabinet-maker who inventories prebuilt cabinets but applies the finish color or varnish stain only after the customer chooses it is utilizing the _____ type of manufacturing.
    a. hybrid
    b. assemble-to-order
    c. make-to-stock
    d. make-to-order
    e. project

20. _____ was one of the first management disciplines to exist in many U.S. colleges and universities.
    a. Operations management
    b. Scientific management
    c. Industrial management
    d. Operations research
    e. Management science

21. The five primary activities of the value chain are
    a. inbound logistics, operations, outbound logistics, marketing/sales, and customer service.
    b. firm infrastructure, operations, outbound logistics, marketing/sales, and customer service.
    c. inbound logistics, operations, outbound logistics, technology development, and customer service.
    d. procurement, technology development, human resource management, firm infrastructure, and margin.
    e. procurement, operations, logistics, research and development, and customer service.

22. After World War II, industrial management was overshadowed as an academic discipline by
    a. management science.
    b. scientific management.
    c. industrial management.
    d. operations management.
    e. manufacturing operations.

23. Which of the following ways can increase productivity?
    a. using the same amount of inputs to produce more output
    b. using a smaller amount of inputs to produce the same amount of output
    c. using a larger amount of inputs to produce less output
    d. all of the above
    e. only a and b

24. Andree's Art, sculpts statues upon commission by a buyer. Andree's Art would most likely utilize which type of production operation?
    a. continuous-flow production
    b. job shop production
    c. line-flow production
    d. project manufacturing
    e. batch production system

25. Which of the following is a support activity of the value chain?
    a. procurement
    b. customer service
    c. margin
    d. inbound logistics
    e. operations

26. Which of the following is a primary activity of the value chain?
    a. procurement
    b. margin
    c. human resource management
    d. technology development
    e. inbound logistics

27. _____ is most flexible and _____ is the least flexible production operation type.
    a. Project manufacturing; line-flow production
    b. Line-flow production; project manufacturing
    c. Line-flow production; job shop production
    d. Job shop production; project manufacturing
    e. Continuous-flow production; project manufacturing

28. Which of the following are inputs into the production process?
    a. services
    b. auxiliary services
    c. technology
    d. productivity
    e. all of the above

29. What graphically delineates the similarities and differences that exist among the various types of basic production processes?
    a. value chain
    b. operations typology schedule
    c. BCG matrix
    d. product-process matrix
    e. business screen portfolio

30. Which of the following statements are FALSE about just-in-time production?
    a. High quality is important to just-in-time production.
    b. A key goal is to produce exactly what is needed.
    c. Just-in-time production is not concerned with waste.
    d. All of the above statements are true.
    e. All of the above statements are false.

SHORT ANSWER QUESTIONS

1. What skills do successful operations managers possess?

12   Chapter 1 - Manufacturing Operations

2. What is product flexibility? What are the most and least flexible types of manufacturing operations?

3. What is the product-process matrix? What happens if a company is "off the diagonal?"

4. What is the value chain? Discuss the two broad groups of value activities?

5. What is time-based competition? What are the two driving forces of time-based competition?

CHAPTER 2
SERVICE OPERATIONS

INTRODUCTION

DEFINING SERVICES
Comparing Service and Manufacturing Operations
Classifying Service and Manufacturing Operations

CHARACTERISTICS OF SERVICE OPERATIONS
High Consumer Contact
Consumer Participation in the Service Process
Perishability of Services
Site Selection Dictated By Consumer's Location
Labor Intensiveness
Variable, Nonstandard Output
Intangibility of the Service Output
Difficulty of Measuring Service Output
OPERATIONS MANAGEMENT IN PRACTICE 2.1: Hotel Automation: Technology versus Personal Service
Difficulty of Measuring Service Quality

STRATEGIC APPROACHES TO SERVICE OPERATIONS MANAGEMENT
The Service Process Matrix
The Strategic Service Vision
OPERATIONS MANAGEMENT IN PRACTICE 2.2: Service Master - Stressing Dignity to its Workers

SERVICE SECTOR TRENDS
Increased International Competition in Services
GLOBAL OPERATIONS MANAGEMENT 2.3: Global Consulting - Becoming More Competitive in the World Economy
Improving Productivity and Competitiveness in Services
OPERATIONS MANAGEMENT IN PRACTICE 2.4: On-Line Banking - Will It Finally Become a Reality?
Technology and Automation in Services
OPERATIONS MANAGEMENT IN PRACTICE 2.5: J.C. Penny - Riding the Third Wave of Information Technology
Adequacy of Service Jobs
Greater Quality Emphasis in Services

CHAPTER SUMMARY

1. The service sector includes all economic activity other than agriculture, mining, construction and manufacturing.

2. Services currently account for approximately seventy-four percent of all U.S. jobs, and generate about seventy-six percent of the gross domestic product.

3. Services are defined as economic activities that produce a place, time, form or psychological utility for the consumer.

   a. Large discount stores provide place utility where a large number and variety of products can be purchased.

   b. A car wash or oil change store provides time utility; time we would otherwise spend doing these chores.

   c. A bank statement provides form utility, information in a form we can understand.

   d. A sporting event, rock concert, etc. provides psychological utility.

4. Goods and services are not completely distinct, but instead are the two end points on a continuum. At one end, you receive very little service and have little contact with the service provider (a self-service grocery); in the middle are restaurants and auto repair shops where service becomes more important; and at the other end, you have pure service in a customized fashion (a typical motel).

5. Five major types of services have developed in response to the stages and economic conditions through which various societies have passed, they are:

   a. Unskilled personal services (e.g., housekeeping services, street vending, etc.)

   b. Skilled personal services (e.g., wholesale and retail merchants services, repair and maintenance, etc.)

   c. Industrial services (e.g., legal and accounting firms, banks, real estate brokers, etc.)

   d. Mass consumer services (e.g., airlines, hotels, entertainment, etc.)

   e. High-technology business services (e.g., information services, consulting, etc.)

6. Service operations generally do not produce tangible outputs, but they can still be classified much like manufacturing operations; according to the degree of standardization of their service. Four classifications are:

   a. Project (e.g., lawyers, doctors, architects)

   b. Job shop (e.g., custom tailor)

   c. Flow shop (e.g., automated car wash)

d. Process (e.g., police and fire protection)

7. Characteristics of services that must be understood by the operations manager to define the competitive environment in which service operations take place are:

   a. High customer contact - services tend to have high levels of customer contact.

   b. Participation in the service process - the customer is often actively involved in the service process.

   c. Perishability of services - an operations manager in the service sector generally does not have the ability to inventory services.

   d. Site selection dictated by consumer location - since many service organizations have direct contact with their customers, they must be located relatively near these consumers.

   e. Labor intensiveness - in most service companies, labor is the major competitive resource because the service employees interact directly with the customer.

   f. Variable, nonstandard output - in many service situations, the service output is variable, because the customers' needs vary while the service is occurring.

   g. Intangibility of the service output - service firms generally produce intangible, perishable products.

   h. Difficulty of measuring service productivity - productivity measures in service firms should include a measure of the quality of the service that is received.

   i. Difficulty of measuring service quality - the quality of a service is determined by the match between customers expectations and perceptions of the service.

8. Two broad strategic approaches to service operations management are the service process matrix and strategic service vision.

   a. The service process matrix contends that there are two elements that can be used to classify different kinds of service businesses, the first element is labor intensity, defined as the ratio of the labor cost incurred to the value of the plant and equipment. The second major element is a joint element that combines the degree to which the consumer interacts with the service process and the degree to which the service is customized for the consumer.
   Classifying service firms as either "high" or "low" on these two dimensions results in a two by two matrix with four quadrants called: "service factories" (low labor intensity, low interaction/customization), "service shops" (low labor intensity, high interaction/customization), "mass services" (high labor intensity, low in interaction/customization) and "professional services" (high labor intensity, high interaction/ customization).
   Strategically, service businesses need to determine the quadrant of the service process matrix they are in and pay close attention to all of the managerial challenges that apply.

   b. The strategic service vision is based on integrating marketing and operations into one function involving four basic strategic elements: (1) target market segments; (2) service concept;

(3) operating strategy; and (4) service delivery. These four strategic elements are welded together by three interactive elements: (1) positioning; (2) value-cost leveraging; and (3) service systems integration.

Finding target market segments requires identifying common characteristics and needs of important market segments and determining the strengths of various competitors. Specifying a service concept involves establishing expectations of the service in the minds of customers and employees. The target market and the service concept are linked by the service organizations positioning of itself in the competitive environment of a selected market.

An operating strategy is developed next in which the role of operations, finance, marketing, quality, productivity and the cost of service are addressed. The service concept and the operating strategy are then linked by a value-cost leveraging process which requires decisions on standardization versus customization, quality control, etc. The service systems integration is the final linkage that ensures that the overall service strategy can be met by the proposed service delivery system.

9. The United States exhibits the characteristics of a postindustrial society, in which service operations are of major importance. Some important trends in the service sector of our economy are: increased international competition in services, emphasis on improving productivity and competitiveness in services, more reliance on technology and automation in services, emphasis on improving productivity and competitiveness in services, more reliance on technology and automation in services, a concern about the adequacy of service jobs and a greater quality emphasis in services.

a. International competition in services is increasing and some U.S. service businesses are becoming increasingly vulnerable to foreign acquisitions primarily because of technological advances.

b. While services employ many people, they do not use them very productively. Historically, service sector productivity has remained relatively flat, making relatively small gains. The reason for this slow growth in service productivity has been attributed to: business cycles; changing service industry mix, inadequate education and training; and financial services industry problems.

c. Services are more reliant on technology and automation than many of us think. The service sector is a major market for high technology and automation. Technology may be applied at four different points in the service process: processing the customer; processing the customer's materials, processing information, and creating new services.

d. Ninety percent of all new jobs created since 1969 have been in the service sector, with the fastest growing job categories those being the better paying - professional and technical type. Statistics show that service jobs in the private sector now pay almost the same as manufacturing jobs.

e. Improvement of quality is becoming a major objective in services throughout the United States. The increased quality emphasis in services has come about from the realization that survival much less growth, in the service sector will be a function of quality. Service companies also recognize that it is much cheaper to keep the customer through good service quality than it is to acquire a new one.

KEY TERMS

a. continuous flow
b. goods
c. high-technology business services
d. industrial services
e. industrial society
f. job shop
g. line flow
h. mass consumer services
i. operating strategy
j. positioning
k. postindustrial society
l. preindustrial society
m. project
n. services concept
o. services delivery system
p. services process matrix
q. service sector
r. service systems integration
s. services
t. skilled personal services
u. target market segments
v. unskilled personal services
w. value-cost leveraging

DEFINITIONS

Directions: Select from the key terms list, the word or phrase being defined below.

_____ 1. role of people, technology, equipment layout and procedures in the service process.

_____ 2. raw materials that have been transformed into finished end products.

_____ 3. process requiring decisions on standardization versus customization, managing supply and demand and controlling quality.

_____ 4. identification of common characteristics and important needs of markets, and strengths of various competitors.

_____ 5. initial type of service activity in developing societies.

_____ 6. to provide a service where several interrelated, complicated tasks must be done, in some specific sequence.

_____ 7. service provided by skilled artisans, shop keepers, wholesale and retail merchants, repair and maintenance people and financial clerks.

_____ 8. all economic activity other than agriculture, mining, construction, and manufacturing.

_____ 9. the strategic element where operating strategy is linked to the service delivery system.

_____ 10. process that will allow the categorization of service businesses as being "high" or "low" in terms of labor intensity and degree of interaction/customization.

_____ 11. establishing expectations of the service in the minds of customers and employees.

_____ 12. much of the world's population who are engaged primarily in agriculture, mining, fishing and forestry, using human and animal labor and basic tools.

_____ 13. quality of life, measured by services such as health, education and recreation, becomes the standard of living goal.

_____ 14. manufacturing is the predominate activity, and technology is employed in a factory environment.

MULTIPLE CHOICE QUESTIONS

1. Services are activities that provide for
   a. time utility.
   b. raw material processing.
   c. fabrication.
   d. farming.
   e. manufactured goods.

2. The monthly statement you receive from your bank provides
   a. psychological utility.
   b. form utility.
   c. place utility.
   d. time utility.
   e. none of the above.

3. A Jiffy-Lube Oil Change Store provides which of the following?
   a. place utility
   b. form utility
   c. psychological utility
   d. function utility
   e. time utility

4. Housekeeping services, military conscription and street vending are examples of
   a. mass consumer services.
   b. high-technology business services.
   c. industrial services.
   d. unskilled personal services.
   e. semi-skilled personal services.

5. Industrial services are characterized by which of the following type services?
   a. auto-rental companies
   b. real estate brokerage firms
   c. retail merchants
   d. airline companies
   e. repair firms

6. "Pure manufacturing" occurs in organizations where
   a. a tangible good is produced.
   b. little contact with the consumer occurs.
   c. substantial contact with the customer occurs.
   d. both a and b.
   e. both a and c.

7. A project is best described as having
   a. long duration with custom product.
   b. short duration with standard product.
   c. long duration with standard product.
   d. short duration with custom product.
   e. none of the above.

8. A job shop is best described as having
   a. short duration with low volume.
   b. long duration with low volume.
   c. short duration with high volume.
   d. long duration with high volume.
   e. long duration with medium volume.

9. A service example of a line-flow configuration is a
   a. software development company.
   b. gourmet restaurant.
   c. sign making shop.
   d. cereal plant.
   e. fast-food restaurant.

10. An example of a continuous flow service is a(n)
    a. automatic teller machine.
    b. oil change shop.
    c. ship building.
    d. consulting.
    e. gourmet restaurant.

11. Job shops are best described as having
    a. low volume with standard product.
    b. high volume with custom products.
    c. low volume with custom products.
    d. long duration with custom products.
    e. short duration with standard product.

12. Customer participation in the service process requires
    a. greater emphasis on inventory control.
    b. more attention placed on technological requirements.
    c. increased emphasis on quality control.
    d. more attention placed on the location and atmosphere of the business.
    e. none of the above.

13. A service company can deal with the perishability of its service by
    a. requiring reservations.
    b. adjusting service capacity.
    c. forcing customers to wait.
    d. all of the above.
    e. only a and b.

14. Which of the following is NOT an attribute involved in improving service quality?
    a. tangibles
    b. reliability
    c. responsiveness
    d. access
    e. empathy

15. An example of a high labor-intensive business is a(n)
    a. law office.
    b. airline.
    c. hospital.
    d. fast food restaurant.
    e. auto dealer.

16. According to the Service Process Matrix, a hospital is an example of a
    a. mass service.
    b. service shop.
    c. professional service.
    d. service factory.
    e. none of the above.

17. According to the Service Process Matrix, a service characterized as "high" labor intensity and "low" degree of interaction/customization would be a
    a. service shop.
    b. mass service.
    c. professional service.
    d. service factory.
    e. none of the above.

18. The strategic service vision involves which of the following elements?
    a. service delivery
    b. service concept
    c. target market segments
    d. operating strategy
    e. all of the above

19. The target market and service concept are linked by
    a. positioning.
    b. operating strategy.
    c. value-cost leveraging.
    d. service delivery system.
    e. service-systems integration.

20. Which of the following are NOT characteristics of a preindustrial society?
    a. little available technology
    b. low productivity
    c. engaged in agriculture, mining, fishing and forestry
    d. focus on the importance of the individual
    e. predominate use of animal labor and basic hand tools

21. United States services are becoming vulnerable to increased foreign competition primarily because of
    a. the devaluation of the dollar.
    b. international trade deficits.
    c. technological advances.
    d. transborder data flows.
    e. labor problems.

22. Which activity is NOT part of the service sector?
    a. transportation
    b. public administration
    c. retail trade
    d. agriculture
    e. entertainment

23. An example of a "pure service" is
    a. a restaurant meal.
    b. a fast-food meal.
    c. installed carpeting.
    d. motel services.
    e. all of the above.

24. Satellite communications is an example of
    a. unskilled personal services.
    b. skilled personal services.
    c. industrial services.
    d. mass consumer services.
    e. high-technology business services.

25. Consumers receive _____ when attending a baseball game.
    a. form utility
    b. psychological utility
    c. place utility
    d. time utility
    e. none of the above

26. Which of the following are reasons attributed to slower growth in service productivity?
    a. lack of technological advances
    b. fluctuating business cycle
    c. inadequate education and training
    d. all of the above
    e. only b and c

27. Which of the following is a characteristic of an industrial society?
    a. goal of high quality of life
    b. life of subsistence
    c. the individual's role is sublimated to the overall objective of making goods efficiently
    d. little technology is available
    e. manufacturing is the predominant activity

22   Chapter 2 - Service Operations

28. Which of the following statements are FALSE about service operations as compared to manufacturing operations?
   a. Service operations have a relatively high degree of customer contact.
   b. Service operations generally need to pay more attention to location.
   c. Service operations require less customer involvement.
   d. Service operations generally need to pay more attention to atmosphere.
   e. All of the above are false

29. There are only twenty people at the fifty-seat movie theater; this best relates to the service characteristic of
   a. perishability.
   b. intangibility.
   c. heterogeneity.
   d. reliability.
   e. variability.

30. McDonald's requires its employees to wear uniforms. McDonald's is most concerned about which dimension of service quality?
   a. responsiveness
   b. assurance
   c. empathy
   d. reliability
   e. tangibles

SHORT ANSWER QUESTIONS

1. What are the five dimensions of service quality?

2. Briefly describe the Service Process Matrix. Explain how businesses in other quadrants have moved to the service factory.

3. Discuss the four types of service operations. Provide an example of each.

4. What are unique characteristics of service operations?

5. Discuss the strategic service vision.

CHAPTER 3
OPERATIONS STRATEGY

INTRODUCTION

BUSINESS-LEVEL STRATEGIC PLANNING
Functional Area Involvement in Business-Level Strategic Planning
The Generic Business Strategies
OPERATIONS MANAGEMENT IN PRACTICE 3.1: Strategic Positioning at Haskell of Pittsburgh

OPERATIONS STRATEGIC PLANNING
Operations as a Competitive Weapon
Operations Competitive Priorities
GLOBAL OPERATIONS MANAGEMENT 3.2: Competitive Priorities at Meiji Seika Kaisha, Ltd. (Pharmaceutical Manufacturing at Odawara)
Strategic Operations Choices

CATEGORIES OF STRATEGIC OPERATIONS DECISIONS
Product or Service Planning
Process Design and Technology Management
Long-range Capacity Planning and Facility Location
Quality Management
Manufacturing or Service Organization
Human Resource Management
Operations Planning and Control

VERTICAL LINKAGES: THE VALUE CHAIN REVISITED
Vertical Integration and Outsourcing
Supply Chain Management
Assembler-Supplier Relationships in Japan

GLOBAL INTEGRATION OF OPERATIONS
GLOBAL OPERATIONS MANAGEMENT 3.3: Global Integration of Operations at Xerox

CHAPTER SUMMARY

1. The purpose of strategic planning is to ensure the long-run profitability of a business organization. Strategic planning requires recognizing the basic structure of business organizations which consists of three levels: (1) the corporate level, (2) the business level, and (3) the functional or product level.

2. Corporate-level strategic planning is concerned with developing an overall plan to effectively guide the corporation as a whole. It provides the framework within which individual strategic business units (SBUs) accomplish their own strategic planning.

3. Business-level strategic planning is concerned with strategic choices which enable the SBU or firm to successfully compete in its external environment. Planning at this level encompasses specifying the firm's

strategic objectives and the methods for accomplishing these goals. As corporate-level strategic planning provides a framework for business-level strategic planning, business-level strategic planning guides the strategic planning process at the functional or product level. The strategic planning hierarchy suggests that operations strategic planning is best understood within the context of business-level strategic planning.

4. The goal of business-level strategic planning is to effectively relate a business unit of a company to its external environment.

   a. The first step in business level strategic planning is to analyze the firm's external environment. The external environment has two parts: (1) the industry environment in which the firm competes and (2) the firm's macroenvironment.

   b. The manager at the business level must also identify opportunities and threats facing the company within its industry environment. Porter's model develops a framework that helps managers identify the opportunities and threats. The model views the state of competition in an industry as dependent on five competitive forces: (1) the threat of new firms entering the industry, (2) the threat of substitute products and/or services, (3) the bargaining power of buyers, (4) the bargaining power of suppliers, and (5) the rivalry among current competitors.

      (1) A weak competitive force may be viewed as an opportunity since it allows a company to earn greater profits while a strong competitive force can be a threat since it negatively affects profits.

      (2) A firm must also evaluate its strengths and weaknesses. A strength in a certain area does not automatically translate into a competitive advantage for the firm. The strength must be relatively greater than its competitors in a strategically important factor; this is called distinctive competence.

5. The functional level or product level strategic planning is closely linked with business level strategic planning because the functional or product organizations within the firm implement the firm's strategic objectives and determine what tactics or methods should be used to achieve those objectives. Functional areas are responsible for carrying out the broad programs, polices and/or action plans that have been formulated to achieve the firm's strategic goals.

6. The essence of business level strategic planning is taking offensive or defensive actions to create a defensible or advantageous position in an industry to successfully cope with the five competitive forces and thereby realize a superior return on investment for the firm. There are numerous strategies to accomplish this, but at the broadest level there are two basic generic strategies:

   a. Cost leadership - components of a strategy to achieve this include aggressively constructing efficient-scale facilities, vigorously reducing costs from experience, emphasizing operating efficiency, controlling costs and overhead, etc.

   b. Differentiation - this strategy is to create a product/service that is recognized industry wide as being unique. Approaches a company might use for differentiating its products from those of its competitors may include: quality, brand image, superior product performance, innovative product technology, product reliability, etc.

   c. Whether a firm pursues a strategy of differentiation, cost, or some combination thereof, it must determine the specific combination of elements, objectives, or priorities which define its strategy or strategic positioning within its industry. The ultimate purpose of strategic positioning is to focus an organizations resources, capabilities, and energies on building a sustainable advantage over its competitors along one or more dimensions of performance.

7. Operations strategy is a collective pattern of choices that determines the structure, resources and infrastructure of the operations system and is directed toward supporting business level and corporate level strategies.

    a. The strategic objectives for which operations is responsible are called operations priorities (e.g., quality of design, delivery speed, low production cost). These provide the starting point for making strategic choices in operations. Seven major categories in which strategic choices are made are: (1) product or service planning, (2) process design and technology management, (3) long-range capacity planning and facility location, (4) quality management, (5) manufacturing or service organization, (6) human resource management, and (7) operations planning and control.

    b. Once operations competitive priorities have been identified, operations must set measurable goals in relation to each of them relative to current performance. Next, is the implementation of the specific strategies. Finally, after formulating and implementing operations strategies, the measurement and assessment of operations performance must be undertaken.

8. If operations is to become a competitive weapon, it must assume a visible and proactive role in defining the competitive advantage that a firm will pursue. To be effective, operations must share equally with other functions in defining the firm's business strategy as well as in implementing it.

9. The strategic objectives for which operations is primarily responsible (or shares major responsibility with other functional areas) are termed operations competitive priorities. There is considerable consistency among American and European manufacturers as to the relative importance of various competitive priorities. One Manufacturing Futures Survey reported that conformance quality, product reliability, and on-time delivery were the top three priorities for European and American firms, while Japanese firms ranked low price, product reliability and on-time delivery as their top three competitive priorities.

10. To achieve and continually enhance the competitive advantage the firm is seeking, a series of coordinated decisions or operations strategic choices of both a structural and an infrastructural nature are required.

    a. The structural or "bricks and mortar" decisions are of the type that determines what kind of production processes, equipment, total capacity, facility location etc.

    b. The infrastructural decisions refer to the management policies and systems that determine how the "bricks and mortar" are managed. An example of this type decision is product/service planning, quality management policies and systems, human resource policies, etc.

11. Product or service planning is a continuous process for most firms due to the necessity of responding to and anticipating customers' needs, wants, and desires. The importance of this area is heightened by factors such as intense competition, expiration of patents, and rapid technological innovation within an industry.

12. Process pertains to the arrangement or grouping of the resources of production comprising the operations system. The fundamental decision is whether the resources of production will be product-focused or process-focused, or some combination of the two.

13. Long-range capacity planning is concerned with the sizing and timing of capacity changes in relation to demand changes. A distinction must be made between a capacity decision and a capacity strategy. A capacity decision would be triggered by a capital authorization request for an expansion of capacity. A capacity strategy would place each capacity decision in the context of a longer-term sequence of such decisions that relate to the firm's overall strategic plan. Facility location is concerned with where operations capacity will be located. Location decisions as well as capacity decisions can provide substantial support to the companies strategic objectives.

14. According to the Manufacturing Futures Survey of 1996, it is clear that quality is a fundamental competitive priority for U.S., European, and Japanese firms. Quality management is concerned with the quality strategies, programs, methods and organizational culture that a firm employs to achieve its quality objectives.

15. The way in which a manufacturing unit is organized has important strategic implications. Companies are recognizing the critical effects of organizational structure on their ability to compete and are moving to create the structure they need.

16. Human resource management is another area of critical strategic importance. World-class competitors place great emphasis on human resource management and on the training and motivation of their workers. A motivated and highly trained work force can aid a company in achieving all of its strategic objectives. A key attribute of world-class competitors is innovative human asset management that encourages excellence, teamwork, and accelerated learning and rewards employees for their direct contributions.

17. Operations planning and control systems are important components of a company's infrastructure. They have critical strategic implications although they are tactical in nature.

18. The value chain consists of value activities that are interrelated by linkages between the way one value activity is performed and the cost or performance of another value activity. Such linkages exist not only *within* a firm's value chain but also *between* a firm's value chain and the value chains of its suppliers and distribution channels. These linkages are called vertical linkages.

19. Vertical linkages are frequently overlooked. Companies may vertically integrate (either backward (suppliers) or forward (distribution channels)) to improve coordination and optimization of vertical linkages. New management approaches and information technology are also making it easier to coordinate their activities and as a result, outsourcing is becoming more common in many industries.

20. The supply chain is the connected series of value activities that is concerned with planning, coordinating and controlling materials, parts and finished products from suppliers to the final customer. The supply chain is characterized by two distinct flows; materials and information.

   a. Supply chain management is the way in which vertical linkages are managed regardless of whether the relationship is with an outside supplier or in-house division. The objective is to synchronize the requirements of the final customer with the flow of materials and information throughout the supply chain to affect a balance between high customer service and cost.

   b. The effective management of the supply chain is customer driven. This means the firm must penetrate deep into its customer organizations to understand their products cultures, markets, and organizations to make sure it is attuned to its customer's needs and requirements.

21. Assembler-supplier relationships in Japan are an integral part of the JIT/TQM production system. Under JIT/TQM production, components are delivered by suppliers directly to the assembly line either hourly or several times a day with no inspection of incoming parts.

   a. At the start of product development the Japanese assembler selects all necessary suppliers. The leading Japanese producers involve fewer than 300 suppliers in each project (compared with 1,000 to 2,500 for Western manufacturers). The number of suppliers involved is much smaller than for Western producers because Japanese producers assign a whole component (e.g. complete seat) to what they call a first-tier supplier.

   b. A first tier supplier has a team of second-tier suppliers. Second tier suppliers are assigned the job of fabricating individual parts. These suppliers are generally manufacturing specialists.

   c. Once parts are in production, the Japanese use a method called value analysis to achieve further cost reductions. Value analysis is a method for comprehensively analyzing the costs of each manufacturing step to identify the steps that have a critical effect on cost and figure out how to make the product less expensively.

22. One big advantage of competing internationally is learning about global competitors before they start taking market share. The successful multinational firms will have to be globally integrated. The North American Free Trade Agreement (NAFTA) and European Community will only increase the pressure to globally integrate. A useful structure for global integration is to declare a global mission, develop a profile of the firm's capabilities and then identify options, pick a plan of action and set specific goals. A firm's management must publicly state the goal of global integration, telling employees, customers and suppliers what the companies global ambitions are and what it will mean for the company.

KEY TERMS

a. business-level strategic planning
b. corporate-level strategic planning
c. cost leadership
d. differentiation
e. distinctive competence
f. factory focus
g. first-tier supplier
h. functional strategic planning
i. global integration of operations
j. Manufacturing Futures Survey
k. operations competitive priorities
l. operations strategic choices
m. operations strategic planning
n. operations strategy
o. product-level strategic planning
p. second-tier supplier
q. strategic operations decision categories
r. strategic planning hierarchy
s. supply chain
t. supply chain management
u. value analysis

DEFINITIONS

Directions: Select from the key terms list the word or phrase being defined below.

_____ 1. strategic choices which enable the SBU or firm to successfully compete in its external environment.

_____ 2. the idea that an organization will perform better with a narrow, clearly defined set of tasks or priorities than with a broad set of tasks.

_____ 3. the connected series of value activities between suppliers and final customers.

_____ 4. the creation of a product/service that is recognized industry-wide as being unique.

_____ 5. when a firm has relatively greater strength than its competitors in a strategically important factor.

_____ 6. developing an overall plan to effectively guide the corporation as a whole.

_____ 7. method for comprehensively analyzing the costs of each manufacturing step, so that cost-critical steps can be identified and targeted for further cost improvement.

_____ 8. generic business strategy that aggressively constructs efficient scale facilities emphasizing operating efficiency, etc.

_____ 9. the strategic objectives for which operations is primarily responsible (or shares major responsibility) with other functional areas.

_____ 10. a philosophy that describes how organizations should manage their various vertical linkages to achieve strategic advantage.

_____ 11. suppliers that are responsible for working as an integral part of the assembler's product development team in developing a new product.

MULTIPLE CHOICE QUESTIONS

1. For multi-business companies, the basic structure consists of which of the following levels?
   a. the corporate level
   b. the business level
   c. the functional level
   d. all of the above
   e. only b and c

2. Corporate level strategic planning is primarily concerned with
   a. strategic choices which enable the SBU to successfully compete in the external environment.
   b. implementing the firm's strategic initiatives and determining what tactics or methods should be used for achieving the firm's goals.
   c. developing an overall plan to effectively guide the corporation as a whole.
   d. the sizing and timing of capacity changes in relation to demand changes.
   e. all of the above.

3. Strategic choices which enable the SBU to successfully compete in its external environment are most closely linked to
   a. business process reengineering.
   b. resource deployment.
   c. business level strategic planning.
   d. corporate level strategic planning.
   e. product level strategic planning.

4. Functional level strategic planning is primarily concerned with
   a. the sizing and timing of capacity changes in relation to demand conditions.
   b. developing an overall plan to effectively guide the corporation as a whole.
   c. implementing the firm's strategic objectives and determining what tactics or methods should be used for achieving those objectives.
   d. strategic choices enabling the SBU to successfully compete in its external environment.
   e. all of the above.

5. ____ provides the framework within which individual business units do their own strategic planning.
   a. Functional level strategic planning
   b. Business level strategic planning
   c. Corporate level strategic planning
   d. All of the above
   e. None of the above

6. Which of the following are NOT components of the cost leadership strategy?
   a. constructing efficient-scale facilities
   b. emphasizing operating efficiency
   c. controlling overhead
   d. innovative product technology
   e. none of the above

7. A sustainable advantage over competitors can be gained from all the following EXCEPT
   a. lower cost.
   b. higher product performance.
   c. more innovative products.
   d. higher profits.
   e. none of the above.

8. If operations is to become a competitive weapon, top management must consult with operations to get its perspective on
   a. major issues facing the business.
   b. strategies being proposed by other functional areas.
   c. options open to operations.
   d. all of the above.
   e. only a and c.

9. Which of the following are referred to as operations competitive priories in the operations literature?
   a. design quality
   b. technological developments
   c. customer service
   d. all of the above
   e. only a and c

10. The 1996 Manufacturing Futures Survey of Japanese manufacturing firms reports the three most important competitive priorities to be
    a. low price, product reliability, and on-time-delivery.
    b. low price, product support, and customization.
    c. reliability/durability, performance quality, and customization.
    d. low price, product support, and fast delivery.
    e. customization, fast delivery, and conformance quality.

11. A series of coordinated decisions of both a structural and an infrastructural nature that are determined after competitive priorities are established are called
    a. product level strategic planning.
    b. operations strategic choices.
    c. supply chain management.
    d. corporate level strategic planning.
    e. strategic positioning.

12. The arrangement or grouping of the resources (machinery, labor) of production pertains to
    a. process model of operations.
    b. process design.
    c. capacity decision.
    d. factory focus.
    e. operations strategy.

13. The type of layout used for high volume production of a few standard products is
    a. product focused.
    b. process focused.
    c. fixed position.
    d. job shop.
    e. none of the above.

14. When a capital authorization request to expand capacity is granted, it triggers a
    a. capacity strategy.
    b. capacity cushion.
    c. capacity decision.
    d. corporate level strategic planning.
    e. none of the above.

15. Building a negative capacity cushion into the capacity plan might provide
    a. high utilization rates.
    b. higher than average return on investment.
    c. slow deterioration in the firm's market position.
    d. all of the above.
    e. only a and b.

16. Which of the following is NOT an important criteria for business location decisions according to the book?
    a. access to markets/distribution centers
    b. access to suppliers and resources
    c. competitive considerations
    d. availability of technology
    e. attractiveness of the site

17. The idea that any organizational entity will perform better when given a narrow, clearly defined set of tasks or priorities than it would when required to perform a broad, somewhat ambiguous set of tasks, is the idea of
    a. business process reengineering.
    b. lean production.
    c. supply chain management.
    d. factory focus.
    e. lean supply.

18. Kaizen means
    a. developing an overall plan to effectively guide the corporation as a whole.
    b. continuous improvement.
    c. having a relatively greater strength than a competitor on a strategically important factor.
    d. strategic planning.
    e. competitive priorities.

19. In Japan, second-tier suppliers are
    a. assigned the job of fabricating individual parts.
    b. a subsidiary of the parent corporation.
    c. responsible for production of a whole component.
    d. under the control of first-tier suppliers.
    e. none of the above.

20. Focusing on product development, purchasing, production, demand management and order fulfillment are all integral to achieving
    a. product/service superiority.
    b. long-term market share.
    c. global integration.
    d. work force harmony.
    e. all of the above.

21. A company's strategic business units are identified at the
    a. functional level.
    b. business level.
    c. horizontal level.
    d. vertical level.
    e. corporate level.

34   Chapter 3 - Operations Strategy

22. The first step in business-level strategic planning is to
   a. analyze the company's external environment.
   b. formulate the company's business strategy.
   c. implement the company's strategy.
   d. establish the company's objectives.
   e. select the strategy formulation team.

23. Which of the following is part of the macroenvironment?
   a. competitors
   b. customers
   c. suppliers
   d. technology
   e. all of the above

24. The steel industry requires high capital investment. This requirement would most influence which of Porter's competitive forces?
   a. the threat of new companies entering the industry
   b. the threat of substitute products
   c. the bargaining power of buyers
   d. the bargaining power of suppliers
   e. capacity influence

25. According to the strategic planning hierarchy, which level of strategic planning influences all other levels?
   a. functional-level strategic planning
   b. product-level strategic planning
   c. business-level strategic planning
   d. corporate-level strategic planning
   e. process-level strategic planning

26. What are Porter's two basic types of generic strategic planning strategies?
   a. factory focus and cost leader
   b. cost leader and differentiation
   c. lean production and business process reengineering
   d. process model approach and niche
   e. distinctive competence and strategic choice

27. Which of the following statements about the generic strategies is(are) TRUE?
   a. Companies that choose the cost leadership strategy ignore quality and service.
   b. Pricing a product relatively low is crucial to the success of the differentiation strategy.
   c. The strategies of cost leader and differentiation are mutually exclusive.
   d. Reducing costs is key to the cost leader strategy.
   e. All of the above.

28. Which of the following would be an example of a measurable goal for the competitive priority of quality of conformance?
    a. reduce the percentage of defective products from 0.01 to 0.005
    b. reduce order lead time from four weeks to one week
    c. increase the percentage of orders delivered on-time from 90 percent to 98 percent
    d. reduce setup time from one hour to 30 minutes on all production lines.
    e. all of the above are examples

29. The Widget Corporation is building a new plant to ensure that it has extra capacity. This strategy is called
    a. strategic positioning.
    b. a capacity strategy.
    c. a capacity cushion.
    d. a positive cushion.
    e. a negative cushion

30. _____ refers to a method for comprehensively analyzing the costs of each manufacturing step with the goal of cost improvement.
    a. Cost reduction
    b. Value analysis
    c. Business process reengineering
    d. Supply chain management
    e. Resource deployment

SHORT ANSWER QUESTIONS

1. Compare and contrast corporate level strategic planning, business level strategic planning and functional level strategic planning.

2. Discuss cost leadership and differentiation as basic types of strategies.

3. Explain the phrase "operations as a competitive weapon."

4. Discuss vertical integration and supply chain management.

5. What are the seven major categories of strategic operations decisions?

CHAPTER 4
FORECASTING DEMAND FOR PRODUCTS AND SERVICES

INTRODUCTION

CHARACTERISTICS OF DEMAND
Factors Influencing Demand
Demand Components

THE FORECASTING PROCESS
Establish Objectives for the Forecast
Determine What to Forecast
Specify the Time Period for the Forecast
Gather and Analyze Data
Select a Forecasting Method
Make the Forecast
Present the Forecast Results
Monitor and Control the Forecast

APPROACHES TO FORECASTING - A PREVIEW

QUALITATIVE FORECASTING METHODS
Naïve Extrapolation
Salesforce Composite
Jury of Executive Opinion
The Delphi Method
GLOBAL OPERATIONS MANAGEMENT 4.1: A Delphi Study of Consumer Attitudes
    Toward Travel in Six Eastern European Countries
Market Research Surveys
OPERATIONS MANAGEMENT IN PRACTICE 4.2: Hewlett-Packard: Sales Forecasting in
    the Fast Lane

QUANTITATIVE FORECASTING METHODS - TIME SERIES ANALYSIS MODELS
Time Series Smoothing
    Simple Average
    Simple Moving Average
    Weighted Moving Average
    Single Exponential Smoothing
    Double Exponential Smoothing
    Other Exponential Smoothing Models
    OPERATIONS MANAGEMENT IN PRACTICE 4.3: Improving Call Center
        Forecasting at L.L. Bean, Inc.
Time Series Decomposition

QUANTITATIVE FORECASTING METHODS - ASSOCIATIVE MODELS
Regression Models
    Simple Linear Regression
    Multiple Linear Regression

OPERATIONS MANAGEMENT IN PRACTICE 4.4: Using Regression Analysis to
Predict the Sales Price of an Apartment Property
Econometric Models

MEASURING FORECASTING ERROR
Absolute Measures of Forecasting Error
Relative Measures of Forecasting Error

MONITORING AND CONTROLLING FORECASTS

USING COMPUTERS IN FORECASTING

CHAPTER SUMMARY

1. Forecasting is a critical element in virtually every significant management decision. It is a statement or inference about the future. Forecasts serve as the basis for long-run corporate planning.

2. There are numerous factors that influence the demand for a product or service, these factors can be classified as internal or external factors:

   a. Internal factors are generally under the control of the organization, examples are: pricing, advertising, sales promotions, product design, packaging and service reputation.

   b. External factors are generally not able to be controlled by the organization, examples are: the general state of the economy and other effects of the business cycle.

3. Common business cycle demand indicators are:

   a. Leading indicators: those time series with turning points that typically precede the peaks and troughs of the general business cycle.

   b. Coincident indicators: those time series with turning points that closely match the turning points of the business cycle.

   c. Lagging indicators: those time series with turning points that typically follow the peaks and troughs of the general business cycle.

4. The demand for any product or service passes through five demand stages called the product life cycle, the period of time encompassing a product's introduction, growth, maturity, decline, and phase-out.

5. The demand for a product or service can be broken down into five major components:

   a. Average: the mean value or central tendency of the time series.

   b. Trend: the general upward or downward movement of demand over time.

   c. Cyclical: refers to the recurrent upward or downward wavelike conditions that occur over time because of general economic or political conditions. Usually longer than one year.

d. Seasonal: short-term, regular fluctuations that are caused by seasonal influences.

e. Random: a series of short, erratic movements that follow no discernible pattern and cannot be forecast.

6. The forecasting process enables the manager to make decisions based on the future value of some variable or the future occurrence of some event. The complete forecasting process can be divided into the following eight steps:

   a. Establish objectives for the forecast: the objectives or purpose of the forecast must be stated clearly at the beginning of the process.

   b. Determine what to forecast: decide if the forecast should be in dollars or in units, for example.

   c. Specify the time period for the forecast: will the forecast cover a short, medium, or long-term time horizon.

   d. Gather and analyze data: data may come from many sources both internal and external.

   e. Select a forecasting method: the two general approaches to forecasting are qualitative (primarily subjective or judgmental in nature) and quantitative (extending historical data into the future or developing associative models). Considerations should include: (1) the type and amount of data available, (2) the underlying pattern of data, (3) the forecast time horizon, (4) the technical ability of the person making the forecast, (5) the use of the forecast, and (6) the attitude of the user in regard to specific forecasting methods.

   f. Make the forecast: most likely this will involve the use of one of numerous computer software packages available.

   g. Present the results: communicate the results to management in an interesting and concise manner.

   h. Monitor and control the forecast: the deviation of the forecast from what actually occurred (forecast error) should be measured and evaluated.

7. Qualitative forecasting methods are perhaps the fastest and simplest ways of making forecasts. They tend to be used when there is not enough time to gather and analyze quantitative data, or when political and economic conditions are changing rapidly and available information may not be available. The most commonly used qualitative forecasting techniques are:

   a. Naïve extrapolation is the simplest of all forecasting methods and assumes the next period will be identical to the current period.

   b. A salesforce composite is the combination of salesforce members' individual forecasts.

   c. A jury of executive opinion is the group opinion of the company's high-level executives.

   d. The Delphi method is a process for obtaining a consensus forecast from a group of "experts" while maintaining their anonymity.

e. Market research surveys can be done either of mass consumers or industrial consumers and are categorized as counting methods.

8. Quantitative forecasting methods use historical data and utilize mathematical and statistical techniques to generate a forecast. There are two major types of quantitative forecasting methods:

a. Time series analysis methods: quantitative models that make forecasts based on the assumption that the past is a good predictor of the future. Time series methods are typically used when there are several years of demand data for the product or service being considered. Examples of time services models are: simple average, simple moving average, weighted moving average, single exponential smoothing, double exponential smoothing, and time series decomposition.

(1) A simple average is an average of all past demand in which all periods have equal weight.

(2) A simple moving average is an average computed for a specified number of recent time periods with all periods having equal weight.

(3) A weighted moving average is a moving average in which more weight is assigned to certain time periods, usually weighting more recent demand data heavier to influence the forecast more than older demand data. The total of all weights usually is equal to one.

(4) Exponential smoothing is a special type of weighted moving average that includes all past observations in the forecast calculation, but assigns greater weight to the most recent observations and less weight to the older ones. Weight applied to these older observations will eventually approach zero. As these observations get older, they impact current period forecasts less and less. The weighting is easily adjusted simply by changing the smoothing constant; α. The smoothing constant, α, is a decimal between 0 and 1. Small values of α would tend to give a very stable forecast with little responsiveness to changes in demand conditions. Large values of α, would tend to give a very responsive forecast to changes in demand conditions, but would also be very unstable with respect to any fluctuations in actual demand patterns.

(5) Double exponential smoothing, or trend-adjusted exponential smoothing, incorporates a trend adjustment into a single exponential smoothing forecast. This makes the technique more versatile as both a short-term and long-term technique.

b. Associative or causal methods: are typically used when the forecast has several years of demand for the product and has exhibited a relationship between the product demand (dependent variable) and other socio-economic factors (independent variable(s)). The forecaster attempts to determine the underlying relationship between the dependent variable and the independent variable(s). Regression models, both simple and multiple, are the most common forms of associative methods.

(1) The method of least squares is used to calculate the coefficients of the regression equation.

(2) Common measures of the accuracy of the fitted regression model are:

(a) The standard error of the estimate; based on the mean square vertical deviations of the actual observations from the fitted regression line.

(b) The correlation coefficient; a relative measure of the association between the independent and dependent variables.

(c) The coefficient of determination; the square of the correlation coefficient, is the ratio of the variation in the data explained by the fitted regression line to the total variation in the data.

9. Forecast error is defined to be the numerical difference between the actual demand in a period and the forecasted demand for that period. Measures of forecast error can be divided into two categories.

a. Absolute measures: the error measurements employed are made in an absolute manner without any consideration given to the underlying level of demand. The most commonly used absolute measures of forecasting error are:

(1) Mean square error (SE)

(2) Standard deviation (SD or σ)

(3) Mean absolute deviation (MAD)

b. Relative measures: the error measurements employed take into account the relative magnitude of the forecasting errors with respect to the underlying demand level. For example, suppose your current forecasting technique is yielding forecasts that are off by 150 units on the average. Is this a large error? Using absolute measures of forecasting error will not reveal any information about the magnitude of this error. Intuitively, the significance of an average 150 unit error would be different if you are forecasting units in the low thousands versus in the hundreds of thousands. The most commonly used relative measures of forecasting error are:

(1) Coefficient of variation (CVAR)

(2) Mean percentage error (MPE)

(3) Mean absolute percentage error (MAPE)

10. To control the forecasting process, forecasts should be monitored. There are three basic methods of monitoring forecasts:

a. Visually comparing actual data and the forecasts

b. Tracking signals: measures whether a forecasting method is biased over time. The tracking signal is defined as the ratio of the cumulative forecast error to the corresponding value of MAD.

c. Control charts: requires the setting of upper and lower limits for individual forecast errors.

11. In practice today, the computer is an extremely important tool for forecasting. A number of large scale computer based forecasting programs are available.

KEY TERMS

a. associative (causal) methods
b. average
c. census
d. coefficient of determination
e. coincident indicators
f. control chart
g. control limits
h. correlation coefficient
i. counting methods
j. cycle
k. Delphi method
l. dependent variable
m. double exponential smoothing
n. econometric model
o. forecast
p. forecast error
q. independent variables
r. intercept
s. judgment methods
t. jury of executive opinion
u. lagging indicators
v. leading indicators
w. least squares
x. market research survey
y. multiple linear regression
z. naïve extrapolation
aa. negative correlation

bb. positive correlation
cc. product life cycle
dd. qualitative forecasting methods
ee. quantitative forecasting methods
ff. random error
gg. regression constant
hh. regression equation
ii. regression model
jj. responsiveness
kk. sales-force composite
ll. sample
mm. scatter diagram
nn. seasonal
oo. simple average
pp. simple exponential smoothing
qq. simple linear regression
rr. simple moving average
ss. slope
tt. single exponential smoothing
uu. standard error of the estimate
vv. stability
ww. time series
xx. time series analysis methods
yy. tracking signal
zz. trend
aaa. Weighted moving average

DEFINITIONS

Directions: Select from the key terms list, the word or phrase being defined below.

_____ 1. methods that allow for personal opinions, guesses and the opinion of others.

_____ 2. a statement or inference about the future.

_____ 3. a time-ordered sequence of observations taken at some regular interval over time.

_____ 4. time series with turning points that typically precede the peaks and troughs of the general business cycle.

_____ 5. time series with turning points that typically follow the peaks and troughs of the general business cycle.

_____ 6. short-term regular fluctuation that is caused by influences such as month of the year, or timing of holidays.

_____ 7. the general upward or downward movement of demand over time.

_____ 8. quantitative models that make forecasts based on the assumption that the past is a good predictor of the future.

_____ 9. mathematical models, such as regression, that relate the effects of product demand to other socio-economic factors.

_____ 10. an average of past demand in which all past periods are equally weighted.

_____ 11. an average computed for a specified number of recent time periods.

_____ 12. a special type of moving average that does not weight each included demand value equally.

_____ 13. data that is collected by means of interviews or a group meeting of executives.

_____ 14. the ratio of the variation in the data explained by the fitted regression line to the total variation in the data.

_____ 15. a measure of the strength of the relationship between two variables

_____ 16. a condition where the independent variable increases while the dependent variable decreases or vice versa.

_____ 17. measures the relationship between a single dependent variable and a single independent variable.

_____ 18. measures whether a forecasting method is biased over time.

MULTIPLE CHOICE QUESTIONS

Directions: Indicate your choice of the best answer to each question.

1. Which of the following areas do NOT need to do forecasting?
    a. marketing
    b. operations
    c. finance
    d. human resources
    e. none of the above

2. Which of the following is NOT an example of an internal factor influencing demand?
    a. backlogs
    b. product life cycle
    c. pricing
    d. advertising
    e. sales promotions

3. Time series data with turning points that closely match the turning points of the business cycle are
   a. lagging indicators.
   b. strategic data.
   c. leading indicators.
   d. tactical data.
   e. coincident indicators.

4. Lagging indicators are those time series with
   a. turning points that typically follow the exponentially smoothed forecast.
   b. turning points that closely match the turning points of the business cycle.
   c. turning points that typically follow the peaks and troughs of the business cycle.
   d. turning points that have seasonal variations.
   e. turning points that typically precede the peaks and troughs of the general business cycle.

5. Leading indicators are those time series with
   a. turning points that typically follow the exponentially smoothed forecast.
   b. turning points that closely match the turning points of the business cycle.
   c. turning points that typically follow the peaks and troughs of the business cycle.
   d. turning points that have seasonal variations.
   e. turning points that typically precede the peaks and troughs of the general business cycle.

6. An example of a lagging indicator is
   a. average manufacturing workweek.
   b. unemployment rate.
   c. new building permits (private housing).
   d. stock price index.
   e. none of the above.

7. Which of the following is NOT one of the five major components of demand for a product or service?
   a. trend
   b. responsiveness
   c. cycle
   d. seasonal
   e. random

8. The average component of demand is
   a. the mean value of the time series.
   b. the recurrent upward or downward wavelike conditions that occur over time.
   c. the upward or downward movement over time.
   d. a regular fluctuation that is a function of weather or the time of year.
   e. short erratic movements that follow no discernible pattern.

9. The seasonal component of demand is
   a. the mean value of the time series.
   b. the recurrent upward or downward wavelike conditions that occur over time.
   c. the upward or downward movement over time.
   d. a regular fluctuation that is a function of weather or the time of year.
   e. short erratic movements that follow no discernible pattern.

10. Random fluctuations in demand can be explained by
    a. the average component.
    b. the seasonal component.
    c. the cycle component.
    d. the trend component.
    e. none of the above.

11. Counting methods are a type of
    a. exponential smoothing.
    b. qualitative forecasting.
    c. moving average.
    d. quantitative forecasting.
    e. time series.

12. Which of the following is NOT a qualitative forecasting method?
    a. Delphi technique
    b. sales force composite
    c. associative methods
    d. jury of executive opinion
    e. market research surveys

13. The forecasting process includes all the following EXCEPT
    a. establish objectives for the forecast.
    b. review all previous forecasts.
    c. gather and analyze data.
    d. make the forecast.
    e. present the forecast results.

14. Which of the following is a possible drawback to the sales force composite method of forecasting?
    a. subject to personal bias
    b. reduces group decision making
    c. anonymity of the respondent
    d. strong personalities tend to dominate the group
    e. difficult to gather results

15. An example of a causal method of forecasting is
    a. moving averages.
    b. exponential smoothing models.
    c. regression models.
    d. time-series extrapolation.
    e. time-series decomposition.

16. Forecasting techniques that attempt to smooth out the data to make the underlying pattern of the data more apparent are
    a. simple averages.
    b. simple moving averages.
    c. weighted moving averages.
    d. all of the above.
    e. none of the above.

17. An advantage of the moving average is
    a. all past demand data is used.
    b. can provide a more stable estimate for demand.
    c. allows the varying of weights applied to past demand data.
    d. α (alpha) can be varied to reflect current demand conditions.
    e. the lower the number of periods used, the more stable the forecast.

18. A smoothing constant, alpha, with a value of 0.0 would result in a forecast
    a. with extreme responsiveness to changes in demand.
    b. unstable with respect to fluctuations in demand.
    c. not being adjusted in any way.
    d. fairly stable with respect to fluctuations in actual demand.
    e. equal to the last actual demand value.

19. Double exponential smoothing is a variation of single exponential smoothing that allows for the incorporation of
    a. random variations.
    b. cyclical fluctuations.
    c. spurious correlation.
    d. trends.
    e. least squares.

20. A forecast that is generated by updating the current forecast by a percentage of the forecast error is called
    a. simple moving average forecast.
    b. qualitative forecast.
    c. weighted moving average.
    d. exponentially smoothed forecast.
    e. time series decomposition.

21. A scatter diagram is used to
    a. determine if multicollinearity exists.
    b. verify a linear relationship between the dependent and independent variables.
    c. search for spurious correlation.
    d. measure forecast accuracy.
    e. selecting an appropriate value for the smoothing constant.

22. Which of the following would NOT be a method to measure forecast accuracy?
    a. MAD
    b. CVAR
    c. MSE
    d. MAPE
    e. none of the above

23. Given the following data, the forecast for 1998 using naïve extrapolation would be ___.

YEAR	DEMAND
1995	16,000
1996	13,500
1997	15,200

a. 14,900
b. 15,200
c. 14,350
d. 14,500
e. none of the above

24. Given the following data, use single exponential smoothing to determine the forecast for 1998.

	Year	Demand	Forecast
$\alpha = 0.5$	1997	4200	3600

a. 3,750
b. 3,900
c. 4,200
d. 4,500
e. 4,560

25. Given the following data, use double exponential smoothing to determine the forecast for 1998.

	Year	Demand	Smoothed Forecast	Smoothed Trend
$\alpha = 0.3$	1996	2,340	2,223	
$\beta = 0.5$	1997	2,457	2,457	176

a. 2,193
b. 2,281
c. 2,457
d. 2,545
e. none of the above

PROBLEMS

PROBLEM SITUATION # 1

Truimph distributors has experienced the following demand for their new remote controlled lawn mower.

Week	Actual Demand
1	10
2	25
3	20
4	10
5	15

26. Using a four week moving average, what is your forecast for week six?
   a. 15
   b. 17.5
   c. 32.5
   d. 25
   e. none of the above

27. What is the exponentially smoothed forecast for week 2, assuming the forecast for week 1 was 16.5 and the smoothing constant is 0.2?
   a. 17.16
   b. 11.3
   c. 15.2
   d. 15.85
   e. none of the above

28. What is the exponentially smoothed forecast for week 6, assuming the forecast for week 5 was 16.5 and the smoothing constant is 0.0?
   a. 10
   b. 15
   c. 15.85
   d. 16.5
   e. none of the above

PROBLEM SITUATION # 2

Art Gowan's microbrewery had forecast sales of $220,000 for the last month. The actual sales turned out to be $250,000.

29. What is the forecast for this month using exponential smoothing and a smoothing constant of 0.3?
   a. $184,000
   b. $235,000
   c. $211,000
   d. $229,000
   e. none of the above

30. If actual sales turnout to be $240,000 this month, what would be the forecast for next month using exponential smoothing with a smoothing constant of 0.3?
   a. $241,000
   b. $232,300
   c. $229,000
   d. $220,400
   e. none of the above

31. If Art had used a smoothing constant of 0.1 in the previous question, what would his forecast be for next month?
   a. $230,100
   b. $218,000
   c. $232,000
   d. $226,000
   e. none of the above

PROBLEM SITUATION # 3

Cape Fear Beer has experienced the following sales volume for their new product, "Rocky Point Lite"

Month	Actual Demand (in kegs)
1	150
2	200
3	200
4	250
5	275
6	300

32. What is the y-intercept of the regression equation?
   a. 275.00
   b. 126.65
   c. 29.29
   d. 45.83
   e. not enough information to calculate

33. What is the complete regression equation?
   a. 229.15 + 29.29X
   b. 29.29 + 126.65X
   c. 29.29 + 229.15X
   d. 126.65 + 29.29X
   e. not enough information to calculate

34. What is the forecast for month 7?
   a. 915.50
   b. 1633.35
   c. 331.70
   d. 434.25
   e. not enough information to calculate

PROBLEM SITUATION # 4

The sales manager for Rainbow Sportswear has gathered the following monthly data on sales of his companies leather sandals.

	Forecast	Actual Demand
April	1000	950
May	1100	1080
June	1200	1230
July	1300	1300

35. What is the MAD for this data?
    a. 24
    b. 25
    c. 95
    d. 33
    e. none of the above

36. What is the MSE for this data?
    a. 250
    b. 950
    c. 240
    d. 330
    e. none of the above

37. What is the MAPE for this data?
    a. 2.5%
    b. 2.4%
    c. 3.3%
    d. 9.5%
    e. none of the above

APPLICATION QUESTIONS

Barry Wray has been renting sailboats by the hour at Wrightsville Beach for the past 6 months. The monthly demand for this service is listed below:

Month	Actual Demand
1	325
2	260
3	281
4	367
5	257
6	298

1. Forecast Barry's demand for month 7 using a simple average of past data.

2. Forecast the demand for month 7 using a five-month moving average.

3. Forecast the demand for month 7 using a three-period weighted moving average, with weights of 0.5, 0.3, and 0.2 (decreasing weights for older data).

4. Forecast the demand for month 7 using exponential smoothing with a smoothing constant of 0.1 and assuming the forecast for period 6 was 300 units.

5. Forecast the demand for month 7 using exponential smoothing with a smoothing constant of 0.9 and assuming the forecast for period 6 was 300 units.

6. Which of the forecast methods calculated in parts 1-5 is the most accurate in forecasting for period 7, assuming that the actual demand in month 7 turned out to be 300 units?

7. Which forecasting method used in parts 2-5 will be most stable in generating future forecasts?

8. Which forecasting method used in parts 2-5 will be most responsive in generating future forecasts?

9. If the data in the original problem was exhibiting an continuing increasing or decreasing trend, would you want a technique that was more responsive or stable?

SHORT ANSWER QUESTIONS

1. Define and discuss internal and external factors influencing demand.

2. List and define the five major components of demand for a product or service.

3. What is the difference between time series and associative forecasting methods?

4. What is the difference between, "absolute" measures of forecast error, and "relative" measures of forecast error?

5. Discuss the use of a Tracking Signal, how is it calculated and operationalized?

CHAPTER 5
PRODUCT PLANNING AND PROCESS DESIGN

INTRODUCTION

ASSESSING CUSTOMERS' NEEDS AND WANTS
Technology-Driven New Product Ideas
OPERATIONS MANAGEMENT IN PRACTICE 5.1: Where You *Really* Need to Hear Customers
New Product Ideas from Market Research
The Voice of the Customer

CUSTOMER SATISFACTION
Selecting Features for Products and Services
Customer-Driven New Product Ideas
Quality Function Deployment
From the House of Quality to Operations Requirements
Application of QFD to New Product Design
Improving Designs Through Simplification and Value Analysis

DESIGN FOR MANUFACTURABILITY
Concurrent Engineering
Implementing Cross-Functional Teams in DFM

PROCESS DESIGN AND LAYOUT FOR MANUFACTURING AND SERVICE SYSTEMS
Projects: Processes that Don't Flow
Intermittent Flow Configurations
Line-Flow Configurations
GLOBAL OPERATIONS MANAGEMENT 5.2: Opel Eisenach GMBH - Creating a High-Productivity Workplace
    Batch Processes
    Assembly Lines
    Continuous Flow Processes
Cellular Manufacturing
Production Line Approach to Service

STRATEGIC ISSUES IN PROCESS DESIGN
Product and Process Innovation
OPERATIONS MANAGEMENT IN PRACTICE 5.3: Merck Fights to Keep Up the Production Pace
The Product-Process Matrix
Designing for the Environment
OPERATIONS MANAGEMENT IN PRACTICE 5.4: ISO 14000 Standards: Ready for Launching

CHAPTER SUMMARY

1. Product planning and process design are strategic decisions made for manufacturing and service operations. The modern environment requires that product planning and process design occur concurrently.

2. The Japanese have made notable contributions in helping American companies accomplish effective product and process design. Most notable is the work of Genichi Taguchi who:

   a. developed experimental methods to achieve improved design,

   b. encouraged that designers should be held accountable for losses due to poor design,

   c. believed organizations should be held accountable for losses to society resulting from the disposal of products no longer useable, and

   d. developed the concept of a "loss function" which can be used to help measure the loss to society from poor design.

In contrast to Taguchi's views of designing for "loss minimization," others see customer satisfaction as the primary objective.

3. Behind the success of most all superior products and services is a process that has been carefully designed to ensure timely, defect-free operations aimed at features the customer wants.

4. While manufacturers strive for "zero defects", service companies must strive for "zero defections". Keeping customers is the best single strategy that a firm can employ against its competition. Keeping customers can be achieved by accessing and responding to customer needs and wants.

5. Long-term success may be achieved by developing new products and services, which are generated by:

   a. Technology

   b. Marketing research

   c. Voice of the customer - technology and marketing research may be incomplete approaches to new product/service design. Listening to the customer and forming close relationships with them may overcome the limitations of the previous two techniques. Sustainable advantage will be created by organizations which recognize that they are in the business not to simply provide new products/services, but because their customers want them to survive, grow and prosper.

6. Customer satisfaction can be defined as meeting or exceeding customer requirements for a product/service:

   a. Features: (does the product/service offer features that are most important to the customer?)

   b. Timeliness: (can the firm respond to customer demand quickly?)

   c. Performance: (is the product/service free of defects?)

7. Firms that listen to their customers are more likely to introduce successful products which require less fine-tuning to the tastes and preferences of the market. The following steps trace the path of a new product/service introduction.

   a. Idea generation

   b. Feature selection

   c. Preliminary design

   d. Prototype development

   e. Test market introduction

   f. Market-wide availability

8. When marketing research questionnaires do not provide sufficient information for product/service ideas, successful Japanese firms use anthropologists to observe and study the customer, rather than asking questions.

9. Quality function deployment (QFD) is a structured technique for translating the voice of the customer into the language of design and manufacturing engineers.

   a. QFD benefits include:

      (1) Fewer changes required after product or service introduction

      (2) Reduced product/service development time

      (3) Reduced costs

      (4) Increased productivity

      (5) Increased customer satisfaction

      (6) Increased market share

      (7) Improved communication within the organization

      (8) Better data to refine the design of future products/services

   b. The QFD technique is performed by constructing a series of sequentially developed matrices:

      (1) House of Quality

      (2) Components matrix

      (3) Process characteristics matrix

(4) Process control matrix

   c. QFD follows six basic steps:

      (1) Voice of the customer - determine what you should be doing in your business

      (2) Competitive analysis - determine how well your product/service is satisfying customer attributes as compared to your competitors

      (3) Voice of the engineer - determine the technical steps and ask how the needs and wants of our customers can be better addressed

      (4) Look for correlations - what relationships exist between the customer attributes and technical requirements.

      (5) Technical comparison with competitors - compare important technical requirement measures to those of the competition.

      (6) Evaluate design trade-offs - examine information related to trade-offs between the technical requirements.

10. Design for manufacturability (DFM) helps ensure the right features and value to meet customer expectations of defect free products and services. Designs can be improved through simplification and value analysis.

11. Shorter development cycles, defined as the time between the release of one model until the release of the next, can be achieved by employing the principle of concurrent engineering.

   a. Concurrent engineering involves overlapping activities in product and process development that were previously performed sequentially. When firms extend concurrent engineering to include supplier involvement, strategies alliances are developed between buyers and sellers that have been shown to be critical to the development of superior quality designs.

   b. Cross-functional teams have been shown to benefit concurrent engineering. Advantages to cross-functional teams include: (1) cycle time improvement, (2) information exchange, and (3) true problem-solving can occur.

   c. Factors that can hinder DFM success include: (1) organizational-level factors such as status parity, (2) number of levels in an organizational chart traversed until all involved individuals have a common manager, (3) project factors, such as, lack of clear goals or high turnover in membership of team, and (4) lack of supplier and customer involvement.

12. The range of process flow configurations in manufacturing and service systems can be grouped into categories according to common features in their flow patterns. These general process types or configurations are useful in comparing the opportunities and challenges presented to management. The various types of processes presented are:

   a. Project: "Processes that don't flow". In a project all materials, workers, information, etc., are brought to the job site. All process activities take place on site. Projects offer a product or service that is unique. Costs are usually higher than they would be if some other production process could have been used. The challenge to managing a project is to coordinate the sequence and timing of activities so that work can proceed efficiently. Examples would be the construction of a bridge or the installation of a new computer and an associated network.

b. Job shops: also called a process oriented layout. Job shops are used when there is a need to process a variety of products or services simultaneously, the number of units produced is small, and flexibility and efficiency are required.

(1) Workstations are laid out according to the type of process performed. Some workstations will tend to be idle while other have a backlog of work to be completed.

(2) Primary advantage for job shops is the flexibility to process a wide variety of products or services.

(3) Significant disadvantage for job shops is the cost per unit being processed. Costs tend to be higher because of increased material handling, increased time required to process, and underutilization of the facilities.

(4) The primary challenge for management is the determination of the order in which the jobs are to be processed. An order may spend a considerable amount of time waiting its turn for processing, this move-and-wait nature of a job shop has given rise to the term intermittent production.

(5) Examples of job shops would be a restaurant kitchen, your local hospital, or a woodworking or metal cutting shop.

c. Line flow configurations or flow shops: also called product oriented layouts. Flow shop configurations are used in dealing with higher volumes of output.

(1) Flow shops are laid out by the order in which the processing steps must be accomplished for the product or service.

(2) Primary advantage of the flow shop is the lower per unit cost.

(3) Primary disadvantage of this approach is the lack of flexibility to adapt to changes in markets or customer wishes.

(4) Examples of flow shops would be automobiles (discrete processing) or petroleum products (continuous flow processing).

d. Batch processing: a hybrid of the job shop and flow shop configurations. In these operations, there is less flexibility than the job shop but more efficiency. This increased efficiency is gained primarily from reduced product variety, higher volume and more dominant material flows. Examples of batch processing would be traditional steel manufacturing or ice cream production.

e. Assembly lines: used when product or service variety is very low, volume is high, dominant material flow patterns exist and production can be performed using repetitive or sequential activities. Examples of assembly lines would be chicken being cut into parts for packaging or the assembly of semiconductors.

f. Continuous flow processes: when the flow of material never stops. In this type process, production continues twenty-four hours per day, seven days a week. Workers and managers monitor and adjust the flow of material to ensure the process is stable and uninterrupted. Examples of continuous flow process are petro-chemical refineries and nuclear power plants.

g. Cellular manufacturing: the manufacturing cell, or cell concept groups the various products produced in a job shop according to common features. The parts families produced by this grouping are assigned to various manufacturing cells.

h. The production line approach to service attempts to reduce the variety of products offered and standardize the methods of operation. McDonald's restaurant is a good example of this approach, they have a limited menu and very rigid operating procedures.

13. To select the appropriate process configuration to adopt in a manufacturing or service operation, a manager must review the product life cycle, the product-process matrix, and various environmental factors.

a. The product life cycle indicates how the volume of products/services demanded tends to change during the introductory, growth, maturity, and decline periods. When products/services are new, production costs are high, volumes are low, and the growth of sales is slow. The maximum rate of demand at maturity, and the length of time that the product retains that position are all important elements in selecting process technologies.

b. The product-process matrix illustrates the linkage between process pattern and product mix and volume. Various process configurations are listed on a diagonal in the body of the matrix. Given the mix and volume considerations and the pattern of flow of products through the process, the most efficient configuration is specified.

c. Organizations must consider the reality regarding the limits of the environment to absorb and process chemical and biological wastes when designing production systems. While some waste is usually inevitable in a manufactured product, reducing the level of waste through effective product/process design will lower facility operating costs. Many companies are actively involved in securing certification in the new ISO14000 environmental standards.

KEY TERMS

a. assembly line
b. batch process
c. cellular manufacturing
d. concurrent engineering
e. continuous flow process
f. cross-functional team
g. customer satisfaction
h. defect
i. design for manufacturability
j. flexible manufacturing systems
k. flow shop
l. House of Quality

m. intermittent production
n. job shop
o. parts families
p. process-oriented layout
q. product life cycle
r. product-oriented layout
s. product-process matrix
t. project
u. quality function deployment
v. repetitive process
w. strategic alliance
x. value analysis

DEFINITIONS

Directions: Select from the key terms list, the word or phrase being defined below.

_____ 1. when production can be performed using repetitive, or sequential activities.

_____ 2. workstations are arranged according to the type of process performed.

_____ 3. long-term contract between suppliers and buyers.

_____ 4. the overlapping of activities in product and process development.

_____ 5. a process used by product designers to assess the characteristics of a product.

_____ 6. illustrating the linkage between process pattern and product mix/volume.

_____ 7. hybrid of the job shop and flow shop configurations.

_____ 8. process configuration used when there is a need to process a variety of product or service types simultaneous, flexibility is required and the number of units to produce is small.

_____ 9. the move-and-wait nature of this type configuration gives it this name.

_____ 10. structured technique for translating the voice of the customer into the language of design and manufacturing engineers.

_____ 11. meeting or exceeding customer requirements.

_____ 12. responsive systems that operate with flow line efficiency, job shop variety and small batch sizes.

_____ 13. layout determined by the order in which processing steps must be accomplished for the product or service.

_____ 14. a production process where there are no discrete units of production.

_____ 15. a production environment where all resources are moved to the job site.

_____ 16. any deviation from the customer's expectations.

_____ 17. indicates how volume of products demanded changes over various periods of time.

MULTIPLE CHOICE QUESTIONS

Directions: Indicate your choice of the best answer to each question.

1. Genichi Taguchi is most noted for
    a. developing quality function deployment.
    b. developing the concept of a "loss function".
    c. experimental methods to achieve improved design.
    d. creating the House of Quality.
    e. both b and c.

2. Successful products and services have which of the following traits?
    a. timely production
    b. error free production
    c. desirable features
    d. all of the above
    e. both b and c

3. While manufacturers strive for "zero defects" service companies must strive for
    a. time basis of service.
    b. greater flexibility.
    c. zero defections.
    d. marketing effectiveness.
    e. new product development.

4. Sustainable competitive advantage will be created by
    a. customers wanting the business to grow and prosper.
    b. low labor costs.
    c. size or market share.
    d. new product introductions.
    e. all of the above.

5. Meeting or exceeding requirements for a product or service is known as
    a. competitive advantage.
    b. quality function deployment.
    c. customer satisfaction.
    d. voice of the customer.
    e. process design.

6. Once preliminary designs are formed, the next stage of product development is
    a. feature selection.
    b. prototype development.
    c. test market introduction.
    d. feature refinement.
    e. market-wide general availability.

7. Which of the following are NOT matrices involved in the construction of the QFD technique?
   a. process control matrix
   b. process characteristics matrix
   c. components matrix
   d. design attributes matrix
   e. House of Quality

8. Which of the following is NOT a step in developing the House of Quality?
   a. the voice of the customer
   b. competitive analysis
   c. supplier capability analysis
   d. discover correlations
   e. evaluate design trade-offs

9. The House of Quality gives the manager
   a. a better understanding of the needs and expectations of the customer.
   b. some measure of how well the customer thinks you are performing.
   c. the technical requirements which work together to provide some level of customer satisfaction.
   d. an idea of the relationship between the organizations technical requirements and the needs and. expectations of the customer.
   e. all of the above.

10. A benefit of concurrent engineering is
    a. free exchange of information.
    b. true problem-solving can occur.
    c. cycle time improvement.
    d. all of the above.
    e. only a and c.

11. Factors that may hinder the success of Design For Manufacturability can include
    a. organizational-level factors.
    b. project factors.
    c. supplier factors.
    d. customer factors.
    e. all of the above.

12. Projects are characterized as
    a. general purpose machinery, flexibility.
    b. relatively high volumes, general purpose equipment.
    c. continuous flow, large volumes.
    d. low volume, unique demand.
    e. intermittent production, flexibility.

13. Intermittent flow configurations are also known as
    a. flow shops.
    b. job shops.
    c. assembly line.
    d. continuous flow.
    e. projects.

14. A job shop configuration would be used when
    a. there is a need for flexibility and volume is small.
    b. there is a need to eliminate or greatly reduce change over time.
    c. there is a need for flexibility and volume is high.
    d. there is a need to produce a high volume of standardized products.
    e. there is a need for high volume and low cost product.

15. The type of configuration where work stations are laid out according to the type process performed is called
    a. batch.
    b. job shop.
    c. project.
    d. flexible manufacturing.
    e. flow shop.

16. Product oriented layouts are also known as
    a. continuous.
    b. batch.
    c. project.
    d. flow shop.
    e. job shop.

17. The type of configuration where the arrangement of the process is determined by the order in which processing steps must be accomplished for the product or service is known as
    a. flexible manufacturing.
    b. product oriented layout.
    c. process oriented layout.
    d. job shop.
    e. continuous layout.

18. The type of process configuration which is a hybrid of the job shop and flow shop configurations is
    a. continuous.
    b. batch process.
    c. assembly line.
    d. project.
    e. process layout.

19. The type of production where the product or service variety is very low, volume is high and dominant material flow patterns are present is
    a. assembly line.
    b. process layout.
    c. batch process.
    d. continuous flow.
    e. project.

20. In what type of process configuration are you never able to see discrete units of the product?
    a. batch
    b. cellular
    c. project
    d. continuous flow
    e. process layouts

21. Which of the following would be considered continuous-flow operations?
    a. nuclear power plants
    b. oil refinery
    c. sugar refineries
    d. paper mills
    e. all of the above

22. A production concept that groups together the various products produced in a job shop according to common features including size, processing steps, and materials is known as
    a. batch production.
    b. product layout.
    c. cellular manufacturing.
    d. continuous production.
    e. project manufacturing.

23. One of the primary outcomes of the production line approach to service is
    a. quality.
    b. flexibility.
    c. consistency.
    d. timeliness.
    e. accuracy.

24. "Product" innovation tends to be highest in which phase of the product life cycle?
    a. introduction
    b. growth
    c. maturity
    d. decline
    e. cannot be determined

25. Flexible manufacturing systems
    a. are designed to operate with flow line efficiency and high variety.
    b. are applicable for job shops only and not assembly operations.
    c. are applicable for flow line systems.
    d. all of the above.
    e. none of the above.

26. Firms that operate below the diagonal on the product process matrix have
    a. less flexibility and lower cost.
    b. greater flexibility and lower cost.
    c. greater flexibility and higher cost.
    d. less flexibility and higher cost.
    e. none of the above.

27. Quality function deployment was developed in _____ in the 1970s.
    a. Japan
    b. Russia
    c. Germany
    d. United States
    e. none of the above

28. The "competitive analysis" step of the House of Quality is created based on
    a. a detailed analysis of competitor's product.
    b. a detailed analysis of your own product.
    c. the customer's perception of your product as compared to the competition.
    d. an analysis of differences between your product and competition's product.
    e. benchmarking studies of competition.

29. The process used to allocate parts to various cells within a cellular manufacturing environment is referred to as
    a. cellular division.
    b. parts allocation.
    c. parts families.
    d. parts sorting.
    e. parts alignment.

30. Mutually beneficial relationships that are established between organizations to address strategic issues are called strategic
    a. partnerships.
    b. alliances.
    c. teamwork.
    d. unions.
    e. cooperation.

SHORT ANSWER QUESTIONS

1. Briefly describe the process of introducing a new product in the marketplace.

2. Describe the benefits of using quality function deployment to assist in design efforts.

3. What are the six steps of QFD? What is accomplished at each step?

4. Compare and contrast projects, intermittent flow configurations, line-flow configurations, and cellular manufacturing.

5. What is the Product-Process Matrix and how is it used?

CHAPTER 6
LONG-RANGE CAPACITY PLANNING AND FACILITY LOCATION

INTRODUCTION

AN OVERVIEW OF CAPACITY PLANNING
    The Importance of Capacity Planning
    Defining and Measuring Capacity
    Measuring System Effectiveness
    Focused Facilities
    OPERATIONS MANAGEMENT IN PRACTICE 6.1: The Focused Factory - Another Concept for Continuous Improvement in Manufacturing

CAPACITY STRATEGIES
    Capacity Cushions
    Strategic Timing of Capacity Changes
    Sizing Capacity Changes
    OPERATIONS MANAGEMENT IN PRACTICE 6.2: High Volume Production - The Key to Success

MAKING CAPACITY PLANNING DECISIONS
    Steps in the Capacity Planning Process
    Using Decision Trees In Capacity Planning
    OPERATIONS MANAGEMENT IN PRACTICE 6.3: A Plant Conversion Solves a Plant Capacity Problem

AN OVERVIEW OF LOCATION DECISIONS
    Why Location Decisions Are Important
    Location Options
    A General Approach to Making Location Decisions

FACTORS AFFECTING LOCATION DECISIONS
    Regional, Community, and Site Considerations
    Dominant Facility Location Factors in Manufacturing
    Dominant Facility Location Factors in Services
    OPERATIONS MANAGEMENT IN PRACTICE 6.4: The Charlotte Panthers Choose a Preseason Training Facility

MAKING THE SINGLE-FACILITY LOCATION DECISION
    Detailed Cost Analysis
    Factor Rating Systems
    Center of Gravity Method
    Locational Cost-Volume-Profit Analysis

MAKING MULTIPLE-FACILITY LOCATION DECISIONS
    Plant Charters Approach
    Transportation Method
    Heuristics

Simulation
Optimization Methods
OPERATIONS MANAGEMENT IN PRACTICE 6.5: Analyzing Alternative Locations and Service Areas for the American Red Cross

STRATEGIC TRENDS IN LOCATION DECISIONS
Business Park Proliferation
Factories: Research and Development Linkages
Globalization of Production
GLOBAL OPERATIONS MANAGEMENT 6.6: NAFTA Opens a New World of Market Opportunities
The Sun Belt Phenomenon
GLOBAL OPERATIONS MANAGEMENT 6.7: Why BMW Cruised Into Spartenburg

CHAPTER SUMMARY

1. Long-range capacity planning and facility location are two intertwined strategies.

   a. Long-range capacity planning addresses the questions: (1) How much a plant should produce; (2) How big a facility should be; and (3) What level of service a company should provide.

   b. Facility location decisions address the question: Where should the facility(ies) be located.

2. Capacity and location decisions are circular in nature. Capacity planning is required when a company decides to make a new product, offer a new service, make more of an existing product, or provide more of an existing service. Demand for products or services is a function of location, so the location decision is tied to the capacity decision.

3. Producers tend to locate facilities close to both their suppliers and their customers, so they can more quickly obtain raw materials and deliver products. Service companies typically try to locate near their customers to achieve a competitive advantage and to create a time and place utility.

4. Capacity planning is among the first decisions that a company has to make. If a company has too much capacity, inventory levels tend to rise or work force and equipment may be under utilized. If a company has too little capacity, it can lose customers to competitors or be forced to use subcontracting.

5. Capacity is defined as the productive capability of a facility. It is usually measured as a quantity of output per unit of time. In some situations when product mix is very diverse, capacity is sometimes defined using input measures rather than outputs.

   a. Common capacity references are to the maximum productive capability of a facility. Other ways of viewing "maximum" capacity are:

      (1) Design capacity - target output rate, or maximum capacity for which the production facility was designed

      (2) Effective capacity - maximum rate of output achievable given various constraints

(3) Actual capacity - reflects the rate of output that is actually achieved. It is normally less than both design and effective capacity because of machine breakdowns, worker absenteeism, etc.

b. Various ways of measuring capacity are useful in evaluating the effectiveness of the production system. Two such measures are:

(1) capacity utilization - a measure of how much a facility is being used.

(2) capacity efficiency - a measure of how well the production system is being used.

6. Skinner proposed that a production facility is most efficient when it concentrates on a fairly limited set of production objectives. This is operationalized through the use of several small facilities, each serving a single market rather than one large facility attempting to satisfy all demand. This concept called the focused factory can also be operationalized through the use of creating plants within plants.

7. A capacity strategy is a key element of a firm's overall manufacturing strategy. A capacity strategy provides a longer-term perspective in which individual, short-term capacity decisions can be viewed.

a. Three basic aspects of capacity strategy are:

(1) Capacity cushions - are the amount by which the average utilization rate falls below 100%

(2) Timing of capacity changes - assuming that demand will grow steadily and that capacity will be added in "chunks", three timing strategies can be utilized,

(a) Anticipate and lead demand
(b) Closely follow demand
(c) Lag demand

b. The level of capacity for which the average unit cost is at a minimum is called the best operating level. At low levels of output, fixed costs must be absorbed by only a few units, which results in a high average unit cost of output. As output increase, average unit cost decreases until some minimum average unit cost is achieved. Beyond that point average unit costs will again increase.

c. Historically, many companies have utilized the concept of economies of scale; as a facility size becomes larger and production volume increases, the average unit cost for its output drops. Average unit cost continues to decrease until the facility becomes so large that diseconomies of scale occur.

8. There are five major reasons why firms initiate capacity planning projects: (1) increasing demand, (2) decreasing demand, (3) major technological changes, (4) changes in the firm's external environment, (5) competitive positioning.

a. The following steps need to be executed to perform effective capacity planning.

(1) Audit and evaluate existing capacity and facilities

(2) Forecast capacity or facilities requirements

(3) Define alternatives for meeting requirements

(4) Perform financial analyses of each alternative

(5) Assess key qualitative issues for each alternative

(6) Select alternative to pursue

(7) Implement the chosen alternative

(8) Audit and review actual results

b. A decision tree is a graphical model of a set of decision alternatives and their consequences. The use of decision trees in capacity planning provides a clear picture of capacity decisions and their outcomes over time. It allows managers to see exactly what is happening at each stage of the decision making process by showing its logical progression.

9. Making a decision on where to locate a facility is a key element in the strategic planning process for all types of organizations, from "mom-and-pop" stores to a Japanese auto manufacturer. Location decisions are among the first problems considered for new companies and an on-going problem for existing companies.

a. Location decisions are made infrequently, usually in response to a major capacity problem.

b. Location decisions have a long-term impact on both revenues and operating costs. A location decision, once made, cannot be easily changed.

c. Managers have several broad options available for making location decisions, under the assumption that additional capacity is needed. Four basic options are:

(1) Do nothing - use internal capacity adjustment techniques, such as, additional shifts, overtime, etc.

(2) Expand existing facility - only viable if expansion is possible at the existing location.

(3) Maintain the existing facility, and add an additional facility elsewhere - this will create a system of facilities.

(4) Close existing facility and move to another location - the most costly option.

d. A general approach to making location decisions consists of six broad steps:

(1) Perform a company oriented needs assessment.

(2) Determine strategies for making location decisions.

(3) Search for a feasible region using both objective and subjective criteria.

(4) Develop location alternatives.

(5) Evaluate and compare the location alternatives.

(6) Select a specific location site.

10. A location decision is made by selecting, in turn, a region, a community within the region, and a site within the community. The search process begins broadly and then is narrowed and focused. The broad search or evaluating regions and communities is termed "macro analysis" and the narrow search, the evaluation of specific sites is called "micro analysis".

   a. Regional decisions depend on the size and scope of the company. For a multinational company, the region may be an entire continent or several countries. For a large U.S. company, it may be a section of the United States, the Southwest, Northeast, etc. The region decision can be influenced by factors such as, market proximity, raw material proximately, transportation accessibility, labor supply, climate, etc.

   b. Once the region is selected, a specific community within that region must be chosen. Community location decisions are influenced by labor supply, wage levels, tax structures, living standards, community attitudes, etc.

   c. After choosing the community, the exact site within the community must be selected. Site selection decisions are influenced by, transportation access, land availability, availability of services, zoning restrictions, taxes, etc.

11. Research indicates that five groups of factors dominate location decisions for new manufacturing plants.

   a. Favorable labor climate - this would entail availability, prevailing wage rates, labor productivity, work attitudes, union activity, etc.

   b. Proximity to markets - this is particularly true for products that are heavy or bulky or involve high outbound finished goods transportation rates.

   c. Quality of life - executives from highly technical industries consider this the most important factor. Examples of quality of life factors are, quality schools, good recreational facilities, etc.

   d. Proximity to suppliers and resources - supplier proximity was rated lower than market proximity, an exception to this is for industries that transport bulky or heavy raw materials.

   e. Proximity to the parent companies facilities - this factor arose because of the many supply and communication linkages that exist in companies having multiple facilities.

12. For service industries, being close to customers is a primary factor influencing location: nine dominant factors relate to service facility location.

   a. Customer based - service facilities should be in close proximity to customers.

   b. Cost based - a location where operating costs are the lowest becomes the dominant consideration for some service companies such as wholesalers or specialty shops.

c. Competitor based - some service business locations are based on being close to their competitors.

d. Support services - location decisions are sometimes based on the proximity of support services.

e. Geographic/environmental - certain services must be located in specific geographic regions, e.g. ski resorts.

f. Business climate - what is the climate of business in a particular city, state, etc.

g. Communication based - some services tend to locate in large, highly developed cities that have excellent communication facilities.

h. Transportation based - a good transportation network may be the deciding factor in a service location decision.

i. Personal desires of the CEO - where the CEO wants to be may be the only reason for a service locating where it does.

13. Making the single facility location decision, whether it is a manufacturing or service facility can be approached using various techniques.

   a. Detailed cost analysis - this is the most direct method, each alternative site can be evaluated by performing detailed cost analysis.

   b. Factor rating systems - widely used technique that allows operations managers to incorporate their personal opinions as well as quantitative information.

   c. Center of gravity method - this is most often used to locate distribution warehouses. It incorporates the existing facilities, distances between them, location of markets, and volume of goods to be shipped.

   d. Locational cost-volume-profit analysis - this technique uses the demand volume, fixed costs, and variable costs to determine an optimal location.

14. Making the multiple facility location decision is more difficult than the single facility location decision. The possibility of multiple locations increases the complexity of facilities but also their locations, and the amount of interaction with existing and new facilities. The various techniques used to solve this problem are:

   a. Plant charters approach - organizations that have multiple plants have indicated that they use four distinct multiplant strategies, or "charters" under which these plants operate.

      (1) Product plant - produces a certain product line, or family of products, for distribution anywhere.

      (2) Market area plant - produces most of the products with distribution confined to the surrounding geographic area.

(3) Process plant - produces a certain segment of the full production process.

(4) General purpose plant - this is a flexible operation that can be assigned any number of responsibilities.

b. Transportation method - transportation method of linear program can be used to determine the minimum cost transportation routes.

c. Heuristics - are general guidelines or "rules of thumb" that can be used to obtain feasible, but not necessarily optimal solutions to problems.

d. Simulation - this is the process of developing a descriptive model of a particular problem and then conducting experiments using the model to determine performance measures for the problem.

e. Optimization methods - encompass a wide range of techniques designed to produce a set of "best" locations or "best" location - allocation decisions.

15. Four major trends in location decisions can be identified:

a. Business park proliferation - locating in business parks of many varieties is becoming an attractive alternative for firms.

b. Factories: research and development linkages - many U.S. firms are now planning to relocate their research and development facilities closer to the factory floor.

c. Globalization of production - operations managers are now thinking in terms of a world market for location.

d. The Sun Belt phenomenon - there is a noticeable trend of industry movement to states characterized as the "Sun Belt states".

KEY TERMS

a. actual capacity
b. actual output rate
c. allocation problem
d. best operating level
e. bottleneck
f. capacity
g. capacity cushion
h. capacity efficiency
i. capacity planning
j. capacity utilization
j. center of gravity method
l. decision tree
m. design capacity
n. diseconomies of scale
o. economies of scale
p. effective capacity

q. facility layout problem
r. facility location
s. factor rating systems
t. general purpose plant
u. heuristics
v. location problem
w. location-allocation problem
x. locational cost-volume analysis
y. locational cost-volume-profit analysis
z. market area plant
aa. optimization methods
bb. plant charters
cc. process plant
dd. product plant
ee. simulation
ff. transportation method

Chapter 6 - Long-Range Capacity Planning and Facility Location

DEFINITIONS

Directions: Select from the key terms list, the word or phrase being defined below.

_____ 1. the measure of quantity of output over time.

_____ 2. the rate of output that is truly achieved.

_____ 3. the level of capacity for which the average unit cost is at a minimum.

_____ 4. the amount by which the average utilization rate falls below 100%.

_____ 5. maximum capacity, or the target output rate.

_____ 6. as production volume increases, the average unit cost for its output drops.

_____ 7. the determination of a geographic location for a firm's operation.

_____ 8. technique for making location decisions that allows managers to incorporate their personal opinions.

_____ 9. general guidelines or rules of thumb.

_____ 10. a facility that produces a certain segment of the full production process.

_____ 11. a type of facility that produces a certain product line, or family of products for distribution anywhere.

_____ 12. special purpose algorithm that can be used to determine the minimum cost transportation plan.

_____ 13. specifying the level of productive capability of a facility that meets market demand in a cost-effective manner.

_____ 14. graphical model of a set of decision alternative and their consequences.

_____ 15. a factor that limits a facility's capacity to less than either its design capacity or effective capacity.

MULTIPLE CHOICE QUESTIONS

Directions: Indicate your choice of the best answer to each question.

1. Capacity planning involves questions about
   a. where to locate facilities.
   b. how much to produce.
   c. process selection for production.
   d. allocation decisions.
   e. all of the above.

2. If a company has too little capacity
   a. it may lose customers to competitors.
   b. may be forced to use subcontracting.
   c. will incur economies of scale.
   d. all of the above.
   e. only a and b.

3. Which of the following is NOT a measure of capacity?
   a. brake jobs completed per day
   b. calculators produced per month
   c. barrels of beer produced per day
   d. seats available in a classroom
   e. none of the above

4. The term effective capacity refers to the
   a. maximum rate of output, given quality standards, scheduling constraints, work force constraints, etc.
   b. rate of output achieved, given machine breakdowns, worker absenteeism, defects, etc.
   c. target output rate, or maximum productive capability of a facility.
   d. ratio of actual capacity to utilization.
   e. output that will minimize cost and meet forecasted demand.

5. The ratio of actual output to design capacity is
   a. utilization.
   b. actual capacity.
   c. efficiency.
   d. effective capacity.
   e. effectiveness.

6. Skinner's plant within plants concept is an example of
   a. flexible manufacturing.
   b. market area plant.
   c. focused factory.
   d. cellular manufacturing.
   e. heuristics.

7. Capacity strategy is typically based on a series of assumptions about
   a. predicted growth and variability of primary demand.
   b. costs of operating and building different sized plants.
   c. the likely behavior of competitors.
   d. all of the above.
   e. only a and b.

8. If plant utilization is 89%, the capacity cushion is ____.
   a. 5%
   b. 11%
   c. 50%
   d. 89%
   e. 100%

9. The rate of output that is achieved, due to machine breakdown, worker absenteeism, defects, and material shortages is
   a. design capacity.
   b. utilization rate.
   c. actual capacity.
   d. efficiency rate.
   e. effective capacity.

10. Which of the following describes the capacity timing strategy that anticipates and leads demand?
    a. positive capacity cushion
    b. capacity is used as a competitive weapon
    c. matching of capacity to forecasted demand
    d. all of the above
    e. only a and b

11. The capacity planning strategy of simply trying to have the right amount of capacity over time is to
    a. lag demand.
    b. simulate demand.
    c. anticipate and lead demand.
    d. closely follow demand.
    e. none of the above.

12. Which of the following describes the lag demand capacity timing strategy?
    a. matching of production capacity to forecasted demand
    b. higher return on investment
    c. positive capacity cushion
    d. all of the above
    e. only a and c

13. The best operating level is defined as
    a. level of capacity for which the average unit cost is at a minimum.
    b. the level of output that minimizes total costs.
    c. desired capacity level.
    d. level of capacity that satisfies demand.
    e. level of capacity for which marginal unit cost is at a minimum.

14. Which of the following is NOT a step in capacity planning?
    a. audit and evaluate existing capacity and facilities
    b. forecast capacity/facilities requirements
    c. define alternatives for meeting requirements
    d. identify optimal operating levels
    e. select alternative to be pursued

15. Which of the following is NOT true concerning facility location decisions?
    a. occurs in response to a major capacity problem
    b. decisions are made frequently
    c. used to expand markets
    d. occurs in response to shifts in customer demand
    e. occurs in response to changing labor conditions

16. As a facilities size becomes larger and its production volume increases, the average unit cost for its output drops, is an example of
    a. best operating level.
    b. economies of scale.
    c. capacity cushion.
    d. effective capacity.
    e. diseconomies of scale.

17. In facility location decisions, "micro analysis" refers to
    a. region decisions.
    b. community decisions.
    c. site decisions.
    d. universal decisions.
    e. both b and c.

18. Labor supply would most strongly influence
    a. region decisions.
    b. community decisions.
    c. site decisions.
    d. all of the above.
    e. both a and b.

19. In location decisions, which of the following are community considerations?
    a. raw material proximity.
    b. recreational opportunities.
    c. climate.
    d. zoning.
    e. all of the above.

20. Which of the following are NOT site related factors in facility location analysis?
    a. land availability
    b. labor supply
    c. air and water pollution restrictions
    d. zoning
    e. fire and police protection

21. A technique for making location decisions that allow managers to incorporate their personal opinions as well as quantitative information is the
    a. detailed cost analysis.
    b. factor rating system.
    c. center of gravity method.
    d. transportation method.
    e. Bender's decomposition approach.

22. Which of the following is NOT one of the plant charters approaches for firms having multiple facilities?
    a. product plant
    b. cellular plant
    c. market area plant
    d. process plant
    e. general purpose plant

23. Which of the following is NOT an example of a market area plant?
    a. frozen foods
    b. soft drink bottlers
    c. staple foods
    d. glass containers
    e. some furniture

24. General "rules of thumb" that are used to obtain feasible, but not necessarily optimal solutions are
    a. decision trees.
    b. factor rating scales.
    c. simulations.
    d. heuristics.
    e. linear programming.

25. Which of the following is NOT a major location trend identified in the text?
    a. movement to the suburbs
    b. business park proliferation
    c. factory/research and development linkages
    d. globalization of operations
    e. Sun Belt phenomenon

PROBLEMS

PROBLEM SITUATION # 1

Karen Shannon, COO of Neon, Inc. has constructed the following graph comparing average unit cost with output rate.

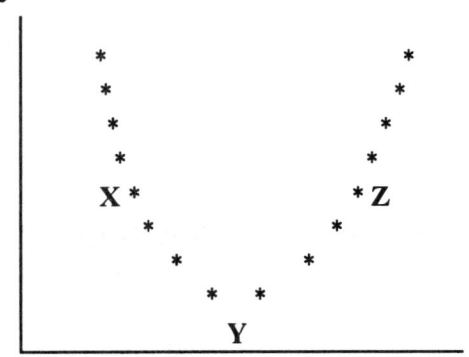

Average Unit Cost vs Output Rate (U-shaped curve with points X on left side, Y at bottom, Z on right side)

26. On the graph, point X would most closely reflect
    a. economies of scale.
    b. diseconomies of scale.
    c. bottlenecks.
    d. best operating level.
    e. actual capacity.

27. On the graph, point Y would most closely reflect
    a. economies of scale.
    b. diseconomies of scale.
    c. design capacity.
    d. best operating level.
    e. actual capacity.

28. On the graph, point Z would most closely reflect
    a. economies of scale.
    b. diseconomies of scale.
    c. design capacity.
    d. best operating level.
    e. actual capacity.

PROBLEM SITUATION # 2

Mathieu's Marble factory has collected the following information on its operation:

Design Capacity = 1,700 units/month
Effective Capacity = 1,200 units/month
Actual Capacity = 900 units/month

29. The Marble factory is operating with a capacity cushion of ____.
    a. .47
    b. .53
    c. .71
    d. .75
    e. none of the above

30. What is the capacity utilization of this facility?
    a. .47
    b. .53
    c. .71
    d. .75
    e. none of the above

31. What is the capacity efficiency of this factory?
    a. .47
    b. .53
    c. .71
    d. .75
    e. none of the above

PROBLEM SITUATION # 3

Performance Shipping Company is attempting to improve customer service by establishing a new transportation terminal. The current locations and volume shipped are:

Location	X	Y	Volume/month
Greenville	2	10	1,200
Fayetteville	9	7	900
Wilmington	11	3	1,500
Lumberton	7	4	2,000

32. Using the center of gravity method, what are the coordinates for the new location?
    a. 1.33, 5.50
    b. 5.50, 7.32
    c. 7.32, 1.33
    d. 7.32, 5.50
    e. none of the above

33. If the data gathered was incorrect, and the corrected monthly volume for Wilmington was 1,850, what would be the new location?
    a. 5.69, 8.00
    b. 7.32, 5.69
    c. 7.54, 5.35
    d. 8.00, 5.50
    e. none of the above

34. If the data given in the original problem was incorrect, and the corrected data showed a 16% increase in the volume at Greenville, what would the new Y coordinate be?
    a. 5.35
    b. 5.50
    c. 5.53
    d. 5.65
    e. none of the above

PROBLEM SITUATION # 4

A manufacturer of cellular phones is preparing to move his operation to a larger facility to accommodate increasing demand. Data concerning the two options available are as follows:

Location	Fixed Costs per year	Variable Costs per unit
A	$100,000	$72.00
B	$142,000	$50.00

35. The manufacturer would choose Location A at a volume level of _____.
    a. 1,900
    b. 1,950
    c. 2,150
    d. 2,500
    e. none of the above

84   Chapter 6 - Long-Range Capacity Planning and Facility Location

36. At what level of volume would the manufacturer choose location B?
    a. 1,850
    b. 1,900
    c. 1,905
    d. 1,910
    e. none of the above

37. At what level of volume would the manufacturer be indifferent between the two locations?
    a. 1,800
    b. 1,850
    c. 1,909
    d. 1,950
    e. 2,010

APPLICATION QUESTIONS

Shelia Karter is reviewing various factors concerning the relocation of her shirt manufacturing plant. She has collected the following data and constructed the Factor Rating scale shown.

Location Factor	Factor Weight	Factor Score Locations A	B	C
Market Proximity	30	8	7	9
Raw material Proximity	20	7	9	6
Labor supply	40	7	6	6
Climate	10	9	5	8

Key: 1 = poor, 10 = excellent

1. What is the weighted average score for location A?

2. What is the weighted average score for location B?

3. What is the weighted average score for location C?

4. Which location would she prefer based on the factor rating system developed? Why?

5. What factor score for location A's climate would make her indifferent between locations A and C?

6. An error was made in data collection, and the corrected factor score for location A is: labor supply = 6. What would be the revised weighted average score for location A.?

7. Suppose that in addition to the error identified in question 6 above, other errors were made. Suppose the corrected scores for location B are: raw material proximity = 10 and climate = 6. Which location would she now prefer? Why?

SHORT ANSWER QUESTIONS

1. What is the difference between design capacity, effective capacity, and actual capacity?

2. Why is the idea of a capacity cushion important in developing long-term capacity strategy?

3. Describe the three capacity-timing strategies.

4. Why are facility location decisions so important?

5. What are the dominant facility location factors for a manufacturing facility? For a service facility?

CHAPTER 7
MANAGING QUALITY

INTRODUCTION

QUALITY IN HISTORICAL PERSPECTIVE

QUALITY MANAGEMENT AS A STRATEGIC ISSUE
OPERATION MANAGEMENT IN PRACTICE 7.1: The Ritz-Carlton Hotel Co.
ISO9000 International Standards
Role of Quality in Manufacturing Strategy
GLOBAL OPERATIONS MANAGEMENT 7.2: A Global Comparison of Quality Capabilities
Malcolm Baldrige National Quality Award
OPERATIONS MANAGEMENT IN PRACTICE 7.3: 1996 Baldrige Award Winners

QUALITY MANAGEMENT LEADERSHIP
W. Edwards Deming
Joseph M. Juran
Philip B. Crosby

DEFINITIONS OF QUALITY
Quality as Excellence
Quality as Conformance to Specifications
Quality as Fitness for Use
Quality as Value for the Price

QUALITY-RELATED PRODUCT CHARACTERISTICS

QUALITY-RELATED SERVICE CHARACTERISTICS

COSTS OF QUALITY
Classifying the Costs of Quality
Interaction of Quality Costs

TOTAL QUALITY MANAGEMENT
TQM Requirements
TQM Implementation Process
Barriers to Implementing TQM

BUSINESS PROCESS REENGINEERING
OPERATIONS MANAGEMENT IN PRACTICE 7.4: Reengineering Taco Bell

CHAPTER SUMMARY

1. Intense competition from Japan and Western Europe forced American businesses to take a closer look at their current business practices. They found that the solution to the international quality challenge might be to manage the strategic quality activities of the firm to enhance competitive position.

2. Garvin explains the history of the American quality movement as a sequential changing of focus over time. He labels these significant phases in quality practice as the eras of:

   a. Inspection - this initial phase was the result of a need for replaceable parts from a stock of spares. This was achieved by the use of a "master part" to which all other manufactured parts were visually compared.

   b. Statistical quality control - W.A. Shewhart developed techniques for predicting the quality of manufactured goods by using statistical techniques to infer the characteristics of an entire population of items from the inspection of a sample of the items. His work was oriented toward process control through inspection and resulted in the development of the first process control charts. Further refinements resulted in the development of models of the average outgoing quality limit (AOQL) so that acceptance sampling procedures could extend beyond a test for a particular lot to a generalization about the entire manufacturing process.

   c. Quality assurance - the work of Juran and Feigenbaum asserted that quality was the responsibility of all workers and managers. The emphasis was on the entire production chain, from design to market, and the contribution of functional groups especially designers, in preventing quality failures.

   d. Strategic quality management - more recently, quality is understood to be a strategic issue which effects everyone and every process within an organization. U.S. firms are recognizing that competitive advantage can result from using the quality of products and services to increase international market share. This requires shifting the company orientation from conforming to design specifications of the product or service to conforming to customers' needs and expectations. In practice, these firms seek to exceed customer expectations.

3. A series of international standards have been created by the International Organization of Standards in conjunction with other international standards organizations to broadly define the components of quality in different industries. This series is known as ISO9000. Being certified under the ISO9000 standards does not necessarily mean that a company produces a top quality product. ISO9000 guarantees consistency not quality, and it is not customer focused. There are four elements of the standard.

   a. ISO9001 - the broadest element in the series. This element provides quality standards in organizations that design, produce, service and install products.

   b. ISO9002 - this is the same as ISO9001 except that is does not include the design and service of products.

   c. ISO9003 - this element is even more limited since it contains no standards for production and would be more suited to a warehousing operation.

   d. ISO9004 - this is not itself a standard, but rather provides information about how to interpret the other standards.

4. A useful model for thinking about the role of quality within operations strategy involves the concepts of order winners and order qualifiers.

   a. Certain characteristics that must be present in an acceptable combination for a product to be considered "in the running" are considered qualifiers. The presence of these attributes puts the product on a short list of potentially acceptable alternatives.

b. A single criterion that is applied to this list of qualified candidates in order to make a selection is called an order winner. These are dimensions that a customer uses to make a choice among competitors.

c. The challenge to competing firms comes when order winning criteria shift. By redefining quality in the eyes of the customer, the conformance measures of quality will soon be relegated to the category of qualifier, and evaluation of a new definition of quality will be necessary to win orders.

5. The Malcolm Baldrige National Quality Award was established in 1987 to emphasize the government's interest in encouraging and improving quality awareness in this country. Awards are provided annually to as many as two manufacturing companies, two service companies and two small businesses. Nominated companies are evaluated on a lengthy set of criteria. The criteria for the award helps provide guidance for management in their quality improvement efforts even if they have no intention of applying for the award. In the spirit of continuous improvement, the award criteria undergo critical evaluation every two years. This evaluation usually results in some minor adjustments to criteria or point values associated with the criteria. In 1997, rather dramatic changes were made to the criteria as compared to 1996 criteria.

6. W. Edwards Deming is recognized as a worldwide leader in the quality movement. In 1950 with American managers interested or unwilling to exert the effort to systematically improve manufacturing, he went to Japan where he began teaching the principles of statistical quality control to senior Japanese managers. For his efforts, he is credited for helping create the "Japanese industrial miracle". The top quality award in Japan is called the Deming Prize. Deming believed that over 90% of all business problems are management controllable. He also believed that improvements in productivity, innovation, participation and profits would be realized through sincere, focused quality improvement efforts. This overall management philosophy is described in his "14 points".

7. Joseph M. Juran describes the current quality transformation within business as a shift from "little Q" to "big Q". Businesses which practice little Q traditionally focus their quality efforts on the physical product or service provided their ultimate customers. The movement today is toward big Q which extends the application of quality concepts to all functional activities recognizing both internal and external customers. While Deming's activities were more focused on statistical process control, Juran was espousing the concept of total quality control. Juran's quality philosophy is based on three managerial processes,

    a. Quality planning

    b. Quality control

    c. Quality improvement

8. Philip B. Crosby is probably best noted for his book entitled "Quality is Free". He believes that doing things right the first time adds nothing to the cost of a product or service, but doing things wrong is what costs money. Crosby has been an outspoken critic of the Malcolm Baldrige National Quality Award, saying that companies tend to focus too much on winning the award rather than making long-term sustainable improvements in quality. Crosby believes that in order for an organization to change from traditional quality management to an innovative and enduring quality management process, an understanding of his "Four Absolutes of Quality Management" is required:

a. What is quality? (conformance to the requirements)

b. What system is needed to cause quality? (a system of prevention, not detection)

c. What performance standard should be used? (standard is zero defects)

d. What measurement system is required? (cost of conformance and the cost of non-conformance)

9. The way the quality of goods and services is defined continues to evolve. The lack of a clear definition of quality makes it difficult for organizations to measure, control, and manage it. Several definitions are:

a. Quality as "Excellence" - defining quality as the characteristic of attained "excellence" in a product or service is elusive, yet it is the most appropriate definition in some cases. Many product or services convey to the user some sense of personal pleasure or esteem. Perceived product "excellence" can be a significant competitive approach.

b. Quality as "Conformance to Specifications" - this approach to quality measurement attempts to measure the extent to which the product or service conforms to design specifications. No matter how the consumer perceives the product/service, if the product/service meets its design specifications, it is deemed to have achieved its quality objectives. If the design specifications are based on the needs and expectations of the customer, then Crosby's definition of quality "conformance to requirements" would be the same as "conformance to specifications".

c. Quality as "Fitness for Use" - this definition of quality includes the customers intended use for the product. The "fitness" concept requires that the design of the product be appropriate for the conditions and purpose of the user.

d. Quality as "Value for the Price" - this comprehensive definition of quality combines economic and consumer criteria with the fitness, conformance, and excellence concepts. This definition recognizes that our desire for conformance to a requirement is often price sensitive.

10. Closely related to the definitions of quality are the concepts of reliability, durability and serviceability. Each of these may be an important criterion for determining the conformance, fitness or value of a product or service.

a. Product reliability - designers describe this as a measure of a statistically random variable representing the mean time between failures (MTBF).

b. Durability - this is a concept that applies to products that are generally considered to be non-repairable. Durability is measured as the mean time to failure (MTTF).

c. Serviceability - this refers to the ease with which a failed product or machine can be returned to functional condition.

Other often used measures of product quality include: whether the product conforms to design specifications; if it performs as it should; if the features you expect are included with the product; if the aesthetics of the product suitable; and your basic perceptions of the product based on prior knowledge.

11. Accurate assessment of service quality is much more difficult than assessment of product quality. Similar characteristics which customers use to gauge the quality of services are:

   a. Reliability - ability to perform service dependably and accurately.

   b. Tangibles - appearance of physical facilities, equipment, personnel, etc.

   c. Responsiveness - willingness to help customers and provide prompt service.

   d. Assurance - front line personnel's knowledge and courtesy, do they convey trust and confidence.

   e. Empathy - individual care and attention.

These dimensions of service quality are useful in helping operations managers design and implement successful service quality initiatives.

12. The American Society for Quality Control (ASQC) has developed a typology of quality related costs that are in common use. The classification system is useful because operations managers can collect data consistent with this format, and identify the opportunities for controlling quality costs that will have the greatest impact. The four categories are:

   a. Internal failure costs - costs of scrap, rework, reinspection, lost production capacity, etc.

   b. External failure costs - include warranty claims, litigation, repairs and service costs. It also includes intangibles such as cost goodwill and reputation.

   c. Appraisal costs - include inspection costs that occur during material receiving, during manufacture, in laboratory testing, etc.

   d. Prevention costs - conducting design evaluations of new products or services, investments in training, and the design and development of new quality equipment, etc.

13. The best way to minimize failure costs is to ensure that defects are prevented during processing, rather than discovered later. Appraisal costs, almost by definition, will not be affected by the number of non-conforming units produced. Traditionally it has been assumed that the costs associated with prevention increase as the defect rate decreases. A current view contends that prevention costs do not increase marginally, and that systematic approaches to the prevention of defects do not increase cost.

14. A goal for business is to formulate an organization-wide approach to quality improvement. Many such efforts are underway and known by many names. The most commonly used term for these improvement programs is total quality management (TQM). There is essentially no difference between TQM and programs by other names such as total quality control (TQC), continuous quality improvement (CQI) and continuous process improvement (CPI).

   a. Total quality management is an organization-wide approach to total customer satisfaction and continuous process improvement. Experience has reveled several requirements which must be met in adopting TQM.

(1) Strategic quality planning - quality planning must be integrated into overall business planning for the entire organization. It should include a clear vision of what the organization desires to achieve with respect to customer satisfaction and continuous process improvement.

(2) Clear focus on "customer" satisfaction - TQM redefines the customer from traditional quality activities. TQM recognizes both internal and external customers, it focuses on the customer of each and every process.

(3) Continuous improvement of key processes - a process is an established series of steps or operations which together work toward a desired result. TQM works towards the concept of continuous process improvement, rather than setting goals which once achieved provide no more incentive for improvement.

(4) Effective collection and analysis of information - information is critical for success of total quality organization. Effective collection and analysis of information allows decisions to be based more on fact than intuition.

(5) Effective use of teamwork and training - process improvement relies heavily on the use of teams of individuals as problem solvers. Regardless of what you call the teams, it is critical to have workers involved in the process improvement activities.

(6) Effective design of products and services - to insure a total quality organization, the desired level of quality must be designed into the product or service. This helps prevent releasing a marginal product to the customer with all the resulting costs.

(7) Effective leadership - leaders in total quality organizations must help create and communicate a clear vision and at every opportunity demonstrate their personal commitment. Without effective leadership, little will be gained through the quality movement.

15. TQM implementations methods will vary according to the individual organization, one general approach to total quality implementation incorporates the following steps: (1) identify critical business issues, (2) secure top management commitment, (3) provide initial training, (4) identify customer requirements, (5) identify key processes, (6) provide specific skills training, (7) collect and analyze data, (8) implement process changes, (9) commit to continuous improvement of key processes.

16. It is thought that in order for companies to compete in ever changing international markets, total quality must be an integral part of their culture. TQM is not a panacea nor is it easily or quickly implemented in the typical organization. Experience has revealed several barriers to successful implementation. Failure of an organization to realize the full potential of total quality can often be attributed to one of these barriers.

17. Business process reengineering is the fundamental rethinking and radical redesign of business processes to achieve dramatic improvements in strategically important measures of performance. Reengineering a company means throwing out all existing structures, procedures and systems and inventing completely new models of organizing and accomplishing work.

KEY TERMS

a. appraisal costs
b. assurance
c. business process reengineering
d. Philip B. Crosby
e. W. Edwards Deming
f. durability
g. empathy
h. external failure costs
i. inspection
j. internal failure costs
k. ISO9000
l. Joseph M. Juran
m. kaizen
n. Malcolm Baldrige National Quality Award
o. order qualifiers
p. order winners
q. poka-yoke
r. prevention costs
s. process
t. product reliability
u. quality assurance
v. quality circle
w. reliability
x. responsiveness
y. serviceability
z. statistical quality control
aa. strategic quality management
bb. tangibles
cc. total quality management

DEFINITIONS

Directions: Select from the key terms list, the word or phrase being defined below.

_____ 1. costs incurred to assess quality and that include costs of inspecting material upon arrival.

_____ 2. an established series of steps or operations that, when accomplished, lead to a desired result or product.

_____ 3. a term used to describe early team activities for process improvement.

_____ 4. the visual comparison of manufactured parts to a "master part".

_____ 5. a series of international standards for quality.

_____ 6. characteristics of competitive products that must be present in an acceptable combination to be considered "in the running" for consumer purchase.

_____ 7. a criterion that consumers use to make a selection among competing products.

_____ 8. national quality award established to emphasize the government's interest in encouraging and improving quality awareness in this country.

_____ 9. he is credited for creating the "Japanese industrial miracle".

_____ 10. costs incurred to prevent defects from occurring in the first place.

_____ 11. costs incurred with finding and fixing defects found outside the organization.

_____ 12. concept applied to products that are usually considered non-repairable, measured as mean time to failure.

_____ 13. the ease with which a failed product can be returned to functional condition.

_____ 14. the ability to perform the promised service dependably and accurately.

_____ 15. willingness to help customers and provide prompt service.

_____ 16. costs incurred on non-conforming products before they leave the ownership of the firm.

_____ 17. organization-wide approach to total customer satisfaction and continuous process improvement.

_____ 18. quality techniques oriented toward the design of production systems which are nearly fool proof.

_____ 19. Japanese term to denote continuous process improvement.

_____ 20. the fundamental rethinking and radical redesign of business processes.

MULTIPLE CHOICE QUESTIONS

Directions: Indicate your choice of the best answer to each question.

1. The quality revolution in American industry has come about in part because of intense competition from
   a. Japan.
   b. Germany.
   c. Western Europe.
   d. all of the above.
   e. only a and b.

2. The impetus for the quality assurance phase of the quality movement can be linked to
   a. the need for interchangeable parts.
   b. the idea that quality is the responsibility for all workers.
   c. the development of mathematical techniques for predicting the quality of manufactured goods.
   d. the idea that quality can be used as a competitive weapon.
   e. all of the above.

3. The era of inspection's primary emphasis is on
   a. the market and consumer needs.
   b. the entire production chain, from design to market.
   c. product uniformity.
   d. product uniformity with reduced inspection.
   e. all of the above.

4. The primary concern for the era of statistical quality control is
   a. detection.
   b. process control.
   c. coordination.
   d. strategic impact.
   e. none of the above.

5. Methods used in the inspection phase of the quality movement are
   a. programs and systems.
   b. statistical tools and techniques.
   c. goal setting and mobilizing the organization.
   d. gauging and measurement.
   e. all of the above.

6. Responsibility for quality in the Strategic Quality Management era belongs to
   a. all departments, with top management only peripherally involved.
   b. the manufacturing and engineering departments.
   c. the inspection department.
   d. everyone in the organization, with top management exercising strong leadership.
   e. none of the above.

7. The orientation and approach of the Strategic Quality Management era is to
   a. "inspect in" quality.
   b. "manage in" quality.
   c. "control in" quality.
   d. "build in" quality.
   e. none of the above.

8. Which stage of the quality movement attempts to "manage in" quality?
   a. inspection
   b. statistical quality control
   c. quality assurance
   d. strategic quality management
   e. none of the above

9. The element of the ISO9000 series that provides for quality standards in organizations that design, produce, service and install products is
   a. ISO9001.
   b. ISO9002.
   c. ISO9003.
   d. ISO9004.
   e. none of the above.

10. The ISO9002 element provides for
    a. information about how to interpret the various standards.
    b. quality standards in organizations that design, produce, service and install products.
    c. quality standards in organizations that produce and install products.
    d. quality standards in organizations that install or store products.
    e. none of the above.

11. In 1987 to emphasize the government's interest in encouraging and improving quality awareness in this country, an award was established named after
    a. W. Edwards Deming.
    b. Malcolm Baldrige.
    c. Joseph M. Juran.
    d. Armand Feigenbaum.
    e. Philip Crosby.

12. The Malcolm Baldrige National Quality Award can be presented to
    a. manufacturing firms.
    b. service firms.
    c. small businesses.
    d. all of the above.
    e. only a and b.

13. The Malcolm Baldrige National Quality Award criteria
    a. provides guidance for management in their improvement efforts.
    b. provide a mechanism by which companies may assess their individual performance.
    c. compare their organizations with others.
    d. all the above.
    e. only a and b.

14. W. Edwards Deming is often credited with
    a. developing total quality management.
    b. Japanese industrial miracle.
    c. quality is free.
    d. all of the above.
    e. only a and c.

15. Joseph M. Juran's quality control philosophy is based on all the following EXCEPT
    a. choice of unit of measure.
    b. setting goals.
    c. measure actual performance.
    d. diagnose the cause.
    e. interpret the difference.

16. A definition of quality that implies that Timex and Rolex watches have equal quality is
    a. quality as excellence.
    b. quality as conformance to design specification.
    c. quality as fitness for use.
    d. quality as value for price.
    e. none of the above.

17. Which of the following is NOT a term normally used to describe product quality?
    a. reliability
    b. serviceability
    c. responsiveness
    d. durability
    e. none of the above

18. Durability is a concept that applies to products that are generally considered to be
    a. repairable.
    b. expensive.
    c. non-repairable.
    d. high quality.
    e. none of the above.

19. Which of the following is NOT a category of quality related costs developed by the American Society for Quality Control?
    a. internal failure costs
    b. external failure costs
    c. appraisal costs
    d. rework costs
    e. prevention costs

20. Which of the following is an example of external failure costs?
    a. scrap
    b. reinspection
    c. rework
    d. lost goodwill
    e. lost production capacity

21. Appraisal costs include all of the following EXCEPT
    a. costs that occur at incoming material inspection.
    b. costs that occur from inspections during product manufacture.
    c. costs that occur through training programs.
    d. costs that occur during laboratory testing.
    e. costs that occur by the use of outside inspectors.

22. Which of the following is NOT a requirement that must be met in a TQM adopting organization?
    a. strategic quality planning
    b. identify critical business issues
    c. clear focus on customer satisfaction
    d. effective use of teamwork and training
    e. effective design of products and services

23. A statement that describes some future state of excellence is
    a. order winners.
    b. quality assurance.
    c. mission.
    d. strategic alliance.
    e. vision.

24. The term used in Japan to denote continuous improvement is
    a. poka-yoke.
    b. total quality management.
    c. ISO9000.
    d. kaizen.
    e. none of the above.

25. The element of the ISO9000 series that provides for quality standards in organizations that install or store products is
    a. ISO9001.
    b. ISO9002.
    c. ISO9003.
    d. ISO9004.
    e. none of the above.

26. Certain characteristics of competitive products that must be present in an acceptable combination to be considered "in the running" for consumer purchase are
    a. order winners.
    b. assurance.
    c. poka-yoke.
    d. qualifiers.
    e. none of the above.

27. The fundamental rethinking and radical redesign of business processes to achieve dramatic improvements in strategically important measures of performance is
    a. poka-yoke.
    b. kaizen.
    c. total quality management.
    d. ISO9000.
    e. none of the above.

28. The quality characteristic that refers to products generally considered to be non-repairable is
    a. reliability.
    b. durability.
    c. conformance.
    d. serviceability.
    e. none of the above.

29. The suggested approach to implementing TQM begins with
    a. effectively designing products and services.
    b. providing initial training.
    c. identifying critical business issues.
    d. collecting and analyzing data.
    e. identifying customer requirements.

30. According to Philip Crosby, the most appropriate definition of quality is
    a. exceeding needs and expectations of the customer.
    b. conformance to requirements.
    c. conformance to specifications.
    d. fitness for use.
    e. excellence.

SHORT ANSWER QUESTIONS

1. Describe the significant eras in the history of the American quality movement. What was the emphasis in each?

2. What is ISO9000? What are its components?

3. What is the Malcolm Baldrige National Quality Award? How is the award administered? Why do you think that the number of nominations for the award been decreasing over the last several years?

4. Briefly describe the philosophies of W. Edwards Deming, Joseph M. Juran, and Philip B. Crosby.

5. Describe the four categories of quality costs and provide two examples of each.

CHAPTER 8
TECHNOLOGICAL DEVELOPMENTS IN OPERATIONS MANAGEMENT

INTRODUCTION

ROLE OF TECHNOLOGY IN TODAY'S BUSINESS ENVIRONMENT
    Technology and the Environment
    OPERATIONS MANAGEMENT IN PRACTICE 8.1: DuPont Generates Energy from Garbage
    GLOBAL OPERATIONS MANAGEMENT 8.2: Japan Bids for Global Leadership in Clean Industry
    Technology-Focused Strategic Alliances

TRANSFERRING NEW TECHNOLOGY FROM CONCEPT TO REALITY

IMPLEMENTING NEW TECHNOLOGY

FIXED, PROGRAMMABLE, AND FLEXIBLE AUTOMATION

COMPUTER-INTEGRATED MANUFACTURING
    Computer-Aided Design
    Computer-Aided Manufacturing
        Numerically Controlled Machines
        Robotics
        Flexible Manufacturing Systems
        Automatic Identification of Parts

TECHNOLOGICAL IMPROVEMENTS FOR SUPPORT
    Artificial Intelligence: Adaptive Technology for the '90s
    Virtual Reality
    OPERATIONS MANAGEMENT IN PRACTICE 8.3: The Marvels of "Virtual Reality"
    Technological Improvements in Communications
    GLOBAL OPERATIONS MANAGEMENT 8.4: Motorola Plans New Satellite Ventures
        Internet
        Intranets

CHAPTER SUMMARY

1. Much of the change we have witnessed in the world around us can be attributed to technology. Technology is one of the most significant issues facing both manufacturing and service companies today.

    a. Technology can increase productivity by (1) reducing costs, (2) improving quality and (3) improving customer responsiveness.

    b. Many of the technological advances are computer based. Some may seem dated, but they are dated in theory only. It has taken decades in some cases for these advances to be applied and accepted in industry.

2. Technology is the application of scientific knowledge. Every task that is accomplished has some associated level of technology.

   a. A task which involves no new technology is considered a low technology task.

   b. A task which involves several new key technologies integrated together is considered to be a high technology task.

3. In general, the application of technology to manufacturing and service operations is intended to improve organizational performance through: (1) improved product and service quality; (2) lower cost; (3) increased responsiveness; (4) increased responsiveness to customers; (5) more flexibility; (6) improved safety; (7) reduced work-in-process inventories; (8) increased long-term profitability.

   a. It must be stressed that it is not always true that a higher level of technology is preferred to a lower level. The key is that any changes in technology must be a strategic decision. Changes in technology permeate the entire organization and can have profound and long lasting implications on the competitive abilities of the firm.

4. Recent survey results show that consumers overwhelmingly feel that business and industry are not concerned enough with environmental problems. The same survey showed that consumers themselves were extremely environmentally conscious. This consumer optimism is based in part on improvements in technology. These same new technologies are being used to develop new products and processes enabling manufacturers to utilize resources more efficiently and reduce waste.

5. Technology has served as the catalyst for many joint ventures between companies in the U.S. and abroad. These strategic alliances have been organized in an attempt to improve the competitiveness of each member company. Strategic alliances are formed in part to: (1) gain access to needed expertise and (2) gain access to new markets.

6. Technology transfer is the process by which technology is applied in the work place or shared between members of a strategic alliance. In the case of foreign alliance members, technology transfer becomes a serious issue since much of the technology is computer technology and national security interests must be considered.

7. While new technology can be treated as the savior of many U.S. companies, others have been relatively slow in adopting new technology. Reluctance to adopt new technology is often due to several barriers.

   a. One such barrier is economic justification for the new technology. Traditional financial accounting practices are not designed to recognize many advantages of new technology.

   b. Another barrier is that management may fail to understand the capabilities of the new technology. If you fail to understand and prepare for the revolutionary capabilities of these systems, they will become as much an inconvenience as a benefit and a lot more expensive.

   c. Another key barrier is the impact of the new technology on the people of the organization. Technological change is thought by many to have a detrimental effect on the organization.

   d. The results of a study conducted to assess the impact of technological change on an organization identified five fallacies which relate to the belief that advanced technology is bad for people.

Fallacy 1: Job loss is the main human resource impact of technological change.

Fallacy 2: The main impact of technological change is on hourly workers.

Fallacy 3: Job design and other technical issues should be handled by experts

Fallacy 4: New automated systems will reduce the need for interpersonal communications on the factory floor and in the office.

Fallacy 5: Technological change is bad for people.

8. Automation is defined as the substitution of machine work for human physical and mental work. There are three basic types of automation being used in manufacturing and service organizations today:

   a. Fixed automation - used in primarily high volume assembly situations were the sequence of processing steps is fixed. Major drawback is its relative inflexibility.

   b. Programmable automation - used to overcome some of the concerns with the inflexibility of fixed automation. This type of automation allows the production of different product designs as long as the differences are not dramatic. Major drawback is that the production system is usually out of service while reprogramming is taking place.

   c. Flexible automation - an automated production facility which can be adapted to a wider variety of product designs. In addition to their flexibility, changeovers can be accomplished with minimal downtime, therefore products can be produced without the necessity of producing in batches.

9. Computer integrated manufacturing (CIM) or enterprise integration is a formal process by which integration of organizational functions may be achieved. CIM can be viewed as the umbrella structure that ties the entire integration activity together. CIM does not necessarily require automation as some people believe. What is required is computer technology as the mechanism by which integration might be accomplished. While management must do the integrating, the computer will be the tool which allows successful management of the system. There are four very simple managerial factors important to the success of a CIM implementation.

   a. Scoping the CIM program - how much to spend and where?

   b. Setting goals and objectives - what specific measurable results are sought?

   c. Choosing the right planning horizon - short-term or long-term.

   d. Applying sound methodologies - what is the step-by-step process for getting results?

If a fifth factor was added to the above list it would relate to human resource considerations in the firm.

10. Computer-aided design (CAD) is defined as the use of computers in interactive engineering drawing and storage of designs. One of the most important uses of CAD today is to quickly create good product designs which are easy to manufacture. CAD encourages experimentation, yields better quality products and helps products get introduced more quickly.

11. Computer-aided manufacturing (CAM) is defined as the use of computers to program, direct, and control production equipment in the fabrication of manufactured items. Typically, CAM applications would include coordination of many other technologies such as:

   a. Numerically controlled machines (NC) - most basic NC machines use prerecorded coded instructions as a means of control. A new generation of NC machines called computer numerically controlled (CNC) machines are attached to a dedicated minicomputer where the NC coded instructions reside. The most advanced NC machines are the direct numerically controlled (DNC) machines where individual machining stations are networked through a central mainframe computer.

12. Robotics is defined as replacing functions previously done by humans with robots that can either be operated by people or run by computer. Robotics are an integral part of an integrated, automated manufacturing system. Robots provide consistency, precision and quality that humans cannot.

13. Flexibility is a key issue in strategic plan formulation. Flexibility means quickly changing something that is currently being done or changing completely to adjust to new product designs. Traditional fixed automation manufacturing facilities, while efficient, are often very inflexible. Similarly, extremely flexible operations are often very inefficient. To get both efficiency and flexibility, flexible manufacturing systems (FMS) may be the key.

   a. Flexible manufacturing systems (FMS) - consist of a group of processing stations, physically interconnected by an automated material handling and storage system and controlled by a computer. An FMS is capable of processing a variety of different products at the same time at various workstations with essentially no set-up time. In larger facilities using FMS, there is an increased use of automated guided vehicles (AGV) for moving parts to and from FMS cells. A completely integrated FMS could employ an automated storage and retrieval system (AS/RS).

14. Bar coding is the most used and recognized form of automatic identification of parts. Bar coding allows data to be quickly and accurately collected and managed effectively through the use of computer technology. Bar code systems involve three elements, (1) the bar code symbol, (2) the symbol reader, (3) the printing process. Situations where conditions such as temperature, dirt, clutter, etc. make bar coding ineffective, the use of radio frequency (RF) identification is often more useful.

15. Artificial intelligence (AI) is an emerging technology which is based on the computer's expert use of information. Basically, AI is thought of as a general field of study in which several different approaches have been taken.

   a. Expert systems - knowledge-based systems where expert human knowledge is converted to rules for the computer's use. The computer uses the rules to evaluate different situations.

   b. Neural networks - based on biological or mathematical models designed to imitate the way the brain works. Neural networks represent a set of very powerful mathematical techniques for modeling, optimization, and control that "learn" processes directly from historical data.

   c. Fuzzy logic - another adaptive technology that is being used in many equipment and plant applications. Comparing "fuzzy" rules to those in a traditional rules based expert system, it can be seen that fuzzy rules are softer and more intuitive in their specification.

   d. Virtual reality - virtual reality allows the operator to become a participant in the computer program execution. This technology is promising to revolutionize the way people interact with their computers.

16. There have been many other technological advancements recently which have allowed significant company wide improvements.

    a. Electronic data interchange (EDI) - through EDI, key vendors are linked by computer network to a company where up-to-date information is readily shared.

    b. Electronic mail - this had become the preferred communication type in most organizations.

    c. Electronic pagers

    d. Cellular phones

    e. Internet - a physical network of computer systems worldwide

    f. Intranet - internal organization's "internets"

KEY TERMS

a. artificial intelligence (AI)
b. automated guided vehicles (AGV)
c. automated storage and retrieval system (AS/RS)
d. automatic identification of parts
e. automation
f. bar coding
g. cellular telephones
h. computer-aided design (CAD)
i. computer-aided manufacturing (CAM)
j. computer integrated manufacturing (CIM)
k. electronic data interchange (EDI)
l. electronic mail
m. electronic pager
n. enterprise integration
o. expert system
p. fixed automation
q. flexibility
r. flexible automation
s. flexible manufacturing systems (FMS)
t. fuzzy logic
u. Internet
v. Intranet
w. neural network
x. numerically controlled machines (NC)
y. programmable automation
z. radio frequency (RF) identification
aa. robotics
bb. strategic alliance
cc. technology
dd. technology transfer
ee. universal product code (UPC)
ff. virtual reality
gg. World-Wide-Web

DEFINITIONS

Direction: Select from the key term list the word or phrase being defined below.

_____ 1. the application of scientific knowledge.

_____ 2. joint ventures between companies in an attempt to improve competitiveness of each member company.

106   *Chapter 8 - Technological Developments in Operations Management*

_____ 3. the process by which the application of scientific knowledge is applied in the work place or shared by members of a strategic alliance.

_____ 4. the substitution of machine work for human physical and mental work.

_____ 5. a type of automation used primarily in high volume assembly situations.

_____ 6. a type of automation that can be adopted to a wide variety of product designs with changeovers requiring minimal downtime.

_____ 7. the formal process by which integration of organizational functions may be achieved.

_____ 8. the ability to quickly change something that is currently being done or changing completely to adjust to new product designs.

_____ 9. an emerging technology whose goal is to make the computer act more human through its ability to reason and respond.

_____ 10. a knowledge-based system where superior human knowledge is converted to rules for the computers use.

_____ 11. networks that are based on biological or mathematical models designed to imitate the way the brain works.

_____ 12. technology that will allow the operator to become a participant in the computer's program execution.

_____ 13. another term that has been used to reflect the most recent view of CIM.

_____ 14. the use of computers to program, direct, and control production equipment in the fabrication of manufactured items.

_____ 15. the use of computers in interactive engineering drawing and storage of designs.

MULTIPLE CHOICE QUESTIONS

Directions: Indicate your choice of the best answer to each question.

1. Technology can be used to
   a. reduce costs.
   b. improve quality.
   c. improve customer responsiveness.
   d. increase flexibility.
   e. all of the above.

2. The application of scientific knowledge is
   a. strategic alliances.
   b. technology.
   c. automation.
   d. CIM.
   e. strategic alliances.

3. Which of the following is NOT a result of the application of technology?
   a. improved product and service quality
   b. lower cost
   c. more flexibility
   d. improved safety
   e. none of the above

4. Technology can be applied in all industries EXCEPT
   a. medicine.
   b. transportation.
   c. sports.
   d. fast food.
   e. none of the above.

5. Key reasons for strategic alliance failures are
   a. cultural differences.
   b. personality conflicts.
   c. short-term focus.
   d. all of the above.
   e. a and c only.

6. Technology transfer is
   a. the substitution of machine work for human physical and mental work.
   b. the formal process by which integration of organizational functions may be achieved.
   c. the process by which scientific knowledge is applied in the work place.
   d. the use of computers to program, direct and control production equipment.
   e. the application of scientific knowledge.

7. Which of the following is NOT a fallacy associated with advanced technology?
   a. Job loss is the main human resource impact of technological change.
   b. Cost savings may accrue with the implementation of new technology.
   c. Job design and other technical issues should be handled by experts.
   d. Technological change is bad for people.
   e. None of the above.

8. A study conducted by the National Association of Manufacturers found the majority of respondents were currently skillful at using
   a. computer-aided design.
   b. flexible manufacturing systems.
   c. expert systems.
   d. manufacturing cells.
   e. robotics.

9. The substitution of machine work for human physical and mental work is
   a. technology transfer.
   b. automation.
   c. computer integrated manufacturing.
   d. enterprise integration.
   e. flexible automation.

10. Fixed automation would be used primarily
    a. in the production of different product designs as long as the differences are not dramatic.
    b. in production facilities which can be adapted to a wide variety of product designs.
    c. in production facilities using computer-aided manufacturing.
    d. in high volume assembly situations.
    e. none of the above.

11. Relative inflexibility is the major drawback to
    a. expert systems.
    b. fixed automation.
    c. programmable automation.
    d. flexible automation.
    e. all of the above.

12. A major drawback to programmable automation is
    a. production system is usually out of service while changeovers are taking place.
    b. extreme inflexibility.
    c. employee training costs.
    d. lack of production volume.
    e. all of the above.

13. Flexible automation would be used primarily
    a. in the production of different product designs as long as the differences are not dramatic.
    b. in production facilities which can be adapted to a wide variety of product designs.
    c. used primarily in high volume assembly situations where standardized products are produced.
    d. product oriented layouts.
    e. none of the above.

14. A type of automation used in the production of different product designs as long as the differences are not dramatic is
    a. flexible.
    b. programmable.
    c. fixed.
    d. expert systems.
    e. none of the above.

15. Enterprise integration is another term for
    a. expert systems.
    b. automation.
    c. flexible automation.
    d. CIM.
    e. CAD/CAM.

16. In CIM, management must do the integrating, the _____ will be the tool which allows successful management of the system.
    a. expert system
    b. computer
    c. artificial intelligence
    d. fuzzy logic
    e. neural network

17. Which of the following is NOT a managerial factor important to the success of a CIM implementation?
    a. setting goals and objectives
    b. scoping the CIM program
    c. choosing the right planning horizon
    d. applying sound methodologies
    e. none of the above

18. CAD is
    a. the process by which scientific knowledge is applied in the work place.
    b. the use of computers in interactive engineering drawing and storage of designs.
    c. the use of computers to program, direct and control production equipment in the fabrication of manufactured items.
    d. the substitution of machine work for human physical and mental work.
    e. the application of scientific knowledge.

19. The use of CAD encourages
    a. experimentation.
    b. better quality products.
    c. quicker new product introduction.
    d. all of the above.
    e. only b and c.

20. The use of computers to program, direct, and control production equipment in the fabrication of manufactured items is
    a. CAD.
    b. FMS.
    c. CAM.
    d. EDI.
    e. AS/RS.

21. Replacing functions previously done by humans with machines that can either be operated by people or run by computer is known as
    a. automation.
    b. technology transfer.
    c. robotics.
    d. computer-aided manufacturing.
    e. all of the above.

22. Essentially no set up times, small lot sizes and the capability to process a variety of different products best describes
    a. programmable automation.
    b. computer-aided design.
    c. flexible manufacturing systems.
    d. expert system.
    e. none of the above.

23. Which of the following is NOT an example of engineering functions associated with computer-aided design?
    a. geometric modeling
    b. product design
    c. automatic identification of parts
    d. automatic drafting
    e. none of the above

24. A knowledge-based system where superior human knowledge is converted to rules for the computer's use is known as
    a. virtual reality.
    b. fuzzy logic.
    c. an expert system.
    d. a neural network.
    e. artificial intelligence.

25. Adaptive technology that is being used effectively in many equipment and plant control applications where there is a need for developing more realistic constraints used for system optimization is
    a. virtual reality.
    b. fuzzy logic.
    c. an expert system.
    d. a neural network.
    e. artificial intelligence.

26. Technology which allows key vendors to be linked by computer network to a company where up-to-date information may be shared is
    a. an expert system.
    b. electronic mail.
    c. electronic data interchange.
    d. radio frequency identification.
    e. all of the above.

27. The _____ is the physical network of computer systems world-wide.
    a. expert system
    b. neural network
    c. information highway
    d. World-Wide-Web
    e. Internet

28. While on the *Rolling Stone's* website, you click an icon (an access point) to other sites. What is this access point called?
   a. hyperlink
   b. access connect
   c. conlink
   d. transfer protocol (TCP/IP)
   e. URL

29. What is an organization-wide Internet that restricts entry from outside the organization?
   a. neural network
   b. firewall
   c. orgnet
   d. intranet
   e. expert system

30. CIM links the business functions with the _____ function of a manufacturing organization.
   a. production
   b. purchasing
   c. engineering
   d. marketing
   e. research & development

SHORT ANSWER QUESTIONS

1. What is computer-aided manufacturing?

2. What different technologies provide automatic identification of parts? Where and why are they useful?

3. Briefly discuss the barriers to effective implementation of technology.

4. Discuss the differences and similarities between fixed, programmable, and flexible automation.

5. Discuss the importance of flexibility in today's manufacturing and service organizations.

CHAPTER 9
ORGANIZATION AND HUMAN RESOURCES

INTRODUCTION

STRATEGIC HUMAN RESOURCES PLANNING

SOCIOTECHNICAL ORGANIZATIONS
Adaptive Organizational Structures
Keys to Worker Productivity

HUMAN RESOURCE ISSUES OF THE 1990s AND BEYOND
Governmental Regulations
Work Force Diversity
Manager as Leader
Participative Management
Team Activities
OPERATIONS MANAGEMENT IN PRACTICE 9.1: Multidisciplinary Teams at Dettmers Industries
Fear in the Work Place
Training and Development
GLOBAL OPERATIONS MANAGEMENT 9.2: Preparing U.S. Managers for Work Abroad
Benefits, Compensation, Recognition, and Reward
    Benefits
    Compensation
    OPERATIONS MANAGEMENT IN PRACTICE 9.3: Linking Customer Loyalty to Compensation at Pizza Hut
    Recognition and Rewards
The Inevitability of Change

WORK MEASUREMENT
Time Studies
Elemental Standard Times
Predetermined Standard Times

LEARNING EFFECTS ON TIME STANDARD ESTIMATION
The Learning Curve
Uses of Learning Curve Concept

CHAPTER SUMMARY

1. The quality movement and advances in technology both have had significant impact on all organizations. These changes are having the greatest impact on the utilization of human resources.

2. Due to the rapid introduction and use of technology in organizations today, we often refer to them as sociotechnical organizations.

3. The primary reason for the high failure rate of new technology implementation has been the explicit neglect of human resource factors. It is imperative that one consider the human factor in both decisions to purchase and implement new technology.

   a. HR managers can play a significant role in linking human resource management practices with the strategic goals of the firm. An effective organization requires a HR function that is proactive rather than reactive.

   b. The model of strategic human resource management describes the human resource environment which must be prepared to deal with both external and internal pressures which result in changing requirements. The model incorporates external factors, such as; (1) social, (2) economic, (3) technical, (4) business, and (5) political, all of which have an influence on the internal elements of: (1) structure, (2) culture, (3) politics, and (4) strategy. Both the external and internal factors have an impact on the development of strategic human resource management.

4. A school of thought has emerged to help explain the relationship between the social and technical elements of the organization. This school of thought called the sociotechnical organization is thought to have first been used by Eric L. Trist in the 1950s.

   a. Trist found that productivity and morale problems could be solved by simply looking at the human side of the organization.

   b. He learned that personal attitudes and group dynamics were influenced by the technical environment.

   c. This sociotechnical system (STS) view indicates that one must study both the social and technical areas of an organization, as well as their interaction, in order to comprehend and effectively address operational problems.

   d. The history of organizations reveals that the focus has been on controlling employee behavior and not encouraging independent thought or flexibility.

5. The emerging need for flexibility, participation, and teamwork in the organization, has led to a discussion on which organizational structures are best suited for accomplishing these goals.

   a. For stable industries, the hierarchical organization structure may be appropriate.

   b. In dynamic organizations, a traditional organizational structure creates barriers which impede necessary communication and cross functional cooperation. Dynamic organizations need the ability to quickly and efficiently get new products or major changes in products to market, respond to changes in customer desires, etc.

   c. Adaptive organizations are characterized by significant employee involvement through their use of teams, projects and alliances, with the goal of unleashing employee creativity. This structure is similar to the structure used in the construction industry where a team of experts from all needed skills is formed to complete a project.

6. At the root of this organizational evolution toward improved competitiveness is the need for improved productivity; as measured as output per unit of input.

a. The key to improved productivity is to identify the right mix of technological advancements and worker skill for the particular situation. In STS terminology, companies need to find the right social/technical balance.

b. It may be true that a lower level of technology and a better trained and motivated work force will yield better results than a higher level of technology with less emphasis on the work force.

c. Many successful companies have recognized their workers as an intellectual resource and are "exploring" worker potential. Who is in a better position to recognize potential problems and be able to recommend practical solutions to those problems than the workers who have worked in that area for years?

d. These are numerous approaches to enhancing productivity, the text lists a series of actions that a typical organization may choose all or part of to enhance their individual productivity. The list presented closely follows the requirements listed in Chapter 7 for successful Total Quality Management implementations. The similarity of these two lists highlights the necessity for cultural change from the top to the bottom of the organization.

7. Governmental regulation is one of the most significant issues facing HR professionals. One such example is the American With Disabilities Act (ADA). This act requires that disabled employees be granted the same opportunities for advancement, training, compensation, access, etc. as their non-handicapped peers. Another, the Age Discrimination in Employment Act (ADEA) protects workers age 40 and up from age discrimination.

8. Work force diversity is an evolving trend challenging HR managers today. In addition to an aging work force, it is predicted that by the year 2000, African-Americans, Hispanic, and Asian-Americans will make up 53 percent of the new work force entrants and 34 percent of all workers. Recent research shows that managing diversity is not only the ethical thing to do, but can actually be a source of competitive advantage.

9. Redefining the role of managers is another critical issue facing organizations. The traditional command and control style of management may not be successful in the evolving, dynamic organizations of today. An effective manager today must play a myriad of roles. These roles include leader, coach, cheerleader, facilitator, negotiator, team builder, trainer, and motivator.

10. In today's modern organization, action must be taken to encourage participation of the workers in decisions relating to their work environment. This is not an easy task in traditional organizations which are characterized by a lack of trust of management by the workers. What is being proposed here is a cultural change, a paradigm shift from the old way to the new.

11. In an effort for companies to create a participative work environment, many have turned to the use of teamwork as the implementation mechanism. This large scale movement toward more teamwork has been one of the most important human resource developments in the last decade. Evolution of team activities start with:

a. Problem-solving teams - also known as quality circles, have been very effective in supporting employee participation and involvement.

b. Special-purpose teams - are the next level of sophistication. These teams usually have more authority and usually focus on more sophisticated problems or projects.

c. Self-managing work team - the highest level of team activity. The use of these teams is not widespread, but for many companies they are a goal for the future.

12. With all the changes taking place in American industry today, the work force is often in constant fear. That fear is affecting employee job performance and their willingness to participate in productivity enhancing activities. Managers must be willing to acknowledge the presence of fear, identify its root causes, and develop long-term strategies to alleviate the fear.

a. Research has indicated that employees hesitated to speak up at one time or another because they feared some type of repercussion. This research suggest that "cycles of mistrust" exist which are based on negative assumptions and self-protective behavior on the part of the manager and employees which serve to insure a self-fulfilling negative relationship. This cycle can start anywhere, but once started, it will continue until broken by some change occurring in the culture of the organization.

b. One of the greatest issues causing fear throughout U.S. companies today is the move toward corporate downsizing or "rightsizing". This downsizing is affecting all employees from the executive suite to the shop or sales floor. Especially hard hit was middle management, which only accounts for about eight percent of the total jobs, but 22 percent of the losses.

13. Training and development are other major human resource issues of the 1990s. In modern organizations today, increasingly diverse training has become a necessity. Today, successful companies view training as an investment in their future.

a. A particular dilemma in industry relates to the ever increasing need for educated entry level employees. The dilemma lies in what to do about existing employees who have been with the company for 10-15 years.

b. Another issue for the 1990s is the need for cross-cultural training for employees. As companies become more international, employees are transferred from place to place in order to best utilize their resources. It is not only the language that should be learned, but the customs and culture of the country as well.

14. A major difficulty exists in creating the proper learning environment where employees ask to be trained and become members of teams Management must determine what types of incentives will work for their organizations and use those incentives to promote desired behavior.

a. Incentives refer to a family of programs used by management to promote a healthy, productive, creative, and inspired work force. Incentive programs take many forms, such as:

(1) Benefits - company benefits such as medical, dental, life and disability insurance coverage, savings and retirement plans, flextime, job sharing, child and elderly care assistance, vacations and sick leave, etc. When the economy is tight and companies are forced to cut costs wherever they can, the benefit packages come under repeated fire.

(2) Compensation - it is often the compensation plan of an organization which encourages or discourages desired employee behavior. An effective compensation plan is one which recognizes the increased responsibilities management has placed on the workers for quality, training, maintenance, troubleshooting, team activities, etc., and rewards workers for accepting and excelling in those new responsibilities. Today, organizations are moving toward

compensation plans which focus on performance and knowledge.

    (3) Recognition and rewards - it has been shown that management often has trouble deciding what forms of recognition and reward to adopt. Usually the problem is that it doesn't consider the wishes and desires of the work force.

15. Work measurement involves the task of determining what rate of output one may expect from a qualified employee working at a normal pace. Work measurement is crucial for establishing standards. Standards are required to accurately measure productivity improvements.

    a. Time studies - also called stopwatch studies, are the most commonly used of all approaches. Steps for accomplishing a time study are:

        (1) Select the task to be analyzed and identify the worker to be used.

        (2) Discuss with the worker the reason of the analysis, and try to dispel any fears the worker may have. Ask the employee to accomplish the task normally.

        (3) Divide the task into necessary elements.

        (4) Determine the appropriate number of cycles to measure for a particular level of confidence

        (5) Time the task

        (6) Analyze the collected data and determine the standard time.

    b. The standard time is calculated by: first determining the mean task duration time as outlined above, then; adjust the mean time to recognize the performance level of the worker being observed, a performance rating is used to adjust the performance of the worker being measured to what is thought to be normal. A performance rating of .85 indicates the work is working 15 percent slower than normal, similarly, a performance rating of 1.15 would indicate that the worker is working about 15 percent faster than normal. The result of this is:

Normal Time = Observed Time X Performance Rating

    c. This normal time does not take into consideration the normal delays and disruptions common in the workplace. To adjust for these unavoidable delays an allowance factor is included in the time. The allowance factor is stated as a percentage of the normal time stated in decimal form. This will give us the standard time:

Standard Time = Normal Time X (1 + Allowance Factor)

    d. It is often easier to establish standard times for new tasks which may share some of the same elements as previously studied tasks. Therefore it is often helpful to divide a task to be evaluated into elemental parts and evaluate each element. One then only needs to identify the elements of the new task, look up the normal times for the elements, and apply any necessary allowances.

    e. Predetermined standard times is another approach to establishing standard times. Using this method, each task is divided into very detailed micro motions, called therbligs. Normal times for basic

118   Chapter 9 - Organization and Human Resources

micromotions are published in tables, available to the analyst.

16. The concept of learning provides that the time required for humans to perform a task often decreases the more times the task is accomplished. In general, more complex tasks of long duration will be more susceptible to learning effects with more repetitions of the task. The generally accepted learning effect is that the time required to produce successive units decreases by the learning factor each time the cumulative output doubles.

17. Learning curve analysis helps quantify expected improvements over time. The concept is very important in a job shop environment where there is often a significant difference in the time required to do the first unit of a batch and the last unit of the batch. Some cautions which should be noted in the application of learning curves include: (1) the degree of learning that takes place may differ between organizations, work areas, and even workers, (2) the time projections are only estimates and should be so treated, and (3) changes may occur over time that affect the time required to accomplish a task, and hence the cost.

KEY TERMS

a. adaptive organization
b. Age Discrimination in Employment Act (ADEA)
c. Americans with Disabilities Act (ADA)
d. benefits
e. compensation
f. corporate downsizing
g. cross-cultural training
h. cycles of mistrust
i. elemental standard times
j. incentives
k. normal time
l. participative management

m. predetermined standard time
n. problem-solving team
o. quality circle
p. recognition and reward
q. self-managing work team
r. sociotechnical system (STS)
s. special-purpose teams
t. standard times
u. therbligs
v. time studies
w. work measurement
x. work force diversity

DEFINITIONS

Directions: Select from the key terms list, the word or phrase being defined below.

_____ 1. this view indicates that one must study both the social and technical areas of an organization, as well as their interaction, in order to comprehend and efficiently address operational problems.

_____ 2. organization characterized by significant employee involvement, through the use of teams, projects and alliances, with the goal of unleashing employee creativity.

_____ 3. this act requires that disabled employees be given the same opportunities as their non-disabled peers.

_____ 4. demographic changes taking place in the workplace.

_____ 5. management style where workers participate in decisions relating to their work environment.

_____ 6. a quality circle formed to resolve a specific problem.

_____ 7. these teams usually have more authority and usually focus on more sophisticated problems.

_____ 8. the negative assumptions and self-protective behavior on the part of employees and managers which serve to insure a self-fulfilling negative relationship is an example of:

_____ 9. also known as "rightsizing".

_____ 10. family of programs used by management to promote a healthy, productive, creative and inspired work force.

_____ 11. an example of this would be, disability insurance coverage, retirement plans, & child care.

_____ 12. the time we measure employee or process improvements against.

_____ 13. the task of determining what rate of output one many expect from a qualified employee working at a normal pace.

_____ 14. sometimes called stopwatch studies.

_____ 15. another name for micro motions.

MULTIPLE CHOICE QUESTIONS

Directions: Indicate your choice of the best answer to each question.

1. Which of the following are having the greatest impact on the utilization of human resources of the firm?
    a. quality movement
    b. work force diversity
    c. advances in technology
    d. all of the above
    e. only a and c

2. The name "sociotechnical organization" reflects
    a. strategic human resource management in organizations today.
    b. only the social side of an organization.
    c. the rapid introduction and use of technology in organizations today.
    d. only the technical side of an organization.
    e. none of the above.

3. Human factors must be considered
    a. during the decision to purchase new technology.
    b. during the compensation phase of HR planning.
    c. during the decisions relating to implementation of new technology.
    d. all of the above.
    e. only a and c.

4. Which of the following is NOT an HR function?
    a. staffing
    b. evaluating
    c. compensating
    d. training
    e. none of the above

5. Which of the following is NOT an internal force influencing the HR function?
    a. structure
    b. culture
    c. politics
    d. strategy
    e. economic

6. Dynamic organizations need the ability to
    a. quickly get new products to market.
    b. respond to changes in customer desires.
    c. respond to changes in the market place.
    d. deal with frequent problems.
    e. all of the above.

7. Organizations characterized by significant employee involvement through the use of teams and alliances are known as
    a. social organizations.
    b. adaptive organizations.
    c. technical organizations.
    d. sociotechnical organizations.
    e. none of the above.

8. Which of the following are NOT critical issues confronting HR practitioners?
    a. governmental regulation
    b. work force diversity
    c. participative management
    d. training and development
    e. none of the above

9. Which of the following are roles an effective manager must play in a dynamic organization?
    a. leader
    b. coach
    c. cheerleader
    d. all of the above
    e. only a and b

10. The normal evolution of team activities within a firm are
    a. (1) special-purpose teams, (2) problem-solving teams, (3) self-managing work team.
    b. (1) problem-solving teams, (2) special-purpose teams, (3) self-managing work team.
    c. (1) problem-solving teams, (2) self-managing work teams, (3) special-purpose teams.
    d. (1) self-managing work team, (2) problem-solving teams, (3) special-purpose teams.
    e. none of the above.

11. Unions are NOT generally opposed to the formation of
    a. problem-solving teams.
    b. special purpose teams.
    c. self-managing work teams.
    d. cross-functional teams.
    e. all of the above.

12. Which of the following are NOT components of the cycle of mistrust?
    a. negative assumptions
    b. self-protective behavior
    c. observed aggressive behavior
    d. reinforced negative assumptions
    e. none of the above

13. Which of the following is NOT a strategy for a manager interested in creating an environment which is full of enthusiasm and trust?
    a. acknowledge the presence of fear
    b. discuss the undiscussables
    c. challenge worst-case thinking
    d. reduce ambiguous behavior
    e. none of the above

14. One of the greatest issues causing fear throughout U.S. companies today is
    a. work force diversity.
    b. participative management.
    c. corporate downsizing.
    d. negative assumptions.
    e. government regulation.

15. Which of the following is NOT a type of training offered by Motorola University?
    a. computer programming
    b. basic reading
    c. statistical process control
    d. foreign languages
    e. none of the above

16. Performance related incentive programs are
    a. compensation.
    b. benefits.
    c. recognition.
    d. all of the above.
    e. only a and c.

17. Disability insurance would be considered
    a. benefits.
    b. compensation.
    c. recognition.
    d. reward.
    e. none of the above.

18. In a time study, the mean time it takes a worker to complete a task, taking into consideration the performance level of the worker is the
    a. standard time.
    b. normal time.
    c. observed time.
    d. allowance time.
    e. elemental standard time.

19. An adjustment to a workers observed mean time to standardize the worker to one who is thought to be normal is
    a. allowance time.
    b. performance rating.
    c. standard time.
    d. normal time.
    e. therblig.

20. In time studies, an adjustment made to normal time to account for unavoidable delays, results in
    a. normal time.
    b. observed time.
    c. standard time .
    d. allowance time.
    e. elemental standard time.

21. In time studies, rest breaks, machine adjustments, engineering changes, etc. are examples of
    a. standard time.
    b. performance rating.
    c. normal time.
    d. allowance factor.
    e. therbligs.

22. The learning curve is based on the concept that the time required to produce successive units of an item decreases by the learning factor each time the cumulative output
    a. doubles.
    b. increases.
    c. triples.
    d. decreases.
    e. quadruples.

23. The concept of learning effects is MOST important with planning and scheduling
    a. jobs in a job shop.
    b. complex tasks of long duration.
    c. simple tasks of long duration.
    d. day-to-day activities.
    e. all of the above.

PROBLEMS

PROBLEM SITUATION #1

The director of environmental services for a major hotel has determined that the average observed time to clean a guest room is 14.20 minutes. In his quest to set performance standards and measure productivity he wants to answer the following questions:

24. If the worker who was observed taking an average of 14.20 minutes to clean a room was in fact 16 percent faster than the average worker, what is the normal time in minutes?
    a. 11.93
    b. 14.36
    c. 15.05
    d. 16.47
    e. none of the above

25. If the amount of time allotted for unavoidable delays is 20 percent, what is the standard time in minutes for this job?
    a. 13.18
    b. 14.36
    c. 15.05
    d. 19.77
    e. none of the above

26. If upon further investigation, the worker under observation was found to be average, the standard time in minutes for this job would be ____.
    a. 16.47
    b. 17.04
    c. 17.23
    d. 19.77
    e. not enough information to calculate

PROBLEM SITUATION #2

A manufacturer of sunglasses has observed one of his technicians performing the task of final assembly. In a preliminary study, he gathered the following time measurements for this task; 3, 7, 4, 8, 12, 13, 5, 6, (all times are in minutes).

27. What is the observed time for this task in minutes?
    a. 7.25
    b. 9.67
    c. 8.00
    d. 58.00
    e. not enough information to calculate

28. What is the normal time for this task if the worker under observation works at a pace 12 percent slower than an average worker?
   a. 6.38 minutes
   b. 7.25 minutes
   c. 8.84 minutes
   d. 58.00 minutes
   e. not enough information to calculate

29. What would be the standard time for this task if there is a 11% allowance for quality control checks?
   a. 6.38
   b. 7.08
   c. 8.05
   d. 9.81
   e. none of the above

PROBLEM SITUATION #3

A skateboard manufacturer needs to know the standard time for assembling skateboards. A worker is observed for six cycles with the following assembly times recorded in minutes: 7.3, 6.8, 9.1, 8.4, 7.6, 8.1.

30. If the observed worker is assembling skate boards at a pace that is approximately 10 percent slower than an average worker, what is the normal time in minutes?
   a. 7.09
   b. 7.88
   c. 9.10
   d. 42.57
   e. not enough information to calculate

31. What is the observed time?
   a. 7.09
   b. 7.88
   c. 9.10
   d. 42.57
   e. none of the above

32. The manufacturer has determined that there are delays to normal time expressed as a percentage for, rest breaks 3%, engineering changes 7%, and material delays 2%. Given these delays, what is the standard time?
   a. 7.09 minutes
   b. 7.88 minutes
   c. 7.94 minutes
   d. 8.83 minutes
   e. none of the above

PROBLEM SITUATION #4

Elmer Fudd has taken measurements from a worker constructing rabbit traps, yielding the following task times in minutes, 32, 28, 29, 39, 21, 27, 40.

33. How many samples should Mr. Fudd take if he wants his estimate to be within 10 percent of the true value and he desires 99 percent confidence in his estimate?
    a. 7
    b. 20
    c. 23
    d. 32
    e. none of the above

34. The worker building the rabbit traps is thought to be an excellent worker and works at a rate approximately 19 percent faster than an average worker. Based on this, what is the observed time?
    a. 25.00
    b. 27.31
    c. 30.86
    d. 36.72
    e. none of the above

35. What is the normal time for this task, given the workers pace of 19 percent faster than average, and an allowance for unavoidable delays of 22 percent?
    a. 27.16
    b. 27.31
    c. 36.72
    d. 37.65
    e. none of the above

36. What is the standard time for this job?
    a. 32.31
    b. 36.65
    c. 37.65
    d. 44.80
    e. none of the above

PROBLEM SITUATION #5

Computer Excess assembles computer systems for home and small business applications. The first unit of its new product line took 5.8 man-hours to assemble. The company has an order for 800 of this particular model. Based on previous experience, management believes that a 90 percent learning curve will apply to this product.

126 Chapter 9 - Organization and Human Resources

37. How long should it take to assemble the second computer system?
   a. 5.80 man-hours
   b. 5.22 man-hours
   c. 5.18 man-hours
   d. 5.08 man-hours
   e. none of the above

38. How long should it take to assemble the fourth computer system?
   a. 3.124 man-hours
   b. 3.658 man-hours
   c. 4.233 man-hours
   d. 4.698 man-hours
   e. none of the above

39. How long should it take to assemble the first 200 computer systems?
   a. 1,160 man-hours
   b. 965 man-hours
   c. 609 man-hours
   d. 556 man-hours
   e. none of the above

40. How long should it take to assemble the entire order of 800 computer systems?
   a. 5,600.8 man-hours
   b. 4,640.0 man-hours
   c. 3,670.2 man-hours
   d. 1977.8 man-hours
   e. none of the above

41. Over the entire order of 800 units, what will be the average time required to assemble each system?
   a. 2.47 man-hours
   b. 3.56 man-hours
   c. 3.98 man-hours
   d. 4.02 man-hours
   e. none of the above

APPLICATION QUESTIONS

The manager of Cobra Marine desires to develop a time standard for the task of final preparation on new boats sold. In a preliminary study he observed his best worker perform this task over five work cycles, with the following results:

Cycle	1	2	3	4	5
Time (hours)	4.2	5.6	2.0	4.1	4.8

1. What was the observed time in minutes for this worker?

2. If this observed worker accomplished the task at a rate that is 15 percent slower than an average worker, what would be the normal time for this operation?

3. If this observed worker accomplished the task at a rate that is 30 percent faster than an average worker, what would be the normal time for this operation?

4. For the observed worker who accomplished the task at a rate 30 percent faster than an average worker, there is an estimated allowance factor of 10 percent. What would be the standard time?

5. How many observations should this manager make if he wants to be within 10 percent of the true value, and desires 95 percent confidence in his estimate?

SHORT ANSWER QUESTIONS

1. Describe the strategic human resource management model. What are the internal and external forces of the model?

2. What approaches are U.S. companies choosing to enhance their productivity?

3. Compare the traditional command and control management style with participative management.

4. Why are incentives important in today's work place? What are various forms of incentives?

5. What are time studies? Why and how are they done?

CHAPTER 10
GLOBAL SUPPLY CHAIN MANAGEMENT

INTRODUCTION

SUPPLY CHAIN MANAGEMENT FOR STRATEGIC ADVANTAGE

TRADITIONAL LOGISTICS MANAGEMENT
    Logistics System Components
        Supplier Network
        Manufacturing Unit
        Customer Network
    Logistics Component Integration
    Logistical Elements

LOGISTICS ISSUES
    Purchasing
        Make-or-Buy Decision
        Sources of Goods and Services
        International Sourcing
        GLOBAL OPERATIONS MANAGEMENT 10.1: Ford Looks for a Few Good Global
            Suppliers
        Best Value for the Money
        Value Analysis
        Supplier Evaluation
        Ethics in Purchasing
    Transportation
        Legal Forms of Carriers
        Transportation Mode Selection
        Freight Consolidation
    Warehousing
    Customer Service

BRIDGING THE GAP TO SUPPLY CHAIN MANAGEMENT
    OPERATIONS MANAGEMENT IN PRACTICE 10.2: At CAT, They're Driving Supplier
        Integration Into the Design Process
    OPERATIONS MANAGEMENT IN PRACTICE 10.3: Enemies Make Great Logistics Allies
    Variability Along the Supply Chain
    Role of Information Technology in SCM
    Third-Party Logistics Services
    OPERATIONS MANAGEMENT IN PRACTICE 10.4: National Semiconductor Improves
        Supply Chain
    Environmental Sensitivity Along the Supply Chain
    Just-in-Time Logistics

CHAPTER SUMMARY

1. Supply chain management (SCM) is a philosophy that describes how organizations should manage their various supply chains to achieve strategic advantage. To achieve a balance between costs and customer satisfaction, a company's managers must think in terms of a single, integrated chain rather than its individual segments. Effective management of a company's supply chain must be customer driven.

2. A firm's competitiveness is based on its ability to provide goods and services when and where they are needed. Efficient and effective transportation and storage systems, integral elements of business logistics, support this competitiveness. A primary theme is the integrative and multi-functional nature of business logistics. Logistics creates value by changes in time, place, and quantity.

3. The Council of Logistics Management defines business logistics as " the process of planning, implementing, and controlling the efficient, cost-effective flow and storage of goods, services, and related information from point of origin to point of consumption for the purpose of conforming to customer requirements." Business logistics provides linkages from the sources of raw materials to the locations of the final customers. These linkages include other functional areas of the firm.

4. There are three major components of the overall logistics system: physical supply, internal operations, and physical distribution.

    a. Physical supply is responsible for the interface between the firm's operating processes and its suppliers.

    b. Internal operations is responsible for managing the flow of material during the material conversion process.

    c. Physical distribution provides the interfaces between the firm's production or service processes and its customers.

5. Traditional functional organizational structures may not have a single organizational unit for managing the total logistics process. Logistics functions are as a result divided up by traditional functional units such as marketing, purchasing, and production, making integration of the logistics components difficult. Managing the total logistics pipeline has benefits that exceed managing the separate parts. Many firms are directing greater resources toward logistic management and have assigned clear responsibility for logistics integration.

6. A typical list of elements within a total logistics system might include:
    a. Transportation
    b. Facilities
    c. Procurement and purchasing
    d. Packaging & shipping
    e. Warehousing and storage
    f. Inventory planning and control
    g. Demand forecasting
    h. Customer service
    i. Order processing
    j. Salvage and scrap disposal

7. Integrating the logistics elements among themselves often requires that tradeoffs be made among the logistics elements; these tradeoffs arise as the logistics elements have different characteristics and meet objectives to differing degrees.

8. Four areas of logistics management worth detailed study are purchasing, transportation, warehousing, and customer service.

   a. Purchasing is the acquisition of needed goods and services at optimum cost from competent, reliable sources. Several important factors to consider include:

   (1) Make-or-buy decision. Is it better to produce an item in-house or buy it?

      (a) Often a complex, strategic issue.

      (b) Economic considerations are simple: At a specified volume, is it cheaper to make an item internally or to buy it already made?

      (c) Factors other than economics must also be considered.

      (d) Firms may choose to make <u>and</u> buy, for risk reduction and for bargaining power.

   (2) Determining the best sources of goods and services, including both domestic and international sources, is a task done by purchasing. Purchasing is responsible for the selection of sources as well as negotiation of purchase contracts. Criteria for determining "best" include quality, cost, reliability, on-time delivery, and ability to meet requirements. Vertical integration occurs when the supplier firm is another part of the purchasing firm. Recent experience is that vertical integration is too expensive and too risky for some companies.

   (3) International sourcing is more complex, due to cultural differences, language barriers, instability of foreign economic and political systems, and greater uncertainty.

   (4) Best value for the money means to buy goods and services at the "lowest total cost," not necessarily at the "lowest price."

   (5) Value analysis is a disciplined effort to compare the function performed by an item and its cost in an attempt to find a lower-cost alternative.

   (6) Supplier evaluation is based not only on price and quality, but also on other dimensions, such as on-time delivery, responsiveness to changes, technical support, or other measures of performance. The trend today is toward fewer, but higher quality suppliers, who are treated as business partners.

   (7) Ethics in purchasing is important because purchasers wield considerable power over suppliers. Firms often have policies or restrictions on behavior of purchasers.

   b. Transportation costs are a large part of logistics costs. Transportation tasks include determining transportation requirements, selecting carriers, monitoring shipments, expediting shipments when necessary, negotiating with carriers, and evaluating carrier performance.

(1) There are three legal forms of transport services: private, common, and contract carriers.

(a) Private carriers are owned by the shipper and primarily provide in-house transportation services.

(b) Common carriers are regulated firms that serve the general public.

(c) Contract carriers provide transportation services that are tailored to the specific needs of a limited set of customers.

(2) Transportation modes: The five primary modes are rail, truck, air, water, and pipeline.

(a) Rail provides relatively low cost transport service primarily for long haul of commodities in bulk and low in value per pound. Delivery is slower and more variable than truck transportation. Routes and schedules are less flexible than trucking.

(b) Truck transportation moves most manufactured goods in the United States. Trucking offers rapid and reliable delivery times, door-to-door service, and a willingness to handle shipment sizes of less than full truck loads.

(c) Air shipment offers the greatest speed, and is best suited for the movement of items high in value per pound, perishable commodities, and emergency items.

(d) Water transportation dominates transoceanic movement for all but the highest-valued commodities. Because of its slowness, water transportation is preferred when low cost per ton-mile is the goal.

(e) Pipelines provide effective point-to-point shipment of fluids such as petroleum products.

(3) Transportation mode selection: Each mode meets the objectives of cost, capability, flexibility, speed and reliability in different degrees. The primary determinants of the appropriate transportation mode are:

(a) the ability of the shipment to absorb transportation costs

(b) the urgency of delivery

(c) shipment size

(4) Intermodal shipments combine two or more modes of transportation, and is frequently enabled by containerization, in which a container can be mechanically moved from a ship to a trailer chassis to a rail car. Containerization is widely used in transoceanic shipping.

(5) Freight consolidation lowers transportation cost per unit by combining small shipments into a larger shipment at lower rates. Use of consolidation points, where small orders are shipped to be combined with others, is widely practiced in the automobile industry. Consolidation strategies are complex and often involve sophisticated modeling.

c. Warehousing uses inventories to reduce uncertainties associated with delivery rates, manufacturing schedules, and demand. Warehousing may be done by the firm, or outsourced. Typical warehouse functions include:

(1) Receive and inspect goods

(2) Identify goods

(3) Sort and dispatch goods to storage

(4) Hold goods

(5) Recall, select. or pick goods

(6) Organize the shipment

(7) Dispatch the shipment

(8) Prepare inventory records

d. Customer service is all activities performed to support the customer during the supplier-customer exchange; this includes pre-sale, sale and post-sale activities. These services affect customer perceptions and customer satisfaction. Organizations must understand customer needs and expectations, and design an appropriate logistics system. Logistics systems can be of strategic importance, for example, by designing systems around quick resupply concepts to provide high levels of customer service.

9. For global strategic advantage, all elements of the supply chain must be integrated so that communication can flow forward and backward through the chain.

10. Much of the difficulty encountered in effective SCM is the result of variability along the supply chain. There are three basic sources of variability:

   a. variability that occurs in the supply network

   b. variability in a company's manufacturing processes

   c. variability coming from the customer network

11. Information technology that has previously been the missing element required to transform traditional logistics functions into world-class SCM is now available and improving daily.

12. Some companies are now farming-out, or outsourcing, all or part of their logistics functions to third-party organizations. Third-party logistics services are the result of outsourcing all or part of a firm's logistics functions. In an increasingly high-tech world, small companies and geographically dispersed firms have difficulty allocating enough resources to be effective in their logistics activities. Other firms prefer to concentrate efforts on their strengths, and leave the logistics to specialists.

13. Environmental sensitivity means that firms have become increasingly concerned with wastes created by logistics operations. This translates into recycling and reuse of packing materials, reduced use of packing materials, use of more appropriate packing materials, and return of used materials to point of origin.

14. Just-in-time logistics treats inventory as waste, existing only to cover up operating problems. JIT systems treat customers as *pulling* material through systems; the conventional view has been firms *pushing* material through. JIT systems attempt to match the inflow of material to the demand rate of customers. JIT requires innovative approaches for logistics management, since JIT philosophy calls for smaller, more frequent shipments, which are counter to long-established notions of bulk shipments, quantity discounts and economies of scale.

KEY TERMS

a. business logistics
b. freight consolidation
c. internal operations
d. outsourcing
e. physical distribution
f. physical supply
g. purchasing
h. reverse logistics
i. supply chain
j. supply chain management
k. value analysis
l. vertical integration

DEFINITIONS

Directions: Select from the key terms list, the word or phrase being defined below.

_____ 1. the process of combining small shipments into one larger shipment to reduce costs.

_____ 2. the logistics component responsible for the interface between the firm's operating processes and its suppliers.

_____ 3. the logistics component that provides the interfaces between the firm's production or service processes and its customers.

_____ 4. the acquisition of needed goods and services at optimum cost from competent, reliable sources.

_____ 5. a disciplined effort to compare the function performed by an item and its cost in an attempt to find a lower-cost alternative.

_____ 6. the process of contracting out all or part of an organization's logistics functions to a third party organization.

_____ 7. the process of returning goods to their source.

_____ 8. a system through which organizations acquire raw material, produce products, and deliver the products and services to their customers.

_____ 9. the process of bringing the sources of supply for key materials and services within the control of the company.

_____ 10. responsible for managing the in-process material flow during the material conversion process.

_____ 11. Philosophy that describes how organizations should manage their supplier/customer networks to achieve strategic advantage.

MULTIPLE CHOICE QUESTIONS

Directions: Indicate your choice of the best answer to each question.

1. The logistics component responsible for the interface between the firm's operating processes and its customers is
   a. purchasing.
   b. physical supply.
   c. physical distribution.
   d. logistics management.
   e. warehousing.

2. Suppliers interface with operating processes in the _____ logistics component.
   a. transportation
   b. vendor relationships
   c. internal operations
   d. physical supply
   e. physical distribution

3. Producers that might wish to deal with member nations of the EEC should strongly consider _____ supplier certification.
   a. Series Seven
   b. AZU285
   c. MIL-SPEC 405
   d. ISO9000
   e. EEC9000

4. A company that provides transportation services tailored to the needs of a specific set of customers is
   a. a common carrier.
   b. a pipeline.
   c. an outbound logistics specialist.
   d. a contract carrier.
   e. a private carrier.

Chapter 10 - Global Supply Chain Management

5. Freight consolidation is effective
   a. on both inbound as well as outbound shipments.
   b. on inbound shipments only.
   c. on outbound shipments only.
   d. on neither inbound nor outbound shipments.
   e. only when full vertical integration of supply is present.

6. _____ are regulated firms that serve the general public for a specified range of goods and services.
   a. Contract carriers
   b. Pipelines, but not railroads
   c. Independent truckers
   d. Common carriers
   e. Railroads, but not truck lines

7. _____ has always been the missing element needed to transform traditional logistics functions to world-class supply chain management.
   a. Effective leadership
   b. Better vendor relations
   c. Information technology
   d. Freight consolidation
   e. None of the above

8. The overall logistics system is composed of
   a. logistical supply, internal operations, and logistical distribution.
   b. internal operations, logistical distribution and physical distribution.
   c. physical supply, external operations, and physical distribution.
   d. physical supply, internal operations, and physical distribution.
   e. none of the above.

9. The long haul of raw materials and low-valued manufactured goods at relatively low cost is typically the market for
   a. pipelines.
   b. rail transportation.
   c. private carriers.
   d. contract carriers.
   e. Amtrak.

10. According to the textbook, _____ have successfully integrated their logistics management, as evidenced by having vice-presidential level logistics executives.
    a. the nation's railroads
    b. Quaker Oats and Dow Chemical
    c. DuPont and Wal-Mart
    d. General Motors and other automotive firms
    e. almost all Fortune 500 firms

11. In logistics systems, _____ provides the interface between the firm's production or service processes and its customers.
    a. physical supply
    b. supply
    c. internal operations
    d. physical distribution
    e. distribution

12. _____ has(have) been a very effective user of freight consolidation.
    a. The nation's railroads
    b. The American automobile industry
    c. Pipelines
    d. Sears
    e. Wal-Mart

13. Which of the following is NOT a logistics system component?
    a. logistical supply
    b. physical distribution
    c. external operations
    d. neither a nor c is a logistics system components
    e. all of the above are logistics system components

14. Which of the following is NOT a "legal form of carrier"?
    a. common carrier
    b. private carrier
    c. contract carrier
    d. letter carrier
    e. all of the above are legal forms of carriers

15. Which of the following terms is normally associated with containerization?
    a. TOFC (truck trailer on rail flat car)
    b. COFC (container on rail flat car)
    c. intermodal shipments
    d. container ship
    e. all of the above

16. Which of the following is NOT a typical warehousing operation?
    a. receive and inspect goods
    b. sort and dispatch goods to storage
    c. sell goods
    d. recall, select, or pick goods
    e. dispatch the shipment

17. Which of the following is NOT among the "top five" customer service measures?
    a. orders delivered on time
    b. order fill rates
    c. carrier performance
    d. order accuracy
    e. handling of customer complaints

18. Which of the following is NOT considered by the authors as a "strategic trend in logistics management?
    a. third-party logistics services
    b. environmental sensitivity
    c. containerization
    d. just-in-time logistics
    e. integrated logistics management

19. The strategic trend in logistics that includes "reverse logistics" as one of its parts is
    a. vertical integration.
    b. integrated logistics management.
    c. environmental sensitivity.
    d. outsourcing.
    e. just-in-time.

20. _____ and _____ are both examples of intermodal transport.
    a. COFC; TOFC
    b. Vertical integration; common carrier
    c. COFC; LCL
    d. TOFC; pallet pooling
    e. TOFC; ISO9000

21. A system through which organizations acquire raw material, produce products, and deliver the products and services to their customers is known as a
    a. supply chain.
    b. distribution network.
    c. channel system.
    d. distribution channel.
    e. supply system.

22. Which of the following is NOT a major component of an organization's supply chain?
    a. supplier network
    b. transportation network
    c. manufacturing unit
    d. customer network
    e. all of the above are major components

PROBLEMS

PROBLEM SITUATION #1

The XYZ corporation estimates that it will need 400,000 units of part P0045 annually. Currently the company is purchasing these parts from a supplier. The landed cost of parts from this supplier is $3.15 each. Executives at XYZ want to consider internal manufacture of the part and have obtained estimates from their cost accountants. These figures indicate that XYZ would incur annual fixed costs of $1,140,000 and unit variable costs of $2.10. XYZ officials believe that economic analysis is appropriate for this decision.

23. What would be XYZ's annual total cost if it chose to make P0045?
    a. $1,260,000
    b. $1,198,000
    c. $1,980,000
    d. $2,400,000
    e. cannot be determined from information supplied

24. What would be XYZ's annual total cost if it chose to continue buying P0045?
    a. $1,260,000
    b. $1,198,000
    c. $1,980,000
    d. $2,400,000
    e. cannot be determined from information supplied

25. XYZ should choose to _____ P0045 and save _____ over the alternative.
    a. make, $180,000
    b. buy, $720,000
    c. make; $720,000
    d. buy, $180,000
    e. make, $1,220,000

26. XYZ will prefer to make P0045 for any demand level _____ _____ units annually.
    a. below; 400,000
    b. above; 1,198,000
    c. above; 1,085,714
    d. below; 1,085,714
    e. cannot be determined from information supplied

PROBLEM SITUATION #2

Saint Charles Street Renovators is evaluating suppliers of upholstery for the renovation of vintage streetcars. Three potential suppliers have passed all criteria for quality, timeliness and service, but differ with regard to how they want to price the upholstery fabric. Arceneaux Heritage Fabrics asks $12 per yard of fabric, but wants Saint Charles Street Renovators to install the special equipment, at an annual cost of $12,000. Werlein's Traditional Fabrics asks $18 per yard but will buy the equipment itself. Alexandria Reproductions asks $13 per yard, and wants Saint Charles Street Renovators to cover one third of the $15,000 annual cost of special equipment. Each streetcar requires 150 yards; the firm plans to renovate 10 cars next year.

27. If annual demand were 3,000 yards, _____ would be the most expensive supplier and _____ the least expensive.
    a. Arceneaux Heritage Fabrics; Werlein's Traditional Fabrics
    b. Alexandria Reproductions; Werlein's Traditional Fabrics
    c. Arceneaux Heritage Fabrics; Alexandria Reproductions
    d. Werlein's Traditional Fabrics; Alexandria Reproductions
    e. None of the above

28. Saint Charles Street Renovators anticipates annual demand to be 1,500 yards next year. At that demand, the three suppliers would be ranked _____ cheapest, _____ middle, and _____ most expensive.
    a. Arceneaux Heritage Fabrics; Werlein's Traditional Fabrics; Alexandria Reproductions
    b. Alexandria Reproductions; Werlein's Traditional Fabrics; Arceneaux Heritage Fabrics
    c. Arceneaux Heritage Fabrics; Alexandria Reproductions; Werlein's Traditional Fabrics
    d. Werlein's Traditional Fabrics; Alexandria Reproductions; Arceneaux Heritage Fabrics
    e. None of the above

29. Based on expected demand, Saint Charles Street Renovators should choose _____ as the low cost supplier at a total cost of _____.
    a. Alexandria Reproductions; $24,500
    b. Arceneaux Heritage Fabrics; $30,000
    c. Werlein's Traditional Fabrics; $13,800
    d. Alexandria Reproductions; $44,000
    e. none of the above

30. Alexandria Reproductions would be the low cost supplier for annual demands
    a. above 2,000 yards per year.
    b. below 1,000 yards per year.
    c. below 2,000 yards per year.
    d. from 1,000 to 7,000 yards per year.
    e. cannot be determined from the data provided.

APPLICATION QUESTIONS

Delta Pirogue Company has extra productive capacity that can be used to produce fiberglass paddles that the company is now buying for $6 each. If Delta makes the paddles, it will incur material costs of $1.50 per unit, labor costs of $2 per unit and variable overhead costs of $1 per unit. The annual fixed cost associated with the manufacturing capacity is $3,000. Demand over the next year is estimated at 3,000 units.

1. If the company continues to buy the fiberglass paddles from outside, what will be the total cost next year?

2. If the company decides to produce the paddles in-house, what will be the total cost for next year?

3. What should the company do and why?

4. At what annual demand would the company be indifferent between making the paddles in-house and buying them from outside?

5. At what level of annual demand would the company be $1,500 better off by making the paddles in-house versus buying them from outside?

Chapter 10 - Global Supply Chain Management

SHORT ANSWER QUESTIONS

1. What is supply chain management and what is its primary objective?

2. Describe the three major components of a firm's supply chain. What types of issues are addressed by each component?

3. What are the key factors used by organizations to evaluate the performance of their suppliers?

4. What are the five primary modes of transportation? If dependable delivery schedules and low transportation costs were equally important to a firm, which of the five modes of transportation might be selected? Why?

5. Describe the three sources of variability found along a firm's supply chain. Provide examples of variation from each source. What role does information technology play in reducing variability?

CHAPTER 11
AGGREGATE PRODUCTION PLANNING

INTRODUCTION

THE CONCEPT OF AGGREGATION
Products
Labor
Time

AN OVERVIEW OF PRODUCTION-PLANNING ACTIVITIES
Long-range Planning
Medium-range Planning
Short-range Planning
OPERATIONS MANAGEMENT IN PRACTICE 11.1: New Software Systems Speed Up Production Planning

FRAMEWORK FOR AGGREGATE PRODUCTION PLANNING
The Production Planning Environment
Strategies for Aggregate Production Planning

TECHNIQUES FOR AGGREGATE PRODUCTION PLANNING
Trial-and-Error Method
Mathematical Techniques
OPERATIONS MANAGEMENT IN PRACTICE 11.2: Meeting the Semiconductor Wafer Fabrication Challenge Using Simulation
Summary of Aggregate Production-Planning Methods
GLOBAL OPERATIONS MANAGEMENT 11.3: Integrated Production Planning for Poultry Processing at Sadia Concórdia SA

AGGREGATE PLANNING IN SERVICE COMPANIES
GLOBAL OPERATIONS MANAGEMENT 11.4: Aircraft Maintenance Personnel Planning at KLM Royal Dutch Airlines

IMPLEMENTING AGGREGATE PRODUCTION PLANS - MANAGERIAL ISSUES

HIERARCHICAL PRODUCTION PLANNING
OPERATIONS MANAGEMENT IN PRACTICE 11.5: Improved Hierarchical Production Planning at Owens-Corning Fiberglas

CHAPTER SUMMARY

1. Aggregate production planning is medium-term capacity planning that typically encompasses a time horizon of two to eighteen months.

   a. Aggregate production planning lies between long-range planning and short-range planning. It gives direction to the other medium-range planning activity, master production scheduling. Long-range planning includes facilities planning; short-range planning includes scheduling.

Long-range planning is higher than aggregate planning in a firm's organizational structure; short-range planning is lower.

b. Long-range is usually thought of to be from one year to five or ten years; medium-range is from two to eighteen months; and short-range, a few months or less

c. In manufacturing, aggregate production planning results in a production plan. In services, aggregate production planning results in a staffing plan.

d. Aggregate planning is "macro" in nature, focusing on totals (aggregates) rather than on individual items. Aggregation deliberately reduces the level of detail to be dealt with by planners.

e. Aggregation is most commonly by product family, since such products have manufacturing characteristics in common. Other types of aggregation are by labor and by time.

2. Production planning, including aggregate planning, links top management to manufacturing. The production plan summarizes the production resources that are needed to achieve the strategic objectives of the firm.

a. Long-range planning results in organizational goals and objectives. It is strategic planning, and is usually done annually with a horizon of several years into the future.

b. Medium-range planning, usually updated monthly or quarterly, has a time horizon of two to eighteen months. Medium-range planning is constrained by long-range planning decisions. Medium-range planning decisions relate to general levels of work force, output, and inventories, and are aggregated, for example by product families. Medium-range planning includes aggregate production planning and the master production schedule.

c. Short-range planning is generally updated weekly, and has a time horizon of a few weeks or months. Short-range planning is constrained by medium-range decisions. Short-range decisions (like material requirements planning) are highly detailed, disaggregated.

3. The objectives of aggregate production planning are to determine how much to produce during each time period in the intermediate time horizon and how to adjust capacity to meet the production requirements.

a. The adjustable elements of capacity include the size of the work force, the length of the work week, the number of shifts worked, and the extent of subcontracting.

b. Aggregate production planning manipulates variables such as work force levels, production rates, and inventory levels.

(1) Work force level is the number of workers required for production.

(2) Production rate is the number of units produced per time period.

(3) Inventory level is the balance of unused units that are carried forward from the previous period.

4. Aggregate production planning is influenced by a number of internal and external factors.

   a. External factors are generally outside the production planners direct control. External inputs to the production planning process include:

   (1) Actions of competitors

   (2) Raw material availability

   (3) Economic conditions

   (4) Subcontractor capacity

   (5) Government regulators

   (6) Marketplace demand

   b. Internal factors are normally associated with their organizational functional area, and differ in their controllability by the production planner. Internal factors include:

   (1) Engineering, such as labor standards and machine standards

   (2) Finance, such as cost data

   (3) Human resources, such as work force levels and training capacity

   (4) Manufacturing, such as productivity and plant capacities

   (5) Marketing, such as demand forecasts

   (6) Materials management, including inventory levels

5. There are many possible specific numerical objectives for aggregate production planning to attempt to achieve. These objectives often conflict with one another. These conflicts are resolved by trading off one objective for another or by letting one objective, such as "minimize costs," dominate.

6. Companies have several methods to influence the level of product or service demand. These include:

   a. Price incentives

   b. Reservations

   c. Backlogs

   d. Complementary products or services

   e. Advertising/promotion

7. Companies can also modify or influence product or service supply in several ways. These include:

   a. Hiring/firing workers

   b. Overtime/slack time

   c. Part-time/temporary labor

   d. Subcontracting

   e. Cooperative arrangements

   f. Inventories

8. Aggregate production planning methods generally are oriented toward minimizing costs. Companies should consider the following costs when planning aggregate production:

   a. Hiring/firing costs

   b. Overtime/slack time costs

   c. Part-time/temporary labor costs

   d. Subcontracting costs

   e. Cooperative arrangement costs

   f. Inventory carrying costs

   g. Back-order and stock-out costs

9. There are two pure strategies for aggregate production planning: *chase* and *level*.

   a. Pure chase strategy adjusts production rates or work force levels to match demand requirements in each time period within the planning horizon.

   b. Pure level strategy maintains a constant production rate or work force level during each of the time periods within the planning horizon.

   c. A strategy that combines elements of the two pure strategies is a mixed strategy.

10. Techniques used in aggregate planning can be categorized into two types: trial-and-error and mathematical techniques. Despite considerable research into the mathematical models, trial-and-error is more widely used.

   a. Trial-and-error methods explore various options until an acceptable solution is found. The technique is not systematic and does not explore all alternative solutions, and therefore does not ordinarily produce an optimum solution.

b. Numerous mathematical techniques have been proposed for aggregate production planning. These include

   (1) Linear decision rule

   (2) Management coefficients model

   (3) Parametric production planning

   (4) Search decision rule

   (5) Production-switching heuristic

   (6) Linear programming -- simplex method

   (7) Linear programming -- transportation method

   (8) Goal programming

   (9) Mixed integer programming

   (10) Simulation models

c. The transportation method is explained in full detail in this chapter.

11. In practice, firms tend to utilize techniques such as charting and spreadsheets before attempting more sophisticated, computerized models. Which tools are used seem to follow from the firm's culture. Research on the value of mathematical models in aggregate planning suggests that mathematical modeling outperforms traditional techniques (the search decision rule showed the greatest improvement). The lack of explicit cost data was the major reason for using relatively simple aggregate production planning techniques.

12. Aggregate planning is also important for service companies. Since services firms do not produce inventories, aggregate production planning results in staffing plans that call for changing the numbers of employees or subcontracting.

13. Once the aggregate production plan has been finalized it has to be implemented. This involves disaggregating the plan into specific product requirements, building the master production schedule.

14. Managerial issues involved in aggregate planning include

   a. Aggregate production planning has to be tailored to the particular company and the particular situation.

   b. Aggregate production planning may be highly constrained by union contracts or by a company policy that seeks to maintain a level work force.

   c. The use of mathematical techniques for aggregate production planning will likely have to be balanced with managerial judgment and experience.

148   Chapter 11 - Aggregate Production Planning

   d. There may be a tendency to blur the distinction between production planning and production scheduling in some companies.

15. Hierarchical production planning is an alternative to time-horizon based aggregate planning techniques. Hierarchical production planning matches product aggregations to decision-making levels in the organization. The most aggregate data are for top management and top-level decisions, while the most detailed data are provided for low-level, shop floor decisions. Disaggregation should follow organizational lines. Only information that is appropriate should be provided at each aggregation level. A major advantage of hierarchical production planning is that each successive level has a simpler structure, less data, and can be analyzed using simpler models.

KEY TERMS

a. aggregate production planning
b. capacity requirements planning
c. chase strategy
d. goal programming
e. hierarchical production planning
f. inventory level
g. level strategy
h. linear decision rule
i. long-range planning
j. management coefficients model
k. master production schedule
l. material requirements planning (MRP)
m. medium-range planning
n. mixed integer programming

o. mixed strategy
p. parametric production planning
q. production plan
r. production rate
s. production-switching heuristic
t. purchasing planning and control
u. rough-cut capacity planning
v. search decision rule
w. short-range planning
x. simplex method of linear programming
y. simulation models
z. staffing plan
aa. transportation method of linear programming
bb. work force level

DEFINITIONS

Directions: Select from the key terms list, the word or phrase being defined below.

_____ 1. is medium-term capacity planning that typically encompasses a time horizon of two to eighteen months.

_____ 2. is corporate strategic planning and results in a statement of organizational goals and objectives.

_____ 3. is the number of workers required for production.

_____ 4. is the number of units produced per time period.

_____ 5. is the balance of unused units that are carried forward from the previous period.

_____ 6. production rates or work force levels are adjusted to match demand requirements over the planning horizon.

_____ 7. a constant production rate or work force is maintained over the planning horizon.

_____ 8. there are both inventory changes and work force and production rate changes over the planning horizon.

_____ 9. is a set of time-phased staff requirements, taking into consideration customer service needs and perhaps machine limited capacities.

_____ 10. is an heuristic model for aggregate planning in which regression analysis is used to determine appropriate production level and work force rules.

_____ 11. gives an approximation of actual resource requirements to make sure that no capacity constraints are violated.

_____ 12. is an early mathematical model for aggregate planning, which attempted to minimize the non-linear sum of four cost elements.

_____ 13. provides a detailed schedule of when each operation is to be run at each work center.

_____ 14. generates the amounts and dates for the manufacture of specific end products.

_____ 15. is the process of tailoring the planning structure to the organization, rather than linking planning levels to different time horizons.

MULTIPLE CHOICE QUESTIONS

Directions: Indicate your choice of the best answer to each question.

1. Which of the following statements about aggregate production planning is TRUE?
   a. Advertising/promotion and overtime/slacktime are ways of manipulating product or service supply in aggregate planning.
   b. Work station loading and job assignments are examples of aggregate production planning.
   c. Advertising/promotion and overtime/slacktime are ways of manipulating product or service demand in aggregate planning.
   d. Aggregate planning uses the adjustable part of a firm's capacity to effectively meet production requirements.
   e. Both b and d are true.

2. Which of the following statements about aggregate production planning is TRUE?
   a. In aggregate planning, backlogs are a means of manipulating demand while part-time/temporary labor are ways of manipulating product or service supply.
   b. A pure chase strategy allows lower inventories when compared to pure level and hybrid strategies.
   c. In spite of the research into mathematical models, aggregate production planners continue to use trial and error methods when developing their plans.
   d. All of the above are true.
   e. Only b and c are true.

3. Which of the following best describes aggregate production planning?
   a. It is the link between intermediate planning and short-range planning decisions.
   b. It is a set of mathematical modeling techniques for capacity planning.
   c. It is a "macro" attempt to respond to predicted demand.
   d. It includes methods for managing aggregate substances as crushed limestone, clamshell and gravel.
   e. It is primarily manpower planning.

4. Aggregate production planning is capacity planning for
   a. the long-range.
   b. the medium-range.
   c. the short-range.
   d. a few months.
   e. a few years.

5. Which of the following is NOT a method or device for manipulating product or service demand?
   a. subcontracting
   b. backlogs
   c. price incentives
   d. advertising/promotion
   e. all are demand options

6. Which of the following is a method or device for manipulating product or service supply?
   a. advertising/promotion
   b. subcontracting
   c. price incentives
   d. backlogs
   e. none of the above; all are demand options

7. Which of the following is a method or device for manipulating product or service demand?
   a. cooperative arrangements
   b. backlogs
   c. price incentives
   d. subcontracting
   e. both b and c are demand-influencing

8. Which of the following statements regarding aggregate production planning is TRUE?
   a. Aggregate planning uses the fixed part of a firm's capacity to effectively meet production requirements.
   b. Aggregate production planning is short-term capacity planning that typically encompasses a time horizon of two to eighteen months.
   c. Aggregate production planning results a staffing plan for manufacturing environments, a production plan for service situations.
   d. Aggregate planning is a "micro" approach to planning, focusing on overall capacity rather than individual products or services.
   e. None of the above are true.

9. Which of the following statements regarding aggregate production planning is TRUE?
   a. Aggregate production planning is the same as aggregate planning.
   b. Aggregate production planning is medium-term capacity planning that typically encompasses a time horizon of two to eighteen months.
   c. Aggregate production planning results in a production plan for manufacturing environments, a staffing plan for service situations.
   d. Aggregate planning is a "macro" approach to planning, focusing on overall capacity rather than individual products or services.
   e. All of the above are true.

10. Which of the following statements regarding aggregate production planning is TRUE?
    a. In a pure chase strategy, production rates or work force levels are adjusted to match demand requirements over the planning horizon.
    b. Because service firms do not inventory their output, a pure level strategy does not apply.
    c. In a mixed strategy, there are both inventory changes and work force and production rate changes over the planning horizon.
    d. A pure chase strategy allows lower inventories when compared to pure level and mixed strategies.
    e. All of the above are true.

11. _____ is NOT an EXTERNAL input to the production planning environment.
    a. Subcontractor capacity
    b. Actions of competitors
    c. Demand forecasts
    d. Raw material availability
    e. All of the above are external inputs

12. Which of the following is NOT one of the INTERNAL inputs to the production planning environment?
    a. labor standards and machine standards
    b. economic conditions
    c. work force levels and training capacity
    d. productivity data
    e. demand forecasts

13. Which of the following is NOT associated with manipulation of product or service demand?
    a. price incentives
    b. reservations
    c. part-time/temporary labor
    d. complementary products or services
    e. advertising/promotion

14. Which of the following is associated with manipulation of product or service demand?
    a. reservations
    b. overtime/slack time
    c. inventories
    d. subcontracting
    e. cooperative arrangements

Chapter 11 - Aggregate Production Planning

15. Which of the following actions is consistent with following a pure chase strategy?
    a. vary production levels to meet demand requirements
    b. vary work force to meet demand requirements
    c. vary production levels and work force to meet demand requirements
    d. little or no use of inventory to meet demand requirements
    e. all of the above

16. Which of the following is NOT consistent with a pure level strategy?
    a. constant production levels
    b. little or no use of inventory to meet demand requirements
    c. vary production levels and/or work force to meet demand requirements
    d. fixed work force levels
    e. both b and c are inconsistent with level strategy

17. Which of the following statements regarding aggregate production planning is TRUE?
    a. Mathematical modeling is less widely used in firms with heavy investments in computer and modeling technology.
    b. In spite of the research into mathematical models, aggregate production planners continue to use trial and error methods when developing their plans.
    c. One of the most recent mathematical approaches to aggregate production planning was the linear decision rule, developed by Holt, Modigliani, and Simon.
    d. The greatest value of the search decision rule is in serving as a guideline for evaluating various plans and policies.
    e. Bowman's management coefficients model uses simulation techniques to model the aggregate planning process.

18. Which of the following statements regarding aggregate production planning is TRUE?
    a. Hierarchical production planning (HPP) is the term used to describe the process of tailoring the planning structure to the organization.
    b. A major advantage of hierarchical production planning is that each successive level has a simpler structure, less data and can be analyzed using simpler models.
    c. Medium-range planning is corporate strategic planning and results in a statement of organizational goals and objectives.
    d. All of the above are true.
    e. Both a and b are true.

19. Which of the following is NOT an element of medium-range planning?
    a. resource planning
    b. aggregate production planning
    c. strategic planning
    d. master production scheduling
    e. rough-cut capacity planning

20. Which of the following is NOT a mathematical model used for aggregate production planning?
    a. transportation method of linear programming
    b. financial planning
    c. parametric production planning
    d. search decision rule
    e. management coefficients model

PROBLEMS

PROBLEM SITUATION #1

Peter's Peripherals assembles multimedia upgrade kits -- sets of components for adding sound and video to desktop computers. The demand for their kits for the next four quarters is estimated in the table below. Unit manufacturing cost for each kit is $160. Holding costs on each kit is $80 per quarter. Any kit that must be delivered late is assessed a backorder cost of $120. Each worker is capable of finishing 10 kits per quarter. If the company chooses to vary work force levels, it will incur costs of $400 for each additional worker, $600 for each termination. The company currently has 28 employees.

	1997-III	1997-IV	1998-I	1998-II
Demand	280	340	360	300

21. Following a pure chase strategy, production in 1998-II will be _____ kits and will require that _____
    a. 300; six workers be terminated.
    b. 300; six workers be added.
    c. 320; no workers be added.
    d. 240; five workers be terminated.
    e. none of the above

22. Following a pure level strategy, production in 1997-IV will be _____ units, which will result in _____ units of ending inventory at the end of that quarter.
    a. 340; 60
    b. 320; 20
    c. 340; zero
    d. 320; zero

23. In addition to the cost of assembling the kits, the sum of inventory holding costs and backorder costs associated with a pure level strategy would be _____.
    a. zero
    b. $8,800
    c. $4,800
    d. $7,200
    e. cannot be determined from the data provided

154   Chapter 11 - Aggregate Production Planning

24.   In following a pure chase strategy, the company would need to _____ at the start of 1998-I.
       a.   hire two workers
       b.   terminate two workers
       c.   keep the work force steady
       d.   terminate six workers
       e.   increase demand

25.   In addition to the unit manufacturing cost, the work force variation costs of a pure chase strategy would be _____.
       a. $7,200
       b. $3,600
       c. $3,200
       d. $6,800
       e.   none of the above

PROBLEM SOLUTION #2

Pierre Part Pirogue Company makes fiberglass pirogues -- one-person boats used by hunters. Demand for the next six months, and capacities of the plant are shown in the table below. Unit cost on regular time is $80. Overtime cost is 150 percent of regular time cost. Subcontracting is not available. Holding costs are $10 per tank per month; backorders cost the firm $10 per unit per month. Management believes that the transportation algorithm can be used to optimize this scheduling problem.

	January	February	March	April	May	June
Demand	15	10	35	50	40	15
Regular capacity	30	30	30	30	30	30
Overtime capacity	10	10	10	10	10	10

26.   How many units will be produced on regular time in January?
       a.   15
       b.   30
       c.   10
       d.   40
       e.   none of the above

27.   How many units will be produced on overtime over the six-month period?
       a.   0
       b.   60
       c.   180
       d.   240
       e.   none of the above

28. What will be the inventory at the end of March?
    a. 50
    b. 15
    c. 35
    d. 30
    e. 0

29. What will be total production from all sources over the six-month period?
    a. 180
    b. 165
    c. 240
    d. 90
    e. none of the above

30. What will be the total cost of the optimum solution?
    a. $14,400
    b. $13,750
    c. $14,100
    d. none of the above
    e. cannot be determined from the information provided

APPLICATION QUESTIONS

Fourchon Offshore Suppliers makes fiberglass tanks that are manufactured into potable water holding tanks for the living quarters on offshore oil and gas platforms. Demand for the next eight months, and capacities of the plant are shown in the table below. Unit cost on regular time is $260 (new equipment is installed in August which reduces cost to $240). Overtime cost is 150 percent of regular time cost. Subcontracting is available in quantities and prices that vary wildly -- when business is good, the subcontractors have their own work. Holding costs are $40 per tank per month; backorders cost the firm $100 per unit per month. Management believes the transportation algorithm can be used to optimize this scheduling problem.

	April	May	June	July	August	Sept.	Oct.	Nov.
Demand	150	170	120	180	100	70	160	150
Regular capacity	100	100	100	100	125	125	125	125
Overtime capacity	40	40	40	40	40	40	40	40
Subcontract cap.	60	80	100	0	40	60	0	80
Subcontract cost	$400	$400	$400	$500	$450	$400	$500	$400

1. How many units will be produced on regular time in June?

2. How many units will be produced by subcontracting over the eight-month period?

3. What will be the inventory at the end of September?

4. What will be total production from all sources in May?

5. How many units will be made on overtime over the eight-month period?

6. In what month(s) will there be backorders?

7. What will be the maximum inventory over the eight-month period and in what month will it occur?

8. What will be the total cost of the optimum solution?

SHORT ANSWER QUESTIONS

1. What is aggregate planning and why is it important to manufacturers?

2. Production planning has several common objectives. What are those objectives and what conflicts do you see in them?

3. Describe the two "pure" operations strategies for aggregate planning. Why is pure level strategy normally not applicable to the aggregate planning of service firms?

4. There are several managerial issues involved in aggregate production planning including relationships with organized labor. How do you think labor unions would evaluate different aggregate planning options?

5. Trial-and-error methods for aggregate production planning continue to be widely used in spite of the development of alternative approaches. Why do you think managers continue to use "primitive" techniques when more sophisticated approaches are available?

CHAPTER 12
INDEPENDENT DEMAND INVENTORY MANAGEMENT

INTRODUCTION

INDEPENDENT AND DEPENDENT DEMAND

BASIC INVENTORY CONCEPTS
    Types of Inventories
    OPERATIONS MANAGEMENT IN PRACTICE 12.1: Increasing Profits by Squeezing
        Work-in-Process Inventory
    How to Measure Inventory
    Reasons for Holding Inventories
    OPERATIONS MANAGEMENT IN PRACTICE 12.2: Inventory Control - An Important
        Ingredient in Wal-Mart's Recipe for Success
    Inventory Costs
    Classifying Inventory Items
    Inventory Records
    GLOBAL OPERATIONS MANAGEMENT 12.3: Beamscope Canada, Inc. Moves to the On-
        Line Age in Inventory Control and Distribution
    Objectives of Inventory Control

HOW MUCH TO ORDER: ECONOMIC ORDER QUANTITY MODELS
    Economic Order Quantity: Constant Demand, No Shortages
    Economic Order Quantity: Constant Demand, Shortages Allowed
    Economic Order Quantity: Uniform Replenishment Rate, Constant Demand, No Shortages
    Economic Order Quantity: Quantity Discounts
    Sensitivity Analysis for the EOQ Model

WHEN TO ORDER: THE CONTINUOUS REVIEW SYSTEM
    Determining the Reorder Point
    OPERATIONS MANAGEMENT IN PRACTICE 12.4: Delivering the Hits at Musicland
    Service Levels, Safety Stock, and Shortages

WHEN TO ORDER: THE PERIODIC REVIEW SYSTEM

COMPARING THE CONTINUOUS REVIEW AND PERIODIC REVIEW SYSTEMS
    OPERATIONS MANAGEMENT IN PRACTICE 12.5: Reducing Inventory and Improving
        Productivity at Von Duprin, Inc.

CHAPTER SUMMARY

1. An inventory is the stock or the store of an item or a resource used by an organization. Good inventory management is important to all firms, whether manufacturing or service. Four reasons for its importance are

    a. Inventories can be a major commitment of monetary resources.

b. Inventories affect virtually every aspect of daily operations.

c. Inventories can be a major competitive weapon.

d. Inventories are a major control problem in many companies.

2. This chapter explores the concepts and techniques that underlie effective inventory management, through a balance of traditional inventory models and modern inventory topics such as just-in-time.

3. Basics of inventory and inventory management include:

a. A key element is whether an item has independent or dependent demand.

(1) Independent demand items are shipped as end items to customers; items may be finished goods or spare/repair parts. Demand is market-based, and is unrelated to the demand for other items.

(2) Dependent demand items are used in the production of a finished product. Such items may be raw materials, component parts or subassemblies. Demand is not directly market-based; requirements are based on the number needed in each higher-level item where the part is used.

b. There are three accounting categories, or types, of inventories:

(1) Raw materials

(2) Work in process

(3) Finished goods

c. There are three methods for measuring inventory:

(1) Average aggregate inventory value

(2) Weeks of supply

(3) Inventory turnover, or turns

4. Inventory serves various functions in a firm. Firms hold inventories to buffer against uncertainties in supply, in the production process, and in demand. Six types of inventory, based on the motivation for holding it, are:

a. Anticipation stock, to meet customer demand.

b. Safety stock, to protect against stock-outs.

c. Cycle stock, to take advantage of economic order cycles.

d. Buffer stock, to maintain independence of operations.

e. Movement inventory, including work-in-process and in-transit inventory, to allow for smooth and flexible production operations.

f. Hedge inventory, to guard against price increases.

5. There are several costs associated with inventory.

   a. Ordering cost, incurred with each purchase order, is independent of the amount ordered and primarily clerical and administrative in nature.

   b. Setup cost, incurred with each production setup, independent of the number of items to be produced.

   c. Holding, carrying, or storage cost is directly related to the number or value of items held. Includes direct costs such as storage costs, insurance, taxes and, obsolescence, as well as opportunity costs for funds invested in inventory.

   d. Stockout or shortage cost, incurred when demand cannot be met immediately. This cost is either a direct cost of special handling or an implicit cost of lost sales and reduced goodwill. Such costs may depend on the number of units short as well as how long the shortage lasts.

   e. Item cost becomes relevant if a quantity discount is available.

6. ABC analysis determines which items are worth close inventory control. This classification is based on the presumption that a controlling the few most important items produces the vast majority of inventory savings.

   a. "A" Items are tightly controlled, have accurate records, and receive regular review by major decision makers.

   b. "B" Items are less controlled, have good records and regular review.

   c. "C" Items have minimal records, periodic review, simple controls.

7. Accurate inventory records must be maintained. Techniques for maintaining accuracy of records include:

   a. periodic review -- physically count all items on hand.

   b. perpetual inventory -- every transaction is reflected in inventory changes.

   c. cycle counting -- a small percentage of all items counted daily and errors corrected.

8. There are two major objectives of inventory control, which commonly are in conflict. The operations manager's problem is in striking a balance between the two. These objectives are

   a. maximize the level of customer service, and

162   Chapter 12 - Independent Demand Inventory Management

    b. promote production or purchasing efficiency by minimizing the cost of providing an adequate level of customer service.

9. The two basic decisions of inventory management are

    a. When to order? This applies whether ordering units for retail sale or scheduling a manufacturing run.

    b. How much to order? Similarly, this applies to manufacturing as well as other firms.

The two decisions are not independent of one another.

10. Economic order quantity (EOQ) models answer the question of how much to order. All variations of the EOQ models specify an optimal order quantity, which minimizes annual costs associated with maintaining inventories. These models clearly demonstrate the tradeoffs required in inventory management.

    a. Each of the models is based on a set of assumptions. The most restrictive set applies to model (1) below, Basic EOQ with constant demand and no shortages. These assumptions are

        (1) It is applicable to a single product that is continuously reviewed.

        (2) The demand rate for the item is known, and is constant over time.

        (3) The item is produced in lots, or purchased in orders.

        (4) Each order is received in a single delivery.

        (5) The lead time is known and constant.

        (6) Inventory holding cost is based on average inventory.

        (7) Ordering costs or setup costs are constant.

        (8) No backorders are allowed.

        (9) There are no quantity discounts.

11. The four models are

    a. Basic EOQ -- constant demand, no shortages

    b. Basic EOQ -- constant demand, shortages allowed

    c. Uniform replenishment model -- constant demand, no shortages

    d. Quantity discount model, no shortages

12. Problems for each of the four models are explored in considerable detail. What follows are some observations about the general behavior of behavior of economic order quantity models. The chapter summary makes no attempt to detail the mathematical modeling of the text.

   a. Item cost is relevant only in the quantity discount model (d). Item cost times annual demand is a fixed amount in models (a) through (c) and cannot affect the decision.

   b. Although calculus was used to derive the optimizing formulas, it is apparent in models (a) and (c) that optimization occurs where annual ordering costs equal annual holding costs.

   c. Maximum inventory in model (c) is less than the production lot size because some items are used without ever being inventoried. Maximum inventory in model (b) is less than the order quantity because backorders are filled before inventory is created.

   d. Once the EOQ is found, related values can be determined algebraically:

      (1) EOQ divided into annual demand is number of orders per year.

      (2) Length of order cycle is 365 divided by number of orders per year.

   e. The rationale for model (b), EOQ with shortages, is that, if shortage costs are low enough, or carrying costs high enough, it may be cheaper to deliberately incur shortages than to keep inventory. This is especially true for perishable items, and for high value custom items such as RVs.

   f. The rationale for model (d), quantity discounts, is that a discount offered may be sufficient inducement for the decision-maker NOT to choose an EOQ-based solution, that the savings in item cost more than offset the net increase in holding costs plus ordering costs.

   g. Carrying cost appears in most formulas as C_H, whose dimensions are dollars per unit per year. It is normal for carrying cost to be referred to as a percent of the value of an item, implying that C_H is the product of unit price times the carrying cost percent. This is specifically the form of the carrying cost in the quantity discount model.

13. Sensitivity analysis. If the numeric inputs to these models are incorrect, are the results invalid? Generally, so long as the inputs are "close enough" to reality that the calculated optimum behavior is near the true value, the increase of total annual inventory cost is small, perhaps negligible.

14. This section contains two models of when to order, the continuous review system model and the periodic review system model. With one exception, both models deal with uncertainties not present in the economic order quantity models.

   a. In this section, demand per unit time can be variable and the lead time can be variable. These uncertainties mean that shortages (stockouts) can and will occur.

   b. Both models utilize the concept of cycle-service level as the measure of customer service. This measure is used because shortage costs are not known. A high cycle-service level serves as proxy for low shortage costs. Safety stock is inventory carried to assure that the desired service level is reached.

c. There is no risk of shortage until a replenishment decision has been made. Cycle-service level is the percentage of demand that can be satisfied from stock on hand during the period at risk. This is the lead time for continuous review systems; it is the protection interval (the lead time plus the fixed order interval) for periodic review systems.

d. Standard statistical tools are used to calculate the amount of safety stock and the corresponding reorder point in continuous review systems, and to calculate the order quantity in periodic review systems. As in the earlier section, this summary does not duplicate textbook exposition of the models.

15. The continuous review system is also called the reorder point system or the fixed order quantity system. This model places an order for the fixed order quantity Q whenever the inventory level falls to the reorder point R. The time between orders is variable. Four cases are presented. In the first case there is no uncertainty and there will be no stockouts. In the other three cases either demand and/or lead time is variable, and shortages will occur.

16. The periodic review system is also called the fixed order interval system. This model places an order for a variable quantity at a fixed time interval T. The variable order quantity is calculated from expected demand plus safety stock, less inventory on hand. The first two terms in this expression are fixed, but inventory on hand is not. When the time to place orders comes, inventory on hand will be high if demand has been low; inventory on hand will be low if demand has been high.

17. Comparing continuous and periodic systems. Each of the systems described has advantages.

   a. Advantages of continuous review include:

      (1) lower safety stock (from shorter period at risk)

      (2) fixed lot sizes may imply easier quantity discounts

      (3) individual review of items may be desirable for expensive items

   b. Advantages of periodic review include:

      (1) less time consuming, less experience needed to maintain

      (2) allows combining orders to the same supplier

      (3) reduced record keeping cost

KEY TERMS

a. ABC classification
b. anticipation stock
c. average aggregate inventory value
d. back order
e. carrying cost
f. continuous review system
g. cycle counting
h. cycle-service level
i. cycle stock
j. dependent demand
k. economic lot size
l. economic order quantity (EOQ)
m. fill rate
n. finished goods
o. fixed order interval system
p. fixed order quantity system
q. fixed time period system
r. holding cost
s. independent demand
t. in-transit inventory
u. inventory
v. inventory turnover (turns)

w. item cost
x. lead time
y. movement inventories
z. ordering cost
aa. periodic review system
bb. pipeline inventory
cc. quantity discount
dd. raw materials
ee. reorder point
ff. reorder point system (ROP)
gg. safety stock
hh. setup cost
ii. shortage
jj. shortage cost
kk. stockout
ll. stockout cost
mm. storage cost
nn. two-bin system
oo. weeks of supply
pp. work-in-process
qq. work-in-process inventory

DEFINITIONS

Directions: Select from the key terms list, the word or phrase being defined below.

_____ 1. is the stock or the store of an item or a resource used by an organization.

_____ 2. is the order size which minimizes total annual costs of maintaining inventories.

_____ 3. is the percentage of demand that can be satisfied from stock on hand during the period at risk.

_____ 4. is inventory carried to assure that the desired service level is reached.

_____ 5. is inventory carried to take advantage of economic order cycles.

_____ 6. is inventory carried to allow for smooth and flexible operations.

_____ 7. is inventory carried to maintain independence of operations.

_____ 8. is inventory carried to meet anticipated customer demand.

_____ 9. is the cost incurred each time a company places an order with a supplier or a production order with its own shop.

Chapter 12 - Independent Demand Inventory Management

_____ 10. is the cost involved in changing over a machine to produce a different part or item.

_____ 11. is the cost associated with maintaining an inventory until it is used or sold.

_____ 12. is the cost incurred when the demand for an item exceeds its supply.

_____ 13. is a shortage where demand for an item will be satisfied when the item next becomes available.

_____ 14. places an order for the fixed order quantity Q whenever the inventory level falls to the reorder point R.

_____ 15. places an order for a variable quantity at a fixed time interval T.

MULTIPLE CHOICE QUESTIONS

1. Which of the following is NOT a motive for holding inventory?
   a. anticipation stock, to meet customer demand
   b. safety stock, to protect against stock-outs
   c. cycle stock, to take advantage of economic order cycles
   d. movement inventory, to allow for smooth and flexible operations
   e. all of the above are motives for holding inventory

2. Which of the following does NOT favor the importance of effective inventory management?
   a. Inventories can be a major commitment of monetary resources.
   b. Inventories affect virtually every aspect of daily operations.
   c. Inventories can be a major competitive weapon.
   d. Inventories are a major control problem in many companies.
   e. All of the above favor effective inventory management.

3. In a basic EOQ setting, which one of the following statements is FALSE?
   a. If annual demand were to double, the EOQ would also double.
   b. If annual demand were to double, both EOQ and orders per year would increase.
   c. If the ordering cost were to increase, the EOQ would rise.
   d. If the ordering cost were to decrease, the EOQ would fall.
   e. All of the above statements are true.

4. Which of the following statements about ABC analysis is TRUE?
   a. "A" items are tightly controlled, have accurate records, and receive regular review by major decision makers.
   b. ABC analysis is based on the presumption that controlling most items is necessary to produce the vast majority of inventory savings.
   c. "A" items have minimal records, periodic review, and simple controls.
   d. ABC analysis is based on the presumption that all items must be tightly controlled to produce important cost savings.
   e. None of the above statements is true.

5. Which of the following statements about basic EOQ models is TRUE?
   a. If annual demand were to double, the EOQ would also double.
   b. If annual demand were to double, both the EOQ and the number of orders per year would increase.
   c. If the carrying cost were to increase, the EOQ would rise.
   d. If the carrying cost were to double, the EOQ would be cut in half.
   e. None of the above is a true statement.

6. A firm has been ordering a certain item 60 units at a time. The firm estimates that holding cost is $2 per unit per year, and that annual demand is about 180 units per year. The assumptions of the basic EOQ model are thought to apply. For what value of ordering cost would their action be optimal?
   a. 3
   b. 20
   c. 180
   d. none of the above is correct
   e. cannot be determined from data provided

7. A firm has been buying a part in an optimal fashion using EOQ analysis. The supplier has now offered a discount of 2 percent off all units if the firm will make its purchases quarterly. Current data for the problem are: D=1800 units per year; C_H=$1; C_O=25. List price of the part is $6. The firm should _____ the discount, because it would _____ the firm _____.
   a. take; save; $208
   b. refuse; cost; $10,192
   c. refuse; cost; $11,000
   d. take; save; $191
   e. cannot be calculated with information given.

8. A firm stocks a certain item for which inventory management is continuous review; the firm's management has established that the cycle-service level should be 95 percent. Demand averages 180 units per day with a standard deviation of 20 units per day. Lead time is fixed at 5 days. The reorder point for this item is approximately _____.
   a. 974 units
   b. 74 units
   c. 988 units
   d. 88 units
   e. cannot be calculated since the EOQ is not provided

9. A firm manufactures an item for which it has good estimates of backorder cost. The firm has estimated that carrying cost is $5 per unit per year, and that backorder cost is $15 per unit per year. Other data are: annual demand is 500 units; ordering cost is $200. The optimal batch size is _____ and shortage amount is _____.
   a. 200, 0
   b. 230, 57.5
   c. 209.5, 18.25
   d. 400, 100
   e. none of the above

168   Chapter 12 - Independent Demand Inventory Management

10. A firm manufactures a certain part which it uses in a downstream operation. The machine which makes the part can make 1200 per day. The parts are needed in the downstream at the rate of 180 per day. Setup cost is $150 and carrying cost is $0.25 per unit per year. The firm operates 250 days per year. The optimal batch size is approximately ____.
   a. 504 units
   b. 7970 units
   c. 7348 units
   d. 1200 units
   e. none of the above

11. Of the following reasons, which would NOT generally be considered a motive for holding inventories?
   a. hedge against price increases
   b. take advantage of economic order cycles
   c. reduce stockout risks
   d. decouple internal operations
   e. all of the above are valid motives

12. The basic Economic Order Quantity model is directly relevant to which of the following tasks?
   a. coordinating the purchase of several related items
   b. performing fixed order interval calculations
   c. calculating single-period inventory quantities
   d. ordering dependent demand items
   e. none of the above

13. In the Economic Order Quantity model with constant demand and no shortages, if the lead time decreases from 4 days to 1, the EOQ will
   a. increase.
   b. be unchanged.
   c. decrease proportionately.
   d. decrease, but not proportionately.
   e. none of the above.

14. Which one of the following best explains the term "80 percent cycle-service level"?
   a. Approximately 80 percent of demand during the lead time will be satisfied.
   b. The probability is 80 percent that supply will exceed demand during the lead time.
   c. The probability is 80 percent that demand will equal supply during the lead time.
   d. The probability is 20 percent that demand will not exceed supply during the lead time
   e. The risk of a stock out during the lead time is 80 percent.

15. Of the following types of items, which would ordinarily have independent demand?
   a. repair parts
   b. spare parts
   c. finished goods
   d. all of the above
   e. only a and c

16. Of the following types of items, which would NOT ordinarily have independent demand?
    a. raw materials
    b. spare parts
    c. subassemblies
    d. all of the above
    e. only a and c

17. Which of the following statements regarding inventory management is TRUE?
    a. Inventory carrying costs consist of both explicit (direct) cost elements and implicit (opportunity) cost elements.
    b. The major implicit cost of inventory holding cost is the cost of insuring inventory.
    c. When a firm practices cycle-counting, every transaction is reflected in changes in inventory records.
    d. The three accounting categories of inventories are raw materials, work in process, and finished goods.
    e. Both a and d are true.

18. In the most basic EOQ model, if D=72000 per year, C_O=$100, C_H=$10 per unit per year, the Economic Order Quantity is approximately ____.
    a. 350
    b. 600
    c. 1,200
    d. 72,000
    e. 4,160

19. Which of the following statements about quantity discounts is TRUE?
    a. In inventory management, item cost becomes relevant to inventory decisions only when a quantity discount is available.
    b. The smaller is annual demand, the less enticing a discount schedule will be.
    c. The smaller is the ordering cost, the less attractive a discount schedule will be.
    d. If carrying costs are expressed as a percent of value, EOQ is larger at each lower price in the discount schedule.
    e. All of the above are true.

20. The just-in-time manufacturing strategy attempts to shrink setup costs. Regarding economic order quantity calculations, such changes would result in
    a. larger order quantities, ordered less frequently.
    b. lower cycle-service levels.
    c. larger safety stocks.
    d. smaller lot sizes, ordered less frequently.
    e. smaller lot sizes, ordered more frequently.

21. A firm has been ordering a certain item 60 units at a time. The firm estimates that holding cost is $2 per unit per year, and that ordering cost is about $20 per order. The assumptions of the basic EOQ model are thought to apply. For what value of annual demand is their action optimal?
   a. 180
   b. 3600
   c. 1200
   d. 35
   e. cannot be determined from data provided

22. A firm stocks a certain item for which inventory management is continuous review; the firm's management has established that the cycle-service level should be 99 percent. Demand averages 180 units per day with a standard deviation of 30 units per day. Lead time is fixed at 8 days. The reorder point for this item is approximately ____.
   a. 974 units
   b. 1659 units
   c. 1638 units
   d. 1999 units
   e. cannot be calculated since the EOQ is not provided

PROBLEMS

PROBLEM SITUATION #1

A local craft shop has contracted to manufacture an item for sale at the hospitality booth at the local visitors center. The manager of that booth is agreeable to the craft shop delivering finished goods at the shop owner's convenience. The items are relatively small and lightweight; so the primary cost of shipping is the relatively fixed cost of a trip across town. Relevant data for the shop are as follows:

> Annual demand (D) =3500 units
> Ordering (shipping) cost (C_O) = $12 per order
> Holding cost (C_H) = $.50 per unit per year

23. If the shop owner's objective is to minimize total inventory costs, how many should she manufacture and accumulate into her inventory before shipping them to the hospitality booth? All answers have been rounded to whole numbers.
   a. 1296
   b. 292
   c. 410
   d. None of the above is correct.
   e. Cannot be determined; the EOQ model does not apply.

24. If the shop owner practices EOQ inventory management, what will her average inventory be, and what will be her annual holding costs? All answers have been rounded to whole units and dollars.
   a. 205 units; $205 in carrying costs
   b. 410 units, $205 in carrying costs
   c. 205 units; $102.50 in carrying costs
   d. 292 units; $146 in carrying costs
   e. none of the above is correct

25. If the shop owner practices EOQ inventory management, how often will she make the trip to deliver finished goods to the visitors' center?
   a. about 12 times per year (every 30 days)
   b. about 43 times per year (every 8 1/2 days)
   c. whenever the visitors' center needs delivery
   d. about 8 1/2 times per year (every 43 days)
   e. none of the above is correct

26. If the visitors' center has a policy change, and wants deliveries made once a month, how much extra will it cost the craft shop, if it chooses to comply with the request?
   a. the cost of 3 1/2 extra trips to the visitors' center, or $42
   b. there is no extra cost associated with the policy change
   c. $12
   d. $217
   e. none of the above

27. If the visitors' center were to require replenishment once per week, how much extra would it cost the craft shop to comply?
   a. the cost of the extra trips, or $522
   b. $641
   c. $624
   d. $453
   e. $320

172   *Chapter 12 - Independent Demand Inventory Management*

PROBLEM SITUATION #2

A local sheltered workshop manufactures fishing lures which use a subassembly also manufactured at the workshop. While the manufacturing process is continuous, the subassemblies are made in batches. Data on the manufacture of the subassemblies appears below.

>   Annual demand (D) = 73,000 units
>   Setup cost (C_O) = $130 per batch
>   Holding cost (C_H) = $.05 per unit per year
>   Daily subassembly production rate = 1,000
>   Daily subassembly usage rate = 200

28. How large should each batch of subassemblies be?
    a. 21,783 units
    b. 19,483 units
    c. 56 units
    d. 2,280 units
    e. 1,020 units

29. Approximately how many days are required to produce a batch?
    a. five working days
    b. exactly one week
    c. 108.9 days
    d. 21.8 days
    e. none of the above

30. How long is a complete cycle?
    a. five working days
    b. exactly one week
    c. 108.9 days
    d. 21.8 days
    e. none of the above

31. What is the average inventory for this problem?
    a. 10,891 units
    b. 8,713 units
    c. 21,783 units
    d. 9,742 units
    e. none of the above

32. What is the total inventory cost (rounded to nearest dollar) of the optimal behavior in this problem?
   a. $871
   b. $3,650
   c. $436
   d. $974
   e. $487

PROBLEM SITUATION #3

A firm has been buying a part in an optimal fashion using EOQ analysis. The supplier has now offered a discount of 4 percent off all units if the firm will make its purchases quarterly. Current data for the problem are: D=7200 units per year; C_H=$1 per unit per year; C_O=$36 per order. List price of the part is $5.

33. What is the EOQ that represents optimal behavior (before considering the discount)?
   a. 7,200
   b. 200
   c. 720
   d. 24
   e. 576

34. What is the total relevant cost of this optimal behavior?
   a. $720
   b. $360
   c. $7,236
   d. $36,000
   e. $7,200

35. What will be the annual inventory carrying charges if the discount is taken?
   a. $6,912
   b. $1,800
   c. $864
   d. $900
   e. $7,812

36. What is the proposed total relevant cost if the firm takes the discount?
   a. $36,720
   b. $35,604
   c. $34,560
   d. $6,912
   e. $7,956

37. The firm should _____ the discount, because it would _____ the firm _____.
    a. take; save; $1,116
    b. refuse; cost; $1,440
    c. refuse; cost; $35,604
    d. take; save; $36,720
    e. cannot be calculated with information given

PROBLEM SITUATION #4

Davidson Hardware stocks an expensive composite-based plaster patching compound, currently classified "A" which is controlled by continuous review. Demand is variable, with an average of 6 pounds per week and a standard deviation of 2 pounds per week. Lead time is constant at one week. The firm's current management of the product calls for a safety stock of one (1) pound.

38. The current reorder point for this product is _____ pounds.
    a. 5
    b. 7
    c. 6
    d. 8
    e. none of the above

39. The current cycle-service level is _____ .
    a. 0.5
    b. 1.29
    c. 0.8413
    d. 0.6915
    e. none of the above

40. If Davidson wanted to change the safety stock so that the cycle-service level became 90 percent, the new reorder point would be _____.
    a. 6
    b. 9.3
    c. 8.6
    d. 8
    e. none of the above

41. Assume that Davidson has reviewed its inventory classifications, and that this item has been reclassified "B" and that it now managed by periodic review. Review occurs once per quarter. With a 90 percent cycle-service level, the proper order target is _____ units.
    a. 54.7
    b. 93.7
    c. 96.3
    d. 84
    e. none of the above

PROBLEM SITUATION #5

Consider the case where the demand for a product is normally distributed, with **m** = 10 and **s** = 2 units per day. Assume that the lead time is fixed at 5 days. The firm manages this product by continuous review, with the cycle-service level at 90 percent. The inventory manager believes the cost to prepare an order is C_O= $25 and that inventory holding costs are C_H=$ 0.50 per unit per year.

42. The average demand during the lead time is ____.
    a. 45 units
    b. 100 units
    c. 10 units
    d. 50 units
    e. none of the above

43. The variability of demand during the lead time is ____.
    a. 6.32 units
    b. 4.47 units
    c. 10.95 units
    d. 50 units
    e. none of the above

44. If the firm seeks a 90 percent cycle-service level, what will be the appropriate reorder point?
    a. 60 units
    b. 57.4 units
    c. 55.7 units
    d. 51.4 units
    e. none of the above

45. When the amount on hand indicates that a replenishment action should take place, how large should this replenishment order be?
    a. 32 units
    b. 57.4 units
    c. 12 units
    d. 604 units
    e. none of the above

46. The firm's finished inventory rule for this product should be
    a. order 604 units whenever stock falls to 56.
    b. order 604 units approximately 6 times per year.
    c. order 57 units whenever stock falls to 604.
    d. order 604 units whenever stock falls to 64.
    e. every two months, order 604 units.

47. If the lead time was not a fixed five days, but normally distributed with a mean of five days and a standard deviation of 1 day, the revised variability of demand during the lead time would be
   a. 6.32 units.
   b. 4.47 units.
   c. 11 units.
   d. 50 units.
   e. none of the above.

48. In the presence of the added source of variability (lead time has a mean of five days with a standard deviation of one day), the firm's finished inventory rule for this product should be
   a. order 604 units whenever stock falls to 56.
   b. order 773 units approximately 6 times per year.
   c. order 57 units whenever stock falls to 604.
   d. order 604 units whenever stock falls to 64.
   e. order 604 units whenever stock falls to 58.

PROBLEM SITUATION #6

Electronic Toys, Games, and So Forth is studying the items it stocks to determine which need the tightest control, and which may be only loosely controlled. The following table reflects historical sales data for one of its work areas.

Item ID	Item Description	Unit Value	Unit Sales, 1993
PCM433	Multimedia add-on	$240	1,000
PCS210	Flight Simulator	$45	3,000
PCX669	Mouse Pad	$6	2,000
PCC317	Diskette (box of 10)	$9	10,000
MCM100	Microphone	$17	100
GOS255	Legal pad (pack of 6)	$4	250
PCX118	Analog joystick	$25	8,000
GOS646	Transparent tape (6)	$5	300
GOS648	Paper clips (10 boxes)	$2	500
PCS510	CD-ROM reference set	$200	3,000
GOS550	Post-its	$2	7,000
PCP399	Ink jet printer	$550	900

49. The total annual sales (in dollars) from this work area is ____.
   a. 36,050
   b. 1,611,200
   c. 1,791,200
   d. 6,056,400
   e. none of the above

50. Product _____ accounts for the largest sales volume of this group; it accounts for about _____ percent of sales from this group.
    a. PCS510; 33
    b. PCP399; 550
    c. PCC317; 10000
    d. PCP399; 28
    e. none of the above

51. When the twelve products are arranged in order of decreasing annual dollar volume, the top two items account for approximately _____ percent of work area sales.
    a. 33
    b. 61
    c. 27
    d. 68
    e. none of the above

52. If this firm wished for A items to represent approximately 20 percent of all items or 60 percent of all sales, then the A item(s) would be
    a. PCM433 and PCS510.
    b. PCS510.
    c. PCM433, PCS510, and PCP399.
    d. PCS510 and PCP399.
    e. not selected because the percentages cannot be matched exactly.

53. If six items are C item(s), they will account for approximately _____ percent of sales.
    a. 10
    b. 2
    c. 50
    d. 15
    e. 20

54. If this firm wished for C items to represent approximately 50 percent of all items, then the C item(s) would be
    a. Mouse Pad, Microphone, Legal pad, Joystick, Transparent tape, Paper clips and Post-its.
    b. Mouse Pad, Microphone, Legal pad, Transparent tape, Paper clips and Post-its.
    c. Mouse Pad, Microphone, Legal pad, Transparent tape, Paper clips and Ink jet printer.
    d. Mouse Pad, Microphone, Legal pad, Transparent tape, Paper clips, and Multimedia Add-on.
    e. none of the above is correct.

55. When the twelve products are arranged in order of decreasing annual dollar volume, the lowest _____ items account for approximately fourteen percent of work area sales.
   a. eight
   b. four
   c. six
   d. none of the above
   e. cannot be calculated

APPLICATION QUESTIONS

A firm manufactures an item in batches; the manufactured items are placed in stock. The firm has estimated that carrying cost is $8 per unit per year. Other data are: annual demand is 9125 units; ordering cost is $50. The firm currently plans to satisfy all customer demand from stock on hand. Demand is known and constant.

1. What is the size of the manufacturing batch that minimizes costs?

2. For this optimal quantity, how many orders will need to be placed each year to satisfy the annual demand?

3. What would be the average inventory level at this optimal quantity?

4. What would be the total relevant cost of this optimal quantity?

5. The firm is concerned over the relatively high carrying costs, and is considering a policy of planned shortages. If the firm learned that backorder cost is $32 per unit per year, what would be the new optimal quantity?

6. What would be the maximum shortage level based on the optimal shortage level?

7. The length of time during which there will be shortages will be about how many days?

SHORT ANSWER QUESTIONS

1. What are the three types of inventory? What are the reasons for holding each type?

2. What are the reasons that companies hold inventory? If an organization could magically control its complete environment (e.g. suppliers do what they say, machines don't break down, quality is 100 percent, customers do not change their minds and give plenty of lead time, etc.), would there be any need for inventory? Explain.

3. What is the ABC inventory classification? How is it useful for organizations?

4. What is a two-bin inventory system and why is it classed as a continuous review system? Some would say that your checkbook is an example of a two-bin inventory system. How is that so?

5. Compare the continuous review inventory system to the periodic review system. Identify when each is appropriate and what triggers an order in each.

CHAPTER 13
DEPENDENT DEMAND INVENTORY MANAGEMENT: MATERIAL REQUIREMENTS PLANNING

INTRODUCTION
    The Development Of Material Requirements Planning (MRP)
        OPERATIONS MANAGEMENT IN PRACTICE 13.1: MRP at Steelcase

MRP PREREQUISITES
    The Master Production Schedule
    Bills of Material
    Inventory Records

THE MRP PROCESS
    MRP Records
    Timing Conventions
    MRP Record Calculations

AN MRP EXAMPLE
    Low-level Coding
    Gross-to-net Requirements Explosion

IMPORTANT OBSERVATIONS
    Loss of Visibility for Low-level Components
    Minimum Length for the Planning Horizon
    MRP System Nervousness
    Freezing the Master Production Schedule
    Lumpiness of Demand

LOT SIZING
    Lot-for-lot
    Fixed Order Quantity
    Period Order Quantity
    Lot Sizing and MRP System Nervousness
    The Importance of Lot Sizing

USE OF MRP SYSTEMS

SOME PRACTICAL CONSIDERATIONS IN USING MRP
    Uncertainty
    Modular Bills of Material
    Closed Loop MRP
    MRP II -- Manufacturing Resource Planning

IMPLEMENTATION OF MRP
    Existing Systems and the Informal System
    Information Requirements
    Inventory Control

OPERATIONS MANAGEMENT IN PRACTICE 13.2: MRP and the Real Cost of Inventory Losses at Gendex
Keys to Successful Implementation
An MRP Implementation Plan
GLOBAL OPERATIONS MANAGEMENT 13.3: Implementing MRP II at the Raymond Corporation

DISTRIBUTION REQUIREMENTS PLANNING (DRP)

CHAPTER SUMMARY

1. Material requirements planning (MRP) is a production planning system specifically designed to handle dependent demand inventory items. While it was initially seen as an improvement over traditional inventory models, it has become a comprehensive and effective production and planning system.

2. An MRP system requires three types of information. These three inputs determine the following for all components and subassemblies: order quantities, planned order release dates, and order due dates.

    a. Master production schedule (MPS): The MPS is a detailed production schedule for finished goods or end-items.

    b. Bills of materials (BOMs): The BOM identifies all components that are used in the production of an end item, the quantity required, and the order in which the components are assembled.

    c. Inventory records: Accurate and current inventory records are vital to smooth functioning of any MRP system.

3. The MPS is a detailed production schedule for finished goods or end-items. The planning horizon is the length of time for which end item production is planned. It is at least as long as the maximum cumulative production and procurement lead time for the firm's finished products. The aggregate production plan specifies production for product families over an extended time horizon. The master production schedule is a more detailed plan that the aggregate production plan and is typically characterized by a one year planning horizon.

4. A bill of material defines the relationship of components to end items.

    a. Component is any inventory item that is part of a finished product.

    b. Assembly drawings or product structure diagrams are graphical forms of the BOM.

    c. Parent component describes a component at one level in the BOM that is composed of components from the next lower level of the BOM. The lower-level components are called child components.

    d. Commonality is the use of a component or subassembly in more than one component, subassembly or end-item.

5. Inventory records are used to maintain the inventory status of items.

   a. The inventory record for each component contains the item identification number, lot size or lot sizing method, lead time, number currently available, and the quantity and delivery date for units already ordered.

   b. Records may also contain information on safety stock requirements and scrap allowances.

6. MRP Process

   a. MRP records are computerized files containing item identification (such as part number and description), inventory information (such as lot sizing), gross requirements, and resulting MRP calculations (culminating in planned order releases). A tabular style of MRP record, suitable for manual calculations, appears below, similar to the text Figure 13.4.

Part No.											
Part Name:											
LS:	LT:	1	2	3	4	5	6	7	8	9	10
Gross Requirements											
Scheduled Receipts											
Planned Order Receipts											
Available Balance											
Planned Order Releases											

   b. MRP systems divide time into fixed intervals, or time buckets, commonly one week. By convention, orders are placed at the beginning of the bucket, orders are available at the beginning of the bucket, and demand must be satisfied by the end of the bucket.

   c. The following terms are in the order found on a typical MRP record:

   (1) Gross requirements is demand for an inventory item. Gross requirements arise from end items or from components required in end items. Gross requirements must be satisfied from inventory, by purchasing, or by production.

   (2) Scheduled receipts indicate size and due date of orders that have previously been released to the shop floor (or to outside vendors).

   (3) Planned order receipts indicate size and due date for the arrival of planned order releases. Planned order receipts is the same as net requirements.

   (4) Available balance is the inventory level of a component at the end of the current period. (The entry left of period 1 indicates the amount available at the beginning of that period, or the beginning inventory.)

   (5) Planned order releases is planned order receipts, offset for the lead time of the item.

   d. Gross-to-net requirements explosion converts the MPS into component requirements using MRP records.

7. Important observations regarding the use of MRP systems:

   a. Loss of visibility -- Low-level components have a reduced planning horizon because of the cumulative lead time of the end item. As lead time offsets make their way down the product structure, the planning horizon is shortened.

   b. The planning horizon minimum length is the maximum cumulative times for all components and their parents. Otherwise, the MRP calculations will not allow sufficient horizon to plan for the acquisition of the lowest level items in time to meet the MPS.

   c. MRP nervousness is a chain reaction or MRP record changes that result from the modification of the MPS. Lot sizing and firm planned orders are possible stabilizing forces. Firm planned orders are the manual fixing or freezing of orders by a production planner so that they are not automatically changed by the MRP when the MPS is changed. Time fences limit changes for different periods in the MPS by requiring approval from different levels in the company (the more immediate the change, the higher the level for approval).

   d. Freezing the MPS -- preventing changes in the MPS for some distance into the near future, serves to avoid some chaotic conditions, such as very frequent changes that anger suppliers and confuse production floor workers. Its disadvantage is that it lessens the MPS's ability to respond to customer needs. Balance is often achieved with time fences -- the nearer to present time, the higher the level of authority needed to make changes in the MPS.

   e. Lumpiness of demand refers to the unevenness of orders for low level items that derive their demand from higher level parents. Smooth demand for a higher level item may become lumpy gross requirements at lower levels when lot sizing rules are applied.

8. Four lot sizing methods are described. There is no optimal procedure for selecting a lot sizing method.

   a. Lot-for-lot (LFL) means that for every lot of a parent component, one lot for the child component is purchased or produced.

   b. Fixed order quantity (FOQ) may follow from EOQ or quantity discount practices or may follow from the discrete nature of certain supplies (which cannot be economically subdivided). This may produce undesirably large levels of inventory.

   c. Period order quantity (POQ) specifies a time span, not a quantity. POQ uses EOQ and average demand to calculate how many periods to buy for. This reduces the inventory buildup that accompanies EOQ use with very irregular demand.

9. In using MRP systems:

   a. The MRP planner is the person who provides inputs, modifies schedules and executes the MRP plan.

   b. Pegging relates the gross requirements for a component to the parent component that caused the requirement.

c. MRP systems often produce only the exception reports, not all MRP records, in order for planners to focus on those items most needing their attention.

10. Practical considerations in using MRP:

a. While MRP seeks to hold down idle inventories, shortages of parts may badly disrupt plans. Uncertainty in length of lead time or in manufacturing yield may be handled with safety stock or scrap allowances. JIT methods in a later chapter will recommend that such uncertainties be fixed rather than keep inventory to cover them.

b. Modular bills of materials may be desirable to avoid huge numbers of end items, which may be generated by the presence of assembly options such as color and trim variation. MRP in this case schedules not the end items themselves but the modules of which they are made. The final assembly schedule then converts modules into end items.

c. Closed-loop MRP uses timely feedback from vendors, from purchasing, and from the shop floor in order to gauge MRP performance and to develop alternatives when production schedules cannot be met.

d. MRP II enlarges MRP to involve the entire firm, not just manufacturing. For example, it may combine MRP data with accounting data to enable production and accounting information systems to be merged. Or it may allow manufacturing schedules to have a direct bearing on capital requirements and other financial matters.

11. MRP implementation requires a huge effort and impacts all parts of the firm. Problems in MRP implementation are more likely organizational and behavioral rather than technical.

a. There can be resistance to change from the current system.

b. MRP requires lots of timely, accurate data. The MRP system can lose integrity if it cannot control product changes (and the resulting changes in bills of materials) or cannot keep electronic inventory in sync with physical inventory.

c. The keys to successful implementation of MRP parallel those of implementing new information technology systems. Factors required for success include

(1) Top management support

(2) Good system design

(3) Appropriate user-designer interaction

d. Included in chapter is a prescriptive MRP implementation plan, Wallace's Proven Path, which suggests that MRP can be planned and implemented over a year and a half. Wallace notes the importance of education in the implementation process. Wallace believes that assuring inventory and BOM accuracy are the most time consuming steps. Wallace believes that the implementation "cold turkey" strategy is too risky and that the "parallel" strategy is impractical. That leaves pilot project as the appropriate strategy for MRP implementation.

186   Chapter 13 - Dependent Demand Inventory Management: MRP

12. Distribution requirements planning (DRP) extends the logic of MRP into the physical distribution system. DRP assists companies that maintain distribution inventories in field warehouses, distribution centers, etc. by improving the linkages between marketplace requirements and manufacturing activities. DRP is a critical link between the market place, demand forecasting, and master production scheduling.

KEY TERMS

a. bill of material (BOM)
b. closed loop MRP
c. economic order quantity (EOQ)
d. firm planned order (FPO)
e. fixed order quantity (FOQ)
f. gross requirements
g. gross to net requirements explosion
h. inventory records
i. item master file
j. lot-for-lot (LFL)
k. low-level code
l. manufacturing resource planning (MRP II)
m. master production schedule (MPS)
n. material requirements planning (MRP)
o. modular bill of material
p. MRP planner
q. MRP records
r. MRP system nervousness
s. option modules
t. pegging
u. period order quantity (POQ)
v. planned order receipts
w. planned order releases
x. product structure diagram
y. safety lead time
z. safety stock
aa. scheduled receipts
bb. time fences

DEFINITIONS

Directions: Select from the key terms list, the word or phrase being defined below.

_____ 1. the expanded MRP system, that provides feedback from the execution functions to the planning functions.

_____ 2. is an production planning system specifically designed to handle dependent demand inventory items.

_____ 3. is a detailed production schedule for finished goods or end-items.

_____ 4. demand for an inventory item arising from all of its parent items.

_____ 5. a bill of material using option modules.

_____ 6. identifies all components that are used in the production of an end item, the quantity required, and the order in which the components are assembled.

_____ 7. a computer file containing information for each component part.

_____ 8. show when planned order releases are expected to arrive.

_____ 9. an amount of time that may be added to planned lead times to allow for possible delivery delays.

_____ 10. is a comprehensive approach for the effective planning of resources of a manufacturing organization.

_____ 11. an inventory balance of a component part that is not used under normal circumstances.

_____ 12. means that for every lot of a parent component, one lot for the child component is purchased or produced.

_____ 13. is a chain reaction or MRP record changes that result from the modification of the MPS.

_____ 14. are the manual fixing or freezing of orders by a production planner so that they are not automatically changed by the MRP when the MPS is changed.

_____ 15. limit changes for different periods in the MPS by requiring approval from different levels in the company.

_____ 16. specifies the order in which the MRP records should be processed.

_____ 17. is the person who provides inputs, modifies schedules and executes the MRP plan.

_____ 18. relates the gross requirements for a component to the parent component that caused the requirement.

_____ 19. converts the master production schedule into component requirements using MRP records.

MULTIPLE CHOICE QUESTIONS

1. A(n) _____ is a list of all parts and materials needed to assemble one unit of a product.
   a. master schedule
   b. kanban
   c. inventory record file
   d. master production schedule
   e. bill of materials

2. Net requirements in MRP is properly calculated by the expression
   a. gross requirements - scheduled receipts - on hand.
   b. gross requirements - on hand + scheduled receipts.
   c. gross requirements - scheduled receipts.
   d. gross requirements - scheduled receipts - planned order receipts.
   e. none of the above.

3. The phrase "dependent demand" is best described by
   a. demand generated by suppliers to the firm.
   b. estimates of demand using regression analysis.
   c. demand derived from the demand for other products.
   d. demand placed on suppliers by their customers.
   e. just-in-case inventory, or safety stock.

4. _____ is(are) NOT a direct input to material requirements planning?
   a. Aggregate production plan
   b. Bills of materials
   c. Master production schedule
   d. Product structure diagram
   e. All are inputs

5. _____ is the input to MRP containing the quantity on hand, the status of outstanding orders, the lot size (or lot sizing method), and the lead time of a specific item.
   a. Master production schedule
   b. Inventory record
   c. Assembly drawing
   d. Net requirements chart
   e. Bill of materials

6. Which of the following are generally part of an item's inventory record?
   a. number currently available
   b. lead time
   c. item identification number
   d. lot size or lot sizing method
   e. all are part of an inventory record

7. The major direct inputs into the MRP system include which of the following?
   a. master production schedule
   b. sales forecasts
   c. inventory record/inventory file
   d. bills of material
   e. all but b are direct inputs to MRP

8. The master production schedule leads to which of the following outputs?
   a. material requirements plan
   b. final assembly schedule
   c. demand forecasts
   d. rough-cut capacity plans
   e. all but c are results of the MPS

9. The "gross to net requirements explosion" in material requirements planning refers to
   a. reducing gross requirements by the amount available in inventory.
   b. offsetting the net requirements by the lead time.
   c. using the bill of materials to translate planned orders into lower level gross requirements.
   d. the lower "net" prices associated with quantity discounts.
   e. using the master production schedule to determine the number of end items needed.

10. "Pegging" is best described as
    a. linking a part requirement with a specific parent component that caused the requirement.
    b. protecting from changes in international currency exchange rates.
    c. linking one foreign currency to the value of another.
    d. manually placing specific planned order releases into specific time buckets.
    e. none of the above.

11. Which of the following statements regarding material requirements planning is TRUE?
    a. Although the concepts behind MRP are simple, its execution can be complicated.
    b. The contents of an inventory record include (among other data) the item identification number, the lot size or lot sizing method, the quantity and delivery date for units already ordered.
    c. MRP can keep order due dates valid even after the orders have been released to the shop floor.
    d. Whether an order is external (to purchase the material) or internal (a production order), lead time is the time lapse between placing an order and receiving it.
    e. All of the above are true.

12. Which of the following statements regarding material requirements planning is FALSE?
    a. In MRP, gross requirements at one level generate the net requirements at the next lower level.
    b. In MRP, a "bucket" refers to a fixed period of time, such as a week.
    c. In an MRP system, safety stocks are normally maintained at all levels, since this reduces production bottlenecks, stockouts and reduces setup costs.
    d. With low-level coding, all occurrences of an item in the product structure diagram are at the same level.
    e. In MRP, an inventory record is maintained for every raw material, component, assembly, subassembly or end item.

13. MRP is an appropriate management tool for which of the following types of inventory?
    a. finished goods
    b. safety stock
    c. raw materials
    d. work in process
    e. only c and d

14. "Dependent demand" means that demand for an item is dependent on
    a. the unpredictable decisions of customers.
    b. demand for the item's immediate parent in the bill of materials.
    c. demand for the finished good of which the item may be a component.
    d. the ability of vendors to supply the item in a timely fashion.
    e. the normal probability distribution.

15. A bill of material is
    a. is part of each items inventory record.
    b. the same as a parts list.
    c. a list showing the parent-child structure of a product.
    d. a bill, or invoice, from the supplier of an item.
    e. the same as gross requirements for an item.

16. In MRP record calculations, the appearance of a negative available balance in a specific time bucket
    a. signals the need for a planned order release in that period.
    b. proves that the MPS was not feasible.
    c. signals the need for a planned order receipt in that period.
    d. is normal procedure and can be ignored.
    e. none of the above.

17. The MPS calls for 120 units of X. There are currently 30 of X on hand. Each X requires 2 of Z. There are 20 units of Z on hand. The gross requirements for Z are ____.
    a. 240
    b. 210
    c. 180
    d. 160
    e. 70

18. The MPS calls for 60 units of Product A and 50 of B. There are currently 30 of Product A on hand. Each A requires 2 of Part C; each B requires 5 of C. There are 60 units of C available. The net requirements for C are ____.
    a. 310
    b. 250
    c. 710
    d. 370
    e. 500

19. In MRP record calculations, the appearance of a positive value for the gross requirements of an end item in a specific time bucket
    a. signals the need for a scheduled order release in that period.
    b. implies that value was scheduled by the MPS.
    c. signals the need for a planned order schedule in that period.
    d. signals the need for either a planned order receipt or a scheduled order receipt.
    e. both b and d are true.

20. Which of the following statements regarding MRP lot sizing is FALSE?
    a. Lot-for-lot attempts to equate holding costs with carrying costs, in a manner similar to EOQ models.
    b. Lot sizing by fixed order quantity does not include the possible use of economic order quantity.
    c. Period order quantity specifies how many units to order in each time bucket.
    d. Lot-for-lot ordering contributes substantially to "lumpiness" of low-level demand, while fixed order quantity cannot.
    e. All of the above are false.

21. Each A requires 4 of Component B; each B requires 1 of Part C. The lead time for assembly of A is 1 bucket. The lead time for the manufacture of B is 2 buckets. The lead time for the procurement of C is 4 buckets. The planning horizon for A is _____ buckets, while for C it is only _____ buckets.
   a. 7; 3
   b. at least 7; at least 4
   c. 6; 2
   d. at least 6; at least 2
   e. 12; 1

PROBLEMS

PROBLEM SITUATION #1

The large parts of a galvanized tubular steel swing frame kit consist of a ridge pole, 4 legs, and two side braces. Each pair of legs fastens to the ridge with two fastener sets. Each side brace requires two fastener sets for attachment to the legs. Each fastener set includes one zinc-plated bolt, one lock-washer, and one nut.

There is one order outstanding, to make 100 frame kits. There are 260 legs in inventory. There are no other large items in inventory, and no scheduled receipts. Fasteners are available from the small parts area.

22. How many part numbers or ID numbers are required to describe this assembly?
   a. 1
   b. 7
   c. 8
   d. 19
   e. none of the above

23. The absolute part count for this kit is ____.
   a. 15
   b. 100
   c. 19
   d. 31
   e. none of the above

24. The gross requirements for legs will be ____.
   a. 200
   b. 400
   c. 100
   d. indeterminate; the net requirements for frame kits are not known
   e. none of the above

25. If there are 260 legs on hand (and no scheduled receipts), net requirements for legs will be ___.
    a. 140
    b. 35
    c. zero
    d. 400
    e. none of the above

26. If there are no side braces on hand, the net requirements for side braces will be ___.
    a. 100
    b. 400
    c. zero
    d. 2
    e. none of the above

27. To enable the completion of the 100 frame kits with no ending inventory, how many fastener sets should be requisitioned from small parts?
    a. 800
    b. 100
    c. 2400
    d. 400
    e. none of the above

PROBLEM SITUATION #2

A metal stamping and fabricating shop uses an MRP system to plan raw material procurement and work in process staging. One of the products manufactured is a standard flush-mount wall cabinet (about 3" deep, fits between wall studs). The shop practices parts commonality wherever possible. In this product, the same fastener (#8 x 1/2" pan head machine screw) is used throughout the product. The product structure diagram, complete with low-level coding, is shown below.

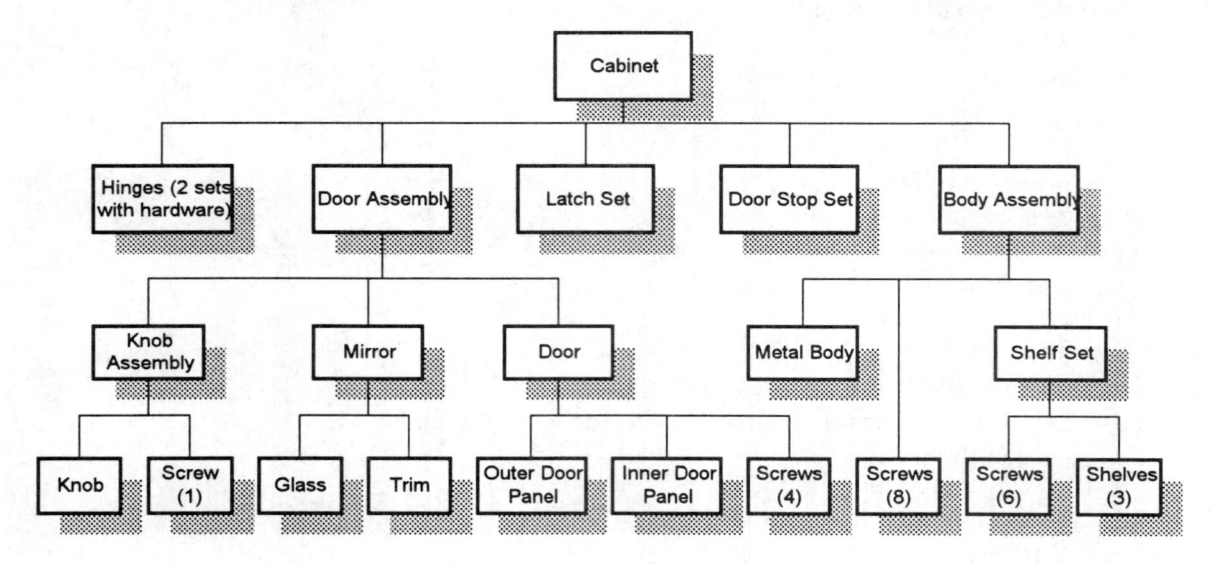

28. If the end item, the cabinet, is at level zero, at what level is the screw?
    a. 1
    b. 2
    c. 3
    d. 4
    e. both 2 and 3

29. How many fasteners will be needed for each cabinet?
    a. 19
    b. 18
    c. 37
    d. 11
    e. 33

30. Which of the following could be a part of the bill of materials for this product?
    a. Knob Assembly
        Knob
        Screw
    b. Shelf (3)
        Screw (6)
    c. Cabinet
        Hinge
    d. Shelves (3)
        Shelf Set
    e. Cabinet
        Mirror

31. Which of the following could NOT be a part of the bill of materials for this product?
    a. Knob Assembly
        Knob
        Screw
    b. Shelf (3)
        Screws (6)
    c. Cabinet
        Door Assembly
    d. Door Assembly
        Outer Door Panel
    e. Cabinet
        Body Assembly
            Shelf Set

32. If there is no inventory of any item except hinges (100 sets) and screws (900), which of the following represent correct (partial) net requirements for a single order for 120 cabinets?
    a. 120 mirrors, 140 hinges, 1380 screws, 360 shelves
    b. 120 mirrors, 240 hinges, 2280 screws, 120 inner door panels
    c. 20 hinges, 120 mirrors, 1380 screws, 120 door stops
    d. 20 hinges, 780 screws, 120 door stops, 120 metal bodies
    e. 140 hinges, 780 screws, 240 latch sets, 120 trim pieces

PROBLEM SITUATION #3

A manufacturer uses modular assembly techniques in assembling and packaging four different multimedia add-on systems. These four models are (a) Office, for intensive business use, (b) Standard, for general purpose use, (c) Economy, the least expensive and least featured package, and (d) Deluxe, the most expensive and most fully featured set. The four models are made up of several input modules including two sound boards (Y is inferior to Z) and two speaker sets (A is better than B). The four product structure diagrams appear on the following page.

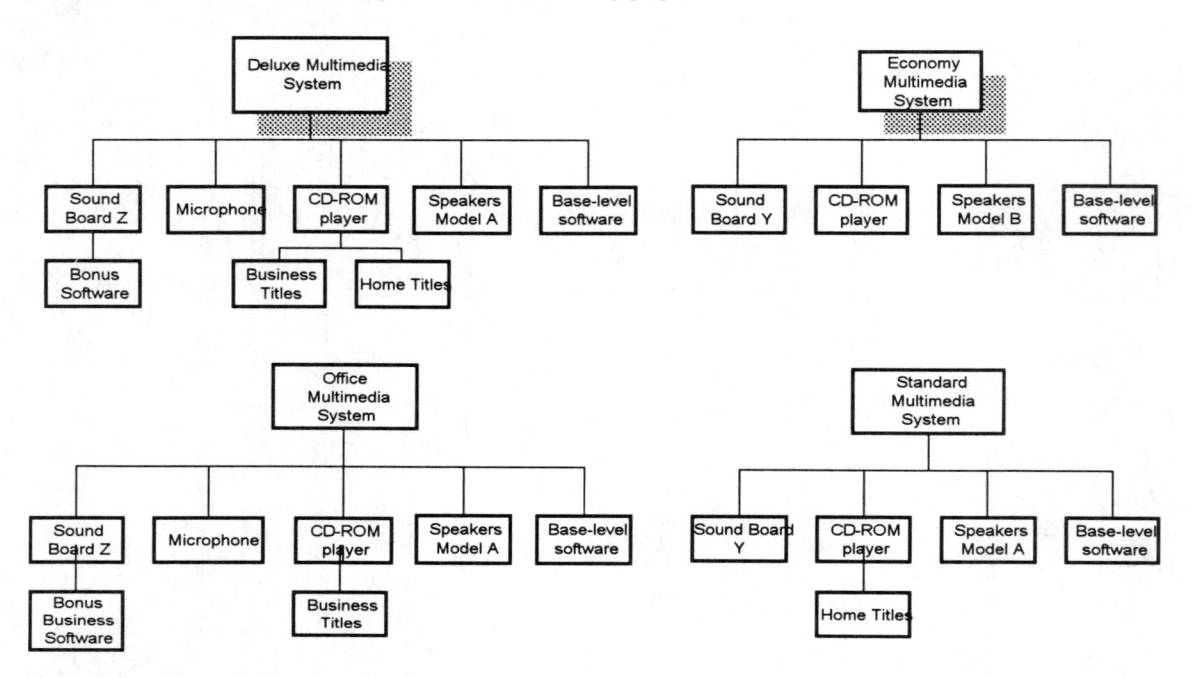

Final assembly requires one week; all components except business titles require one week; business titles require two weeks. The MPS for the next six weeks appears below. The firm has no inventory of any software, components or modules.

Product	Week 1	Week 2	Week 3	Week 4	Week 5	Week 6
Deluxe	10	0	10	0	10	10
Economy	20	10	0	20	0	0
Office	0	10	10	10	10	20
Standard	20	20	20	20	30	20

33. What will be the gross requirements for microphones in week 3?
    a. 10
    b. 20
    c. 30
    d. 50
    e. none of the above

34. What will be the planned order release of microphones in week 3?
    a. 20
    b. 30
    c. 50
    d. 60
    e. none of the above

35. What will be the gross requirements for Speaker A in Week 2?
    a. 20
    b. 30
    c. 40
    d. 50
    e. none of the above

36. What will be the planned order release for home titles in week 1?
    a. 20
    b. 30
    c. 50
    d. 60
    e. none of the above

37. What will be the gross requirements for CD-ROM players in week 2?
    a. 20
    b. 30
    c. 50
    d. 60
    e. none of the above

APPLICATION QUESTIONS

A very simple product (A) consists of a base (B) and a casting (C). The base consists of a base plate (P) and two fasteners (F). There are currently 50 castings and 120 bases on hand. Final assembly takes one week. The casting has a lead time of three weeks. All other parts have one week lead times. There are no scheduled receipts. All components are lot for lot except the fasteners, which are FOQ=400. The MPS requires 100 units of product A in week 5 and 150 in week 8.

1. What are the gross requirements for base (B)?

196   *Chapter 13 - Dependent Demand Inventory Management: MRP*

2. When are the planned order releases for base (B)?

3. What is the available balance of base (B) in week 5?

4. What are the gross requirements for fasteners (F)?

5. What must be the timing and quantity of planned order releases for fasteners (F) in order to meet MPS requirements.

6. The available balance of fastener (F) in week 9 is ____.

7. What must be the timing and quantity of planned order releases for casting (C) in order to meet MPS requirements.

SHORT ANSWER QUESTIONS

1. List the three key inputs to the MRP system. What is the purpose of each and how they are interrelated?

2. What is the difference between a scheduled receipt, a planned order receipt, and a planned order release?

3. Describe the four major problems/issues that must be addressed in MRP systems. Include in your description any possible remedies for the problem/issue.

4. What is "pegging" in an MRP system? What is its purpose and importance?

5. What is MRP II? How does it differ from MRP?

CHAPTER 14
MEDIUM- AND SHORT-RANGE CAPACITY PLANNING

INTRODUCTION
    The Need for Capacity Planning
    Strategic Implications of Capacity Planning

CAPACITY PLANNING AND THE PRODUCTION PLANNING AND SCHEDULING FRAMEWORK
    Capacity Planning as a Trial-and-error Process
    OPERATIONS MANAGEMENT IN PRACTICE 14.1: Capacity Planning Makes the Shop Floor Manageable at Minnesota Wire & Cable Co.

A CAPACITY PLANNING EXAMPLE

ROUGH-CUT CAPACITY PLANNING METHODS
    Capacity Planning using Overall Factors (CPOF)
    Capacity Planning using Capacity Bills (CB)
    Capacity Planning using Resource Profiles (RP)
    Comparison of Rough-cut Methods Results

DETAILED CAPACITY PLANNING
    Capacity Requirements Planning (CRP)
    Using CRP
    OPERATIONS MANAGEMENT IN PRACTICE 14.2: Capacity Planning in a Make-to-Order Environment at Borsig Valve Company

CAPACITY PLANNING AND SERVICE OPERATIONS

CHAPTER SUMMARY

1. Capacity planning techniques are used to evaluate the feasibility of a master production schedule given the (finite) capacity of a company.

2. While medium/short-range planning are tactical tools, the ability of a firm to plan its capacity effectively can contribute to the competitive positioning of the firm, by reducing cost or by improving schedule performance.

3. There are four capacity planning techniques. Each has its own advantages/disadvantages. The first three are all part of rough cut capacity planning; the fourth is detailed capacity planning. The four methods are:

    a. Capacity Planning using Overall Factors (CPOF): This method uses standard capacity factors obtained from accounting records to estimate capacity requirements.

    b. Capacity Planning using Capacity Bills (CB): This approach uses the bill of materials (BOM) and routing and standard time data to determine capacity requirements.

c. Capacity Planning using Resource Profiles (RP): This technique considers component lead time information in addition to the BOM and routing and standard time data to provide time-phased capacity requirements.

d. Capacity Requirements Planning (CRP): CRP uses the material plans generated by MRP to estimate the time-phased capacity requirements of a proposed MPS.

4. There are no optimal models for scheduling production, but scheduling must still take place. MRP in conjunction with capacity planning has proved to be a workable system in many production environments.

5. The three rough-cut techniques differ in their requirements and in their abilities.

a. Capacity Planning using Overall Factors is the simplest of the techniques, but is also the least accurate. It requires information typically easily available within the firm, and the calculation needs are relatively simple. CPOF combines the MPS with standard time data (how much labor does a product need) and work center data (how busy was this center, relative to other centers) to crudely estimate the load on a workstation. CPOF has four shortcomings: (1) Current product mix may differ from the mix that determined work center data; (2) Routing and time phasing (lead time offsets) of activities are not considered; (3) Component lot-sizing is not considered; and (4) Work-in-process inventories are not considered.

b. In Capacity Planning using Capacity Bills, the basic level of detail is the manufacturing operation or activity, as guided by the routing for a component. This detail can be aggregated to the work center level and to the component level. This avoids the problem associated with variation in product mix in the MPS (seen in CPOF), but does not resolve the timing of component orders or the number of setups required by the MPS. MPS data, combined with work center actual requirements per unit (not estimates as in CPOF), result in work center requirements in total.

c. Capacity Planning using Resource Profiles solves the timing problems of the other rough-cut methods, but not the lot-sizing problems. Earlier methods (Overall Factors and Capacity Bills), in a deliberate simplification, did not consider that the requirements for the parts within a component might occur in an earlier period than for the component itself. Resource Profiles combines the bill of materials (as used in Capacity Bills) with lead times for parts to produce an operation setback chart. This chart enables the time phasing of operations on parts of a component. This time phasing is quite similar to the lead time offsets used in MRP, except that the term lead time had been redefined. In this use, lead time includes queue time -- time a component spends waiting for an operation.

6. Capacity Requirements Planning (CRP) is a detailed capacity requirements planning method. It corrects for the omissions and simplifications of the rough-cut methods. For example, this method alone is capable of working with actual lot sizes of components and with actual number of setups. The inputs to CRP which were not used in the rough-cut methods are the scheduled receipts and the planned order receipts of MRP. Since these receipts consider component lot sizing, lot sizing is thus incorporated into the CRP calculations. This exposes the iterative nature of Capacity Requirements Planning, since MRP is an operation "downstream" from capacity requirements planning. This added level of accuracy and realism comes at a price of higher information requirements, more complex

computations, and less ability to experiment with alternative solutions. Also, since lot sizing is now part of the process, lumpiness of demand can be a problem as it was in MRP.

7. If CRP identifies an infeasible MRP, the resulting pattern of changes in the MPS will have effects on the MRP itself. This is the iterative nature of CRP again. These effects can be complex and unstable. A cascade of changes in MRP may result from an adjustment in the MPS. CRP attempts to lessen this thrashing among CRP-MPS-MRP levels by the concept of a firm planned order -- a manual rescheduling to smooth capacity requirements and bring feasibility to the MPS.

8. The capacity planning problem is different and harder to solve in service operations. Service operations have five distinctive characteristics that impact the capacity planning problem.

  a. Customers are participants in the production process.

  b. Server products cannot be stored in inventories.

  c. Service site location is dictated by customers.

  d. The service production process is labor intensive.

  e. The service product is intangible.

KEY TERMS

a. capacity bill
b. Capacity Planning using Capacity Bills (CB)
c. Capacity Planning using Overall Factors (CPOF)
d. Capacity Planning using Resource Profiles (RP)
e. Capacity Requirements Planning (CRP)
f. detailed capacity planning
g. operation setback chart
h. rough-cut capacity planning

DEFINITIONS

Directions: Select from the key terms list, the word or phrase being defined below.

_____ 1. uses the material plans generated by MRP to estimate the time-phased capacity requirements of a proposed MPS.

_____ 2. uses standard capacity factors from accounting records to estimate capacity requirements.

_____ 3. uses the bill of materials (BOM) and routing and standard time data to determine capacity requirements.

_____ 4. considers component lead times in addition to the BOM and routing and standard time data to provide time-phased capacity requirements.

_____ 5. an overall approach to capacity planning that requires a detailed set of inputs for precisely estimating capacity requirements.

_____ 6. an approach to capacity planning that uses simplifying assumptions for approximating capacity requirements based on the MPS.

_____ 7. combines operation lead times with bills of materials to illustrate the time phasing of capacity requirements.

_____ 8. shows the total processing time required for a unit at each work center and in total.

MULTIPLE CHOICE QUESTIONS

1. The capacity planning technique that uses standard capacity factors from accounting records to estimate capacity requirements is
   a. Capacity Planning using Overall Factors.
   b. Capacity Planning using Capacity Bills.
   c. Capacity Planning using Resource Profiles.
   d. Capacity Requirements Planning.
   e. Material Requirements Planning.

2. The rough-cut capacity planning technique that uses the Bill of Materials (BOM) and Routing and Standard Time Data to determine capacity requirements is
   a. Capacity Planning using Overall Factors.
   b. Capacity Planning using Capacity Bills.
   c. Capacity Planning using Resource Profiles.
   d. Capacity Requirements Planning.
   e. Material Requirements Planning.

3. Component lead time information, bills of materials, and routing and standard time data provide time-phased capacity requirements in the capacity planning technique called
   a. Capacity Planning using Overall Factors.
   b. Capacity Planning using Capacity Bills.
   c. Capacity Planning using Resource Profiles.
   d. Capacity Requirements Planning.
   e. Material Requirements Planning.

4. Bills of Materials and Routing and Standard Time Data more accurately determine capacity requirements in the rough-cut capacity planning technique called
   a. Capacity Planning using Overall Factors.
   b. Capacity Planning using Capacity Bills.
   c. Capacity Planning using Resource Profiles.
   d. Capacity Requirements Planning.
   e. Material Requirements Planning.

5. _____ is the capacity planning technique that uses component lead time information, bills of materials, and routing and standard time data provide time-phased capacity requirements.
   a. Capacity Planning using Overall Factors
   b. Capacity Planning using Capacity Bills
   c. Capacity Planning using Resource Profiles
   d. Capacity Requirements Planning
   e. Material Requirements Planning

6. _____ is the capacity planning technique that estimates the time-phased capacity requirements of a proposed MPS using the material plans generated by MRP.
   a. Capacity Planning using Overall Factors
   b. Capacity Planning using Capacity Bills
   c. Capacity Planning using Resource Profiles
   d. Capacity Requirements Planning
   e. Material Requirements Planning

7. The rough-cut capacity planning technique _____ makes use of operation setback charts.
   a. Capacity Planning using Overall Factors
   b. Capacity Planning using Capacity Bills
   c. Capacity Planning using Resource Profiles
   d. Capacity Requirements Planning
   e. Material Requirements Planning

8. Which of the following is a shortcoming of capacity planning using overall factors?
   a. ignores time phasing of component requirements
   b. ignores lot sizing used for component items
   c. does not consider the current status of finished and work in process inventories
   d. is inaccurate if the current product mix differs from the historical product mix
   e. all of the above are shortcomings

9. Which of the following statements regarding the rough-cut capacity planning technique of Overall Factors is TRUE?
   a. Capacity planning using overall factors is inaccurate if the actual product mix differs from the historical product mix at a work center.
   b. Capacity planning using overall factors considers lead time offsets (time phasing) in calculating the demands placed on a work center.
   c. Estimating the labor capacity needed at each work center is a two-step process.
   d. The method of overall factors cannot determine the number of production setups associated with an MPS because it does not consider lot-sizing of components.
   e. Only statement b is false.

10. Which of the following statements about capacity planning is TRUE?
    a. Capacity planning in MRP systems (dependent demand systems) are effective because of the number of analytical models developed in this area.
    b. Two ways that capacity planning can contribute to the competitive positioning of a firm are by reducing costs and by developing new process technologies.
    c. Capacity planning provides a necessary means for developing an MPS that can be executed on the shop floor.
    d. MRP in conjunction with capacity planning provides an optimized solution to the medium-range production scheduling problem.
    e. All of the above are false.

204   Chapter 14 - Medium- and Short-Range Capacity Planning

11. Which of the following is NOT a shortcoming of capacity planning using overall factors?
    a. ignores time phasing of component requirements
    b. does not consider standard time data
    c. does not consider the current status of finished and work in process inventories
    d. is inaccurate if the current product mix differs from the historical product mix
    e. all of the above are shortcomings

12. Which of the following statements regarding capacity planning is TRUE?
    a. Of the three "rough-cut" capacity planning techniques, only Resource Profiles takes time phasing onto account.
    b. Even though the methods of Overall Factors and Capacity Bills use different calculation algorithms, they may calculate the same total capacity requirement.
    c. The method of Capacity Bills considers lot-sizing of components, and can therefore calculate the number and cost of setups.
    d. Capacity planning using resource profiles considers component lead time information in addition to the Bill of Materials and Routing and Standard Time Data to provide time-phased capacity requirements.
    e. All of the above are true.

13. The manufacture of 12-gallon polyethylene water tubs consumed 144 hours last year. Another 240 hours were spent in the making of 30-gallon tubs. There were 800 units of the smaller tub made, but only 600 units of the larger. Standard time for the large tank is ____.
    a. 0.275 hours
    b. 0.4 hours
    c. 1.8 hours
    d. 0.18 hours
    e. none of the above

14. Polyethylene carboys (enclosed tubs with spigots) pass through operations of pouring, blowing, cleaning, and finishing, which historically account for 30, 35, 15, and 20 percent of the company's operating hours. Standard time for small tubs is .2 hours. If the MPS called for 60 small tubs, the estimated time at the cleaning operation is ____.
    a. 18 hours
    b. 3.6 hours
    c. 80 hours
    d. 1.8 hours
    e. 12 hours

15. Wooden curio racks pass through the operations of cut, sand, assemble, and finish, which historically account for 20, 25, 15, and 40 percent of the company's operating hours. Standard time for small racks is 2 hours, while large racks take 4. If the MPS called for 6 small and 2 large tanks, the estimated time at the finishing operation is ____.
    a. 12 hours
    b. 48 hours
    c. 19.2 hours
    d. 8 hours
    e. none of the above

16. The standard setup time for a certain precision casting is 1.2 hours, and standard processing time is .02 hours. If this product is run in lots of 500 units, the total time per unit is ___.
    a. 610 hours
    b. 0.0224 hours
    c. 11.2 hours
    d. 0.02 hours
    e. none of the above

17. The standard processing time for a soft metal casting is .06 hours. If time reduction strategies can cut the standard setup from 2 hours to 1 hour on a constant lot size of 50 units, the total time per unit will fall from _____ to _____.
    a. 2.06 hours; 1.06 hours
    b. 5 hours; 4 hours
    c. 0.04 hours; 0.02 hours
    d. 0.1 hours; 0.08 hours
    e. none of the above

18. The standard setup time for a component is 0.5 hours and its unit processing time is 0.05 hours. What lot size is sufficient to keep the total processing time per unit at or below 0.075 hours per unit?
    a. 20
    b. 10
    c. 4
    d. 200
    e. cannot be determined from the data provided

PROBLEMS

PROBLEM SITUATION #1

A millwright has come under the influence of time-reduction philosophies, and he has cut setup times accordingly. Setup times are now 0.2, 0.4, 0.3, 0.4, 0.4, 0.5 for six activities. At the same time, he has changed all lot sizes to 200 linear feet (a lot size reduction in most cases) to try to be more attuned to his customers. The detail for planning the millwright's capacity bill is in the table below (all times are in hours).

Activity	Setup Time (per batch)	Run time (per lin. ft.)	Batch size (in lin. ft.)
Cut to rough dimension	.2	.005	200
Cut finger joints	.4	.010	200
Joint edges	.3	.050	200
Cut rear chamfer	.4	.004	200
Shaper	.4	.005	200
Finish sander	.5	.007	200

206   Chapter 14 - Medium- and Short-Range Capacity Planning

19. If 1,600 linear feet must be produced next week, _____ hours must be allowed all processing activities (setup and run-time).
   a. 35.2
   b. 3520
   c. about 130
   d. about 147
   e. none of the above

20. The capacity bill for this exterior crown molding suggests that each linear foot of molding will
   a. cost about $0.09.
   b. require 0.092 hours.
   c. require 0.81 hours.
   d. require about 2.28 hours.
   e. none of the above.

21. The capacity bill for this product suggests that the average unit time at the shaper activity will be _____ hours per linear foot.
   a. 0.007
   b. 0.005
   c. 0.407
   d. 0.4
   e. none of the above

22. If 800 linear feet are required for a specific contract, _____ hours will be spent in setup at all activities.
   a. 800
   b. 8.8
   c. over 70
   d. about 64
   e. none of the above

PROBLEM SITUATION #2

A local millwright makes "gingerbread" -- Victorian decorative woodwork -- primarily for the restoration of century-old homes. One popular product is a large exterior crown molding, produced and sold by the linear foot. This molding passes through six activities, each of which requires a setup and a production run. Details are in the following table (all times are in hours).

Activity	Setup Time (per batch)	Run time (per lin. ft.)	Batch size (in lin. ft.)
Cut to rough dimension	.3	.005	800
Cut finger joints	.5	.010	400
Joint edges	.4	.050	400
Cut rear chamfer	.6	.004	200
Shaper	.6	.005	100
Finish sander	.8	.007	100

23. The capacity bill for this exterior crown molding suggests that each linear foot of molding will _____.
    a. cost about $0.10
    b. require about 0.10 hours
    c. require 0.81 hours
    d. require 3.71 hours
    e. none of the above

24. The capacity bill for this product suggests that the average unit time at the shaper activity will be _____ hours per linear foot.
    a. 0.011
    b. 0.005
    c. 0.006
    d. 0.5
    e. 1.1

25. If 3,200 linear feet are required, _____ will be spent in setup at the rough-cut activity.
    a. 1.2 hours
    b. 240 hours
    c. 4 hours
    d. 1,600 hours
    e. none of the above

26. If 3,200 linear feet are required for a specific contract, _____ hours will be spent in setup at all activities.
    a. 2,000
    b. 3.2
    c. over 60
    d. about 320
    e. none of the above

27. If 1,600 linear feet must be produced next week, _____ hours will be required for all processing activities (setup and run-time).
    a. 500
    b. 5,120
    c. about 50
    d. 161
    e. none of the above

PROBLEM SITUATION #3

Last quarter, the records of Zack Benjamin's fiberglass container manufacturing firm indicated that 1480 hours had been recorded in all operations combined in the making of 1,200-gallon potable water tanks. Another 1,830 hours was spent in the making of his other model, a 1,800-gallon tank. Zack produced 80 units of the smaller tank, but only 60 of the larger one. These tanks pass through operations of casting, glassing, cleaning, coating and finishing. Historically, these operations consume 30, 15, 5, 10 and 40 percent of the company's operating hours. The table below contain the MPS for the next six months.

Product	October	November	December	January	February	March
1,200 gallon tank	30	25	30	15	10	20
1,800 gallon tank	10	20	15	20	40	25

28. What is standard time for the smaller tank?
    a. 30.5 hours
    b. 18.5 hours
    c. 1,480 hours
    d. 860 hours
    e. none of the above

29. What is the estimated time in the coating work center in January?
    a. 887.5 hours
    b. 277.5 hours
    c. 140.5 hours
    d. 88.75 hours
    e. none of the above

30. If Zack has at most 1,200 labor hours for all processing tasks combined, which month(s) has(have) estimated requirements beyond that limit?
    a. March
    b. October
    c. February
    d. February and March
    e. no month has estimated requirements over 1,200 hours

31. What are the estimated total processing requirements for October?
    a. 860 hours
    b. 40 units
    c. 1,960 hours
    d. 555 hours
    e. none of the above

32. What are the estimated processing requirements for the 1,200-gallon model in November?
    a. 762.5 hours
    b. 462.5 hours
    c. 25 units
    d. 1,073 hours
    e. none of the above

PROBLEM SITUATION #4

B. B. Arcement works part-time in his home workshop preparing stock for area craft fairs. Among other products, he makes three models of pine bookshelf, Small, Medium, and Large. Standard time for small bookshelves is 80 minutes; medium bookcases, 105 minutes, and large bookcases, 120 minutes. Each bookcase goes through six operations, Cut (all parts to rough dimension), Sand, Assemble, Rout (decorative moldings on edges), Varnish, and Embellishment. Historically, the Cut operation takes up 10 percent of Mr. Arcement's processing time. The historical processing relatives of this operation and the others appear in the table below. Also below is Mr. Arcement's tentative Master Production Schedule for the next six months.

Operation	Percent
Cut	10
Sand	25
Assemble	20
Rout	10
Varnish	20
Embellish	15

Model	April	May	June	July	August	Sept.
Small	5	10	15	5	10	10
Medium	5	5	5	10	10	5
Large	5	0	0	10	0	5

33. The total processing minutes planned at all work centers for April is _____.
    a. 152.5
    b. 1,525
    c. 15
    d. 305
    e. none of the above

34. The processing minutes planned at the Varnish work center in September is _____.
    a. 1925
    b. 20
    c. 385
    d. 400
    e. none of the above

35. The Small bookshelf model will require _____ processing minutes in May.
    a. 800
    b. 400
    c. 525
    d. 1,725
    e. none of the above

36. The Medium bookshelf model will require _____ processing minutes in the Assembly work center in June.
    a. 305
    b. 345
    c. 105
    d. 61
    e. cannot be determined from the data provided

37. If Mr. Arcement has at most 2,000 minutes per month to devote to bookshelves over the span of this MPS, the month(s) of _____ is(are) currently scheduled beyond capacity.
    a. July
    b. September
    c. May
    d. April and September
    e. April through September

38. Over the period covered by the MPS, how many minutes will Mr. Arcement be "assembling" bookcases?
    a. 4,320 minutes
    b. 3,500 minutes
    c. 2,220 minutes
    d. 2,000 minutes
    e. none of the above

APPLICATION QUESTIONS

Doug Issongrafe makes two products at a set of work centers. Both products are curios to be sold at souvenir shops. Each consists of a purchased casting, a made casting, and a purchased base. The purchased casting needs inspection only; the made casting requires a casting operation, then a painting operation. The base requires varnishing. The three components are then assembled (glued together), and the finished product is packed. The table below details lead times and operation times for each activity for each product. The MPS, looking 8 weeks ahead, is also provided.

Work center	Total hours per unit of A	Lead Time (weeks)	Total hours per unit of B	Lead Time (weeks)
Pack	.2	1	.2	1
Assemble	.4	1	.5	1
Paint	.6	1	.4	1
Varnish	.3	1	.2	1
Inspect	.1	1	.1	1
Mold	.8	1	.6	1

Product	Week 1	Week 2	Week 3	Week 4	Week 5	Week 6	Week 7	Week 8
Curio A	10	10	15	15	10	5	0	10
Curio B	5	5	10	5	0	15	10	5

1. What would be the total hours required to process one unit of Curio A through all operations?

2. How many hours of Molding work would be required in week 4 if the Capacity Bill technique was used?

3. How many hours of Assembly work would be required in week 3 if the Capacity Bill technique was used?

4. How many hours of Assembly work would the MPS requirement of 15 units of Curio A in week 6 create, and in which week would the work be created?

5. How many hours of Molding work would be required in week 4 if the Resource Profile technique was used?

6. When using the Resource Profile technique, an MPS requirement in week 8 creates Packing and Molding work center requirements in which weeks?

7. Which work center is the first to experience low-level loss of visibility? Of the eight weeks in the planning horizon covered by the MPS, how long is that work center's horizon?

SHORT ANSWER QUESTIONS

1. What is the purpose of capacity planning with respect to dependent demand inventory management as covered in the previous chapter?

2. What is "rough-cut" capacity planning? What is the difference between rough-cut capacity planning and capacity requirements planning (CRP)?

3. How are capacity planning in manufacturing operations different from capacity planning in service operations?

4. What techniques are used to accomplish rough-cut capacity planning and what are their differences?

5. How can firm planned orders help smooth capacity requirements? Are there any problems with their use? Explain.

CHAPTER 15
SHOP-FLOOR CONTROL

INTRODUCTION
   The Task of the Shop-Floor Control Manager

SHOP-FLOOR CONTROL IN CONTINUOUS AND REPETITIVE OPERATIONS
   Continuous Process Shop-Floor Control
   Repetitive Operation Shop-Floor Control
   Mixed-Model Assembly in Repetitive Manufacturing

SHOP-FLOOR CONTROL IN INTERMITTENT, JOB SHOP OPERATIONS
   Terminology
   Performance Measures in Job Shop Floor Control
      Reduce Setup Times
      Reduce Queue Times
      Reduce Material Handling

SCHEDULING INTERMITTENT, JOB SHOP PROCESSES
   Input-Output Control
   Order Review and Release
   Scheduling and Sequencing
   Gantt Chart Construction
   Johnson's Rule for Fixed Sequence, Two-Machine Problems

DATA COLLECTION AND ORDER DISPOSITION
   OPERATIONS MANAGEMENT IN PRACTICE 15.1: Streamline Manufacturing: Sun
      Microsystems, Inc.

INNOVATIVE CONTROL: THEORY OF CONSTRAINTS
   OPERATIONS MANAGEMENT IN PRACTICE 15.2: Dixie Reengineers Scheduling and
      Increases Profit 300 Percent

CHAPTER SUMMARY

1. Shop floor control (SFC) addresses the challenges of successfully executing complex, sophisticated manufacturing plans. This challenge exists, because of the number and complexity of operations, for continuous and for intermittent operations, for line operations and for flow operations. While attention will be paid to the shop floor problems of continuous flow plants and of assembly line operations and their hybrids, most attention will focus on shop floor control of the job shop.

2. Shop floor control is defined by APICS as "a system for utilizing data from the shop floor to maintain and communicate order status information on shop orders (manufacturing orders) and on work centers."

3. Six sub-functions of shop floor control are:

a. assigning priority of each shop order

b. maintaining work-in-process quantity information

c. conveying shop order status to the office

d. providing actual output data for capacity control purposes

e. providing quantity by location by shop order for work-in-process inventory and accounting purposes

f. providing measurement of efficiency, utilization and productivity of the work force and machines

4. The terminology of shop floor control includes many terms special purpose terms, and is deserving of a special summary section.

a. A job is a unit of production that follows some sequence of operations. Job and order are frequently used interchangeably.

b. A production lot is the number of units in the order that are produced between process setups. The production lot size is usually the same as the order size.

c. Transfer lots are fractions of the production lot passed on to the next work station.

d. Operation processing time is the estimated time required at an operation.

e. Total processing time is the sum of the operation processing times for a job. Total time will be much larger than total processing time. Total time includes processing time and delays.

f. The delay multiplier is the ratio of total time to processing time.

g. Planned lead time is the estimated time that it will take to complete an order including processing time and delays.

h. Flowtime or cycle time is the time that the order takes to flow through the shop.

i. Completion date is the actual time when an operation is completed.

j. Actual flowtime is the difference between the completion date and date the order was released to the shop.

k. Throughput is the total volume of output from a process.

l. The busiest operation that restricts the flow of output is known as the bottleneck operation.

m. Setup time is the time required to setup a machine to process an order.

n. External activities can be accomplished while the machine is still running.

o. Internal activities cannot be accomplished until the machine is stopped.

p. Queue time is time jobs wait in queue for their turn on a machine

q. Routing is the sequence of operations that a job will follow.

r. Alternative routings bypass bottleneck operations.

s. Sequencing is the process of prioritizing jobs that are waiting to be processed.

t. Dispatching rules are the rules used to establish job priorities.

u. A Gantt chart is a common technique to assess the start and finish time of a job.

v. Dynamic arrivals are new jobs that have the potential of resequencing jobs already in the queue.

w. In the first come, first served rule, orders are processed in the sequence in which they arrived.

x. In the shortest processing time rule, gives highest priority to the job with the shortest processing time.

y. In the earliest due date rule, highest job priority goes to the job with the earliest due date.

z. A constraint is anything which limits an organization's ability to improve.

5. The task of the shop floor manager depends upon the type of processing. Capital intensive flow operations require the most specialized training, as such operations rarely shut down. Repetitive manufacturing operations are somewhat less demanding. Job shops require that the shop floor manager be the most broadly trained, the most flexible.

6. In spite of these differences, all three situations have similar performance measures:

   a. How well are resources utilized?

   b. Is output to specifications?

   c. Is output on time?

   d. What is the role of the worker in effective shop floor control?

7. Concerns of shop floor control in continuous and repetitive operations.

   a. Continuous shop floor control -- concern is in maintaining "linearity" by producing a consistent product at a consistent rate of production.

   b. Repetitive shop floor control -- scheduled production is subject to change in response to demand; order control and feedback systems support this flexibility. EDI and similar systems help synchronize resource arrivals with demand.

c. Mixed model -- assembly can be improved by reducing variability in the product. Fewer options makes schedules more predictable. (This did not work for U.S. auto makers.) Another method of improving assembly is to design a shop floor control system that can respond flexibly to a wide range of designs and options.

8. Shop floor control in intermittent, job shop operations is covered in detail in the remainder of the chapter. A hospital emergency room is cited as a good example of a job shop - demand somewhat unpredictable, no two patients with the same problem, a wide range of capabilities needed to treat them, the sequence of operations is jumbled, and the need for prioritizing patients during busy times.

9. Steps in job shop floor control are:

   a. Determine job routings

   b. Estimate time required at each work center

   c. Itemize the materials required

   d. Determine the delivery date. Two versions are: (1) Customer specifies date, can firm produce by that date? (2) Firm specifies date, will customer accept?

10. Several measures of performance in job shop floor control include:

    a. Work-in-process inventory -- smaller is better for several reasons: (1) more WIP represents more funds committed; (2) more WIP may indicate long flowtimes or cycle times (less responsive to customers?); (3) WIP takes up space, leads to congestion and confusion.

    b. Throughput -- more is better.

    c. Utilization -- while high utilization is usually desirable, it can lead to counter-productive decisions. For example, keeping people and machines busy increases WIP.

    d. Lead time -- smaller is better. Strategies to reduce lead time include (1) reduce setup times, (2) reduce queue times, (3) reduce material handling.

11. Scheduling intermittent, job shop processes is accomplished by sequencing -- prioritizing the jobs waiting to be processed. There are few optimizing techniques, but many heuristics for the sequencing task. These heuristics are known as dispatching rules.
    a. Five common dispatching rules are:

       (1) First Come, First Served

       (2) Shortest Processing Time

       (3) Earliest Due Date

       (4) Slack Time Remaining

       (5) Critical Ratio

b. Four measures are commonly used to measure the performance of dispatching rules:

   (1) Average Flowtime

   (2) Average Number of Jobs in the System

   (3) Average Lateness

   (4) Maximum Lateness

c. Dispatching rules are complicated by dynamic arrivals and by multiple operations.

d. A common technique to assess start and finish times that constitute a schedule is the construction of a Gantt chart, a horizontal bar chart that plots the assignment of critical or scarce resources to jobs during a period of time.

12. Johnson's rule is a technique for handling a special class of job shop problems, where each job passes through two stations in the same fixed order. Johnson's rule minimizes the elapsed time to complete work on all jobs.

13. The system should maintain records on location and status of orders, on actual use of material at each work center, and on the status of machines and tooling. This may be automated by barcoding the product.

14. The theory of constraints (TOC) is about identifying bottleneck operations, or constraints, which have fixed capacity and cannot be rushed. These bottleneck operations are critical to determining the throughput of the manufacturing system. The textbook describes a five-step process to minimize the impact of constraints on the organization.

   a. Time lost at a bottleneck operation is time lost to the entire productive system. Time saved at non-bottleneck operations may cause no increase in production.

   b. Theory of constraints uses a vocabulary different from other areas; for example, the term throughput is used in money terms rather than physical terms. The theory of constraints suggests that traditional cost accounting procedures lead managers to incorrect decisions.

   c. "Drum-buffer-rope" is the control system usually associated with TOC. The drum signals the pace of manufacturing as set by the bottleneck operation. The buffer is WIP inventory in front of the bottleneck. The rope ensures synchronization of production steps to the master schedule.

   d. Optimized Production Technology software deals with bottleneck operations.

KEY TERMS

a. alternative routings
b. bottleneck operation
c. completion date
d. cycle time
e. delivery date
f. drum-buffer-rope (DBR)
g. flow time
h. Johnson's Rule
i. lead time
j. operation processing time
k. Optimized Production Technology (OPT)
l. planned lead time
m. synchronous manufacturing
n. theory of constraints (TOC)
o. throughput
p. transfer lots
q. utilization

DEFINITIONS

Directions: Select from the key terms list, the word or phrase being defined below.

_____ 1. the date determined for a job to be completed for the customer.

_____ 2. the percentage of time a resource is being used productively.

_____ 3. are fractions of the production lot passed on to the next work station.

_____ 4. the estimated time required at an operation.

_____ 5. the process of directing the flow of material through a facility so as to maximize utilization of bottleneck operations.

_____ 6. a software package designed to execute the concept of synchronous manufacturing.

_____ 7. the estimated time that it will take to complete an order, including processing time and delays.

_____ 8. the time that the order takes to flow through the shop.

_____ 9. the actual time when an operation is completed.

_____ 10. a process used to reduce queue time and bypass bottleneck operations.

_____ 11. the total volume of output from a process.

_____ 12. the operation with the highest utilization that restricts the flow of product.

_____ 13. minimizes the total elapsed time for a set of jobs that are processed through two workstations in the same fixed order.

_____ 14. a term used to describe the control mechanism associated with synchronous manufacturing.

MULTIPLE CHOICE QUESTIONS

Directions: Indicate your choice of the best answer to each question.

1. _____ is the performance measure that calculates the lateness of the average job.
   a. Average performance
   b. Average flowtime
   c. Average lateness
   d. Maximum lateness
   e. Flowtime performance

2. Which of the following is a criterion used by the authors to measure the performance of scheduling rules?
   a. average number of jobs in the system
   b. minimum flowtime
   c. average slack time remaining
   d. minimum lateness
   e. all of the above are criteria

3. Which of the following statements regarding the theory of constraints is TRUE?
   a. Constraints must be physical only.
   b. Constraints can be physical or metaphysical.
   c. Constraints can be physical or non-physical.
   d. Constraints must be fiscal only.
   e. Constraints can be fiscal or non-fiscal.

4. _____ is a shop floor dispatching rule that relates the time available to complete a job to the amount of work left to be completed.
   a. Shortest processing time
   b. Earliest due date
   c. First come, first served
   d. Critical ratio
   e. None of the above

5. Dispatching by the earliest due date (EDD) rule will
   a. minimize the average flowtime.
   b. minimize the critical ratio.
   c. minimize the average lateness.
   d. minimize maximum lateness.
   e. maximize the minimum flowtime.

6. Which of the following dispatching rules ordinarily tends to give the best results when the criterion is average time for completion of the full sequence of jobs?
   a. shortest processing time
   b. first in, still here (FISH)
   c. first in, first out (FIFO)
   d. first come, first served (FCFS)
   e. slack time remaining

7. The level of customer service in a job shop can be monitored by which of the following criteria?
   a. average flowtime
   b. flowtime
   c. average lateness
   d. WIP inventory
   e. only b and d

8. Which of the following objectives would have the effect of minimizing the work-in-process inventory?
   a. minimizing the average flowtime
   b. minimizing the average lateness
   c. minimizing the average number of jobs
   d. minimizing the flow times
   e. none of the above

9. The time that an order takes to flow through the shop is
   a. value added time.
   b. flowtime or cycle time.
   c. queue time.
   d. total processing time.
   e. operation processing time.

10. _____ is the sum of the operation processing times for a job.
    a. Flowtime or cycle time
    b. Total time
    c. Actual flowtime
    d. Total processing time
    e. Planned lead time

11. Application of the shop floor scheduling rule of shortest processing time generally results in
    a. minimum average flowtime.
    b. minimum average lateness.
    c. maximum average lateness.
    d. minimum maximum lateness.
    e. none of the above.

12. _____ is the estimated time that it will take to complete an order including processing time and delays.
    a. Flowtime or cycle time
    b. Actual flowtime
    c. Queue time
    d. Completion date
    e. Planned lead time

13. In shop floor management, the estimated time required at an operation is
    a. flowtime or cycle time.
    b. actual flowtime.
    c. operation processing time.
    d. total processing time.
    e. value added time.

14. In shop floor management, the busiest operation is known as
    a. the bottleneck operation.
    b. the no-slack time remaining operation.
    c. the critical ratio operation.
    d. the critical operation.
    e. all of the above.

15. In the context of shop floor control, _____ can be accomplished while the machine is still running.
    a. relaxing the bottleneck operation
    b. internal activities
    c. external activities
    d. only production (no maintenance)
    e. transfer lots, but not production lots

16. _____ is the ratio of total time to processing time.
    a. The delay multiplier
    b. Flowtime
    c. The critical ratio
    d. Johnson's ratio
    e. Taylor's efficiency rating

17. _____ is that part of a larger production lot passed on to the next work station while work continues on the remainder of the production lot.
    a. Production lot
    b. Order size
    c. Transfer lot
    d. Critical ratio
    e. Economic production quantity

18. Orders are processed in the sequence in which they arrive if the _____ rule is used to sequence jobs.
    a. earliest due date rule
    b. first come, first served rule
    c. slack time remaining
    d. critical ratio
    e. Johnson's

19. When a set of jobs must pass through two workstations whose sequence is fixed, _____ is the procedure used to optimize the sequence.
    a. earliest due date rule
    b. first come, first served rule
    c. slack time remaining
    d. critical ratio
    e. Johnson's rule

20. Two dispatching rules that consider two variables in determining the priority of jobs are
    a. slack time remaining and critical ratio.
    b. critical ratio and earliest due date.
    c. earliest due date and first come, first served.
    d. Johnson's rule and slack time remaining.
    e. shortest processing time and slack time remaining.

PROBLEMS
PROBLEM SITUATION #1

Morris DeLaune operates a publishing plant, where he produces, inspects, sorts and bundles the lecture notes for students at the nearby medical school. "Mo" has just received the orders shown below. Scheduling in his shop is done by priority decision rules. Today is day 200.

JOB NAME	DUE DATE	PRODUCTION DAYS REQUIRED
Z001	257	22
Z002	267	14
Z003	227	10
Z004	242	18

21. What sequence of jobs would the dispatching rule first come, first served generate?
    a. Z001-Z002-Z003-Z004
    b. Z003-Z002-Z004-Z001
    c. Z003-Z004-Z001-Z002
    d. Z004-Z001-Z003-Z002
    e. none of the above

22. What sequence of jobs would the dispatching rule shortest processing time generate?
    a. Z001-Z002-Z003-Z004
    b. Z003-Z002-Z004-Z001
    c. Z003-Z004-Z001-Z002
    d. Z004-Z001-Z003-Z002
    e. none of the above

23. What sequence of jobs would the dispatching rule slack time remaining generate?
    a. Z001-Z002-Z003-Z004
    b. Z003-Z002-Z004-Z001
    c. Z003-Z004-Z001-Z002
    d. Z004-Z001-Z003-Z002
    e. none of the above

24. The average flowtime from scheduling by first come, first served is ____.
    a. 42 days
    b. 168 days
    c. 64 days
    d. 152 days
    e. 140 days

25. The total flowtime from scheduling by shortest processing time is ____.
    a. 168 days
    b. 140 days
    c. 35 days
    d. 42 days
    e. 64 days

26. The average jobs in system under shortest processing time is ____.
    a. 3.62
    b. 2.19
    c. 3.69
    d. 4
    e. 1

27. The average lateness of earliest due date scheduling is ____.
    a. 38 days
    b. 1.75 days
    c. 64 days
    d. 3.62 days
    e. zero

28. The maximum lateness of shortest processing time is ____.
    a. 7 days
    b. 57 days
    c. 49 days
    d. 22 days
    e. zero

29. The dispatch rule that results in minimum flowtime for this problem is _____; that minimum flowtime is _____ days.
    a. first come, first served; 64
    b. earliest due date; 152
    c. shortest processing time; 140
    d. slack time remaining; 152
    e. shortest processing time; 35

PROBLEM SITUATION #2

Durand Mall has two check stations that are required at the end of every repair task performed by the mall staff. These are the Major Functionality Review (MFR) and the Minor Defect Scan (MDS). The MFR must be performed successfully before the MDS is begun. On Saturday evening, six repair jobs (A-F) are awaiting these two activities. Processing times for the six jobs are given in minutes.

	JOB					
	A	B	C	D	E	F
MFR	46	35	28	22	15	18
MDS	31	58	18	40	17	24

30. Using Johnson's rule, Job _____ will be the first to be scheduled, and it will be placed in _____ position.
    a. B; the first
    b. B; the last
    c. E; the first
    d. E; the last
    e. E; either first or last is optimal.

31. Using Johnson's rule, Job _____ will be the second to be scheduled, and it will be placed in _____ position.
    a. E; second
    b. C; first
    c. F; last
    d. (F; second) and (C; last) tie
    e. B; last

32. Using Johnson's rule, Job _____ will be the last to be scheduled, and it will be placed in _____ position.
    a. B; last
    b. B; fourth
    c. E; first
    d. C; last
    e. none of the above

33. Using Johnson's rule, the optimal sequence of jobs is ____.
    a. E-F-D-B-A-C
    b. A-B-C-D-E-F
    c. E-C-D-B-A-F
    d. E-F-D-C-B-A
    e. none of the above

34. At hour 26, _____ is the activity at MFR, while _____ is the activity at MDS.
    a. F; E
    b. B; D
    c. E; C
    d. F; D
    e. E; F

35. Following optimal assignment of jobs by Johnson's rule, the minimum completion time for all six jobs is ____.
    a. 139
    b. 204
    c. 213
    d. 352
    e. none of the above

APPLICATION QUESTIONS

A firm that specializes in desktop publishing for local charities has agreed to take on the following four jobs. The firm has not decided which dispatching rule to apply in order to prioritize the jobs and fix them into the schedule.

	JOB			
	A	B	C	D
TIME REQUIRED	5	4	3	1
DUE DATE (days from now)	11	10	16	2

1. What sequence of jobs would the critical ratio dispatching rule generate?

226   Chapter 15 - Shop-Floor Control

2. What sequence of jobs would the shortest processing time dispatching rule generate?

3. What sequence of jobs would the earliest due date dispatching rule generate?

4. What sequence of jobs would the slack time remaining dispatching rule generate?

5. What would be the total flowtime from scheduling by shortest processing time?

6. What would be the average flowtime from scheduling by critical ratio?

7. What would be the average number of jobs in the system under first come, first served?

8. What would be the average lateness using earliest due date scheduling?

9. What would be the maximum lateness using shortest processing time?

10. Which dispatching rule results in the minimum flowtime for this problem? What is this minimum flowtime in days?

SHORT ANSWER QUESTIONS

1. What is shop floor control and what are the activities it accomplishes?

2. Consider a hospital emergency room. What kinds of "shop floor" issues would need to be addressed?

3. Describe three measures of job shop performance. Why is each important to the overall effectiveness of the job shop?

4. Describe the application of five dispatching rules. What are the advantages and disadvantages of each? What are the traditional performance measures for dispatching rules?

5. What are the three performance measures proposed under the theory of constraints? Describe why each is important. Describe the control mechanism often associated with the theory of constraints.

CHAPTER 16
JUST-IN-TIME PRODUCTION

INTRODUCTION
    OPERATIONS MANAGEMENT IN PRACTICE 16.1: Labor Unrest and the JIT Production Environment

STRATEGIC EFFECTS OF JUST-IN -TIME PRODUCTION
    Origins of JIT philosophy

TOTAL BUSINESS CYCLE MANAGEMENT

MANAGING MATERIAL FLOWS
    Set-up Reduction and the EOQ Lot Size
    Inventory Reduction Caution

JUST-IN-TIME SYSTEM REQUIREMENTS
    Production Flexibility Along the Supply Chain
    GLOBAL OPERATIONS MANAGEMENT 16.2: Canadian Supplier Speeds Parts Delivery Across the Border
    Schedule Stability and Discipline
    Comprehensive Quality Assurance
    Creating Teams of Competent, Empowered Employees
    JIT Systems and Signals
        Push Versus Pull Production Systems
        JIT Signals and Kanban
        Modifications of the Signaling System
        When to Use Kanban
    Logistics Systems to Support JIT Delivery
        JIT Purchasing
        JIT II®
        OPERATIONS MANAGEMENT IN PRACTICE 16.3: Purchasing Leads the Charge Toward Just-in-Time

IMPLEMENTATION OF JUST-IN-TIME

COORDINATING JIT AND MATERIAL REQUIREMENTS PLANNING

CHAPTER SUMMARY

1. Just-in-time (JIT) is a market driven, waste free production system sufficiently flexible and responsive to changes in market demand to produce exactly what is needed.

2. JIT is not a physical system, but a system of beliefs and attitudes combined with a collection of methods and procedures all shaped into a general management philosophy describing how an operation should be managed. Thus JIT is more than simply an inventory control system and more than just a manufacturing system.

3. Motivations for JIT systems include:

   a. reducing inventory of all types

   b. increasing productivity of direct labor employees

   c. improving utilization of equipment on products that will be deployed quickly

   d. producing well-designed, defect-free products

   e. improving responsiveness to changing markets and customer requirements

4. While most modern application of JIT derives from the work of the Japanese automaker, Toyota, Henry Ford understood and practiced many JIT-like concepts decades earlier.

5. A firm's total-business cycle is the elapsed time from when a customer need is identified until the need is satisfied and payment is received. The total-business cycle is composed of several sub-cycles:

   a. order entry cycle

   b. procurement cycle

   c. production cycle, or work-in-process cycle

   d. packing and shipping cycle

   e. distribution cycle

   f. accounts receivable cycle

6. There is a connection between EOQ models and JIT. If setup cost can be reduced by a factor of four, EOQ is cut in half; another reduction by four, another halving. Average inventory falls proportionate to the fall in EOQ. Research into reduction of setup cost may generate considerable savings.

7. "Rocks in the materials river" and "funnel" are metaphors for the uncertainties, inefficiencies and restrictions that are motivation for keeping "just-in-case" inventory.

   a. In the "rocks" metaphor, the buffer stocks are the high water level that allows the "boat" of operations running smoothly. Reducing/removing the "rocks," such as scrap, rework, long setups, etc., allows for a lower water level -- less inventory.

   b. In the "funnel" metaphor, the only way to get a sustainable increase in the output rate is to expand the neck of the funnel. That is, continually identify those problems which are restricting the flow of work.

   c. In the JIT philosophy, rather than keep inventory for the operational uncertainties, the firm should seek faster responsiveness and flexibility instead.

8. Requirements for JIT systems include:

   a. Production flexibility at every stage of supply. It is not sufficient to have suppliers ship in smaller, more frequent lots, or be ready to ship on demand. This is not sustainable because the suppliers do not gain from the JIT system.

   b. Schedule stability and discipline. There is an inherent stability in a system where the correct amount of each product is produced as needed. If setup costs can be driven so low that "lot size of one" is possible, stability follows because costly interruptions do not occur. Stability may also be enhanced by sales practices that depend less on discounts based on the amount bought at one time.

   c. Comprehensive quality assurance. The costs of scrap and rework are wastes to be eliminated.

   d. Teams of competent, empowered employees. Formation of teams for creative problem solving requires fundamental changes in the role of worker and supervisor. These changes often mean greater responsibility, which must be accompanied by empowerment to take appropriate action.

   e. A signaling system to pull production. Factories in older, "push" systems have seldom needed signals to tell them when to start work; they were continuously working. "Pull" systems do not schedule work in advance, but authorize it. Kanban is one type of signaling system.

   f. A logistics system to support JIT delivery. Using JIT for strategic advantage often requires quick and regular supply from other firms. Close proximity between supplier and firm is often part of the solution.

   (1) JIT purchasing uses multiple criteria to include price, reliability, quality, and flexibility when selecting suppliers. Traditional purchasing relies too heavily on price. JIT purchasing focuses on establishing supplier "partners."

   (2) JIT II® takes the partnering concept one step further. Under this innovative concept, supplier representatives may actually be stationed at the customer's facility. This representative may have total control of maintaining the supply of parts provided by his or her company. The concept is sometimes referred to as "vendor managed inventory (VMI)."

9. General suggestions for the implementation of JIT include

   a. Run a carefully selected pilot project, so the first JIT experience is a success.

   b. Identify key supervisors for JIT reorientation.

   c. Production areas must be well organized and designed (to improve material flow and communication between work centers).

   d. Invite suppliers to observe the JIT system so they can understand the interface required.

10. Four frequently-cited obstacles to JIT implementation are:

   a. cultural resistance to change.

   b. lack of resources, especially training or education.

   c. lack of top management understanding or commitment, especially from management underestimating the magnitude changes necessary for JIT.

   d. Performance measurement; conflicts between team objectives and individual incentive plans.

11. Coordinating JIT and MRP

   a. JIT is a pull system while MRP is a push system, but the two systems can be complementary, not contradictory.

   b. The two systems can be hybridized: JIT/Kanban for daily use parts; MRP for master planning and special orders is one possible example.

   c. JIT-based reductions in production cycle times lead to shorter MRP planning horizons, and thus to increased ability to respond to changing demand.

KEY TERMS

a. conveyance kanban
b. just-in-time systems
c. kanban
d. new product development cycle
e. new strategy development cycle
f. production kanban
g. pull production system
h. push production system
i. short-cycle manufacturing
j. total business cycle
k. vendor managed inventory

DEFINITIONS

Directions: Select from the key terms list, the word or phrase being defined below.

_____ 1. attempt to increase the flexibility and responsiveness between suppliers and customers in order to eliminate waste and improve customer satisfaction and overall competitiveness.

_____ 2. a system of beliefs and attitudes combined with a collection of methods and procedures all shaped into a general management philosophy describing how an operation should be managed.

_____ 3. the elapsed time from when a customer need is identified until the need is satisfied and payment is received.

_____ 4. the situation in JIT II where supplier representatives reside in their customers' facilities and directly manage their inventory for the customer.

_____ 5. Japanese term for "card" that refers to a signaling device used in a pull production system.

_____ 6. Another term (other than JIT) used by some organizations to describe their philosophy of continuously improving cycle times by eliminating waste.

_____ 7. the time required to identify a new need in the marketplace and satisfy that need.

_____ 8. the time required to develop a new strategy and complete its implementation.

_____ 9. authorizes a work center to produce a part.

_____ 10. signals the need to move more parts to that department or work center.

_____ 11. is a traditional production system where work is scheduled in advance with the objective being to ensure high utilization of people and equipment.

_____ 12. is a demand-driven production system in which utilization is sacrificed for flexibility and reductions in inventories, and in which work is authorized when needed.

MULTIPLE CHOICE QUESTIONS

Directions: Indicate your choice of the best answer to each question.

1. Which of the following statements concerning JIT is TRUE?
   a. Alfred P. Sloan in the 1920s understood and practiced many of the concepts considered to be JIT concepts.
   b. Total quality management (TQM) is one manifestation of the operational task of eliminating waste and increasing the productive use of resources.
   c. "Short-cycle manufacturing" describes the philosophy of stopping production before the equipment wears enough to start producing defective units.
   d. The emergence of just-in-time as a leading manufacturing strategy is because time has become the most powerful source of competitive advantage.
   e. All of the above are false.

2. Which of the following statements concerning JIT is FALSE?
   a. "Short-cycle manufacturing" describes the philosophy of continuous improvement of cycle times through waste reduction.
   b. The origin of JIT concepts and methods is generally accepted to be the Japanese auto manufacturer Toyota more than any other single source.
   c. Alfred P. Sloan in the 1920s understood and practiced many of the concepts considered to be JIT concepts.
   d. The emergence of just-in-time as a leading manufacturing strategy is because time has become the most powerful source of competitive advantage.
   e. All of the above are true.

3. Which of the following is NOT one of the sub-cycles of the total-business cycle, the elapsed time from when a customer need is identified until the need is satisfied?
   a. work-in-process cycle
   b. procurement cycle
   c. accounts receivable cycle
   d. acceptance sampling cycle
   e. distribution cycle

4. Which of the following is NOT a motivation for adopting JIT systems?
   a. reduction in inventory of all types
   b. increased productivity of direct labor employees
   c. improved utilization of equipment on products that will be deployed quickly
   d. cost-minimizing logistics systems
   e. improved responsiveness to changing markets and customer requirements

5. Which of the following statements regarding materials and inventory management in JIT is TRUE?
   a. Set-up times should be increased as much as possible in order to realize the most benefit from JIT.
   b. The "ideal" lot size is one.
   c. Purchasing agreements are relatively short-term when just-in-time methods are adopted.
   d. Long term supplier/customer relationships often allow the customer to purchase in large discounted lots and receive frequent small lot deliveries.
   e. Both b and d are true.

6. Which of the following statements concerning JIT philosophy is TRUE?
   a. Just-in-time systems attempt to eliminate waste, improve customer satisfaction and improve overall effectiveness.
   b. "Short-cycle manufacturing" describes the philosophy of continuous improvement of cycle times through waste reduction.
   c. Just-in-time (JIT) is one manifestation of the operational task of eliminating waste and increasing the productive use of resources.
   d. JIT is a system of beliefs and attitudes combined with a collection of methods and procedures all shaped into a general management philosophy describing how an operation should be managed.
   e. All of the above are true.

7. Which of the following is the FIRST of the sub-cycles of the total-business cycle, the elapsed time from when a customer need is identified until the need is satisfied?
   a. distribution cycle
   b. procurement cycle
   c. order entry cycle
   d. accounts receivable cycle
   e. production cycle, or work-in-process cycle

8. Which of the following are among the requirements for implementation of JIT systems?
   a. production flexibility at every stage of supply
   b. stability and flexibility in scheduling
   c. a logistics system to support JIT delivery
   d. teams of competent, empowered employees
   e. all of the above are required for JIT implementation

9. JIT production systems are ordinarily used in
   a. small batch (job shop) production.
   b. continuous processing, such as oil refining.
   c. project situations, such as bridge construction.
   d. repetitive manufacturing.
   e. none of the above.

10. _____ is NOT a characteristic of JIT production systems.
    a. Defect-free quality
    b. Small lots and small setup time
    c. Minimal work in process inventories achieved through independent production schedules
    d. An ideal EOQ of one
    e. All of the above are JIT characteristics

11. Major objectives of JIT production systems include
    a. elimination of all sources of waste.
    b. reduction of all unnecessary inventory.
    c. input into material requirements planning.
    d. reduction of rework and scrap in production.
    e. responses a, b, and d.

12. The modern JIT production concept was developed and popularized by
    a. Allen-Bradley.
    b. Sloan School of Business Administration.
    c. General Motors Company.
    d. Toyota Motor Company.
    e. Henry Ford.

13. Which of the following is NOT an obstacle to JIT implementation?
    a. cultural resistance to change
    b. lack of resources, especially training or education
    c. lack of top management understanding or commitment, especially from management underestimating the magnitude changes necessary for JIT
    d. performance measurement conflicts between team objectives and individual incentive plans
    e. all of the above are obstacles

14. Which of the following is NOT an objective of JIT systems?
    a. improve overall competitiveness
    b. eliminate waste
    c. improve customer satisfaction
    d. increasing the productive use of resources
    e. all of the above are objectives of JIT systems

15. Which of the following statements regarding just-in-time systems is TRUE?
    a. The just-in-time philosophy of defect-free production requires that much time be spent on the inspection of both inputs and outputs.
    b. JIT is a physical system, a collection of methods and procedures, detailing how an operation should be managed.
    c. Just-in-time is a market driven, waste free production system sufficiently flexible and responsive to changes in market demand to produce exactly what is needed.
    d. Just-in-time is concerned with the use of time as measure of effectiveness in efforts to provide adequate customer satisfaction and short-term competitiveness.
    e. None of the above is true.

16. Which of the following statements regarding JIT systems is TRUE?
    a. A firm's total-business cycle is the elapsed time from when a customer need is identified until the need is satisfied and production is completed.
    b. "Just-in-case" is a somewhat derogatory term referring to inventory levels that are unnecessarily high.
    c. Companies that have earned the true benefits from JIT implementation have focused primarily on improving manufacturing operations.
    d. In an ideal JIT operation, the only time material would stop would be while acceptance sampling is being performed.
    e. All of the above are true.

17. The implementation of JIT methods in Japan are in part due to
    a. limited natural resources.
    b. heterogeneity of the Japanese people.
    c. abundant space.
    d. rigid application of the EOQ principles.
    e. legal requirements.

18. Benefits of JIT production include
    a. increased productivity of direct labor employees.
    b. increased finished goods inventories.
    c. improved responsiveness to customers.
    d. decreased utilization of equipment.
    e. increased use of raw materials.

19. Which of the following is NOT a benefit of adopting JIT production?
    a. producing defect-free and well designed products
    b. increased productivity of direct labor employees
    c. decreased utilization of equipment on products that will be deployed quickly
    d. improving the company's responsiveness to changing markets
    e. reducing raw material, work-in-process, and finished goods inventories

20. _____ manufacturing describes the philosophy of continuously improving cycle times by eliminating waste.
   a. Reduced-cycle
   b. Rapid-cycle
   c. Decreased-cycle
   d. Reduction-cycle
   e. Short-cycle

21. The early experiences of _____ provided the Japanese with their concept of JIT.
   a. Henry Ford
   b. Joseph Juran
   c. W. Edwards Deming
   d. Adam Smith
   e. Frederick Taylor

22. The last of the sub-cycles of the total business cycle is the
   a. accounts receivable cycle.
   b. distribution cycle.
   c. production cycle.
   d. packing and shipping cycle.
   e. transfer cycle.

23. Which of the following is NOT a common misunderstanding of JIT?
   a. JIT will increase the productivity of direct labor employees.
   b. JIT may result in producing defect-free products.
   c. JIT is simply an inventory control system.
   d. Both a and b are misunderstandings.
   e. None of the above is a misunderstanding.

24. Which of the following is NOT one of the sub-cycles of the total-business cycle?
   a. acceptance sampling cycle
   b. production cycle
   c. packing and shipping cycle
   d. procurement cycle
   e. accounts receivable cycle

25. Joe works as a supplier representative whose primary function is to manage the inventory provided by his employer. Joe's office is at the customer's facility. This process refers to
   a. a push production system.
   b. vendor managed inventory.
   c. a kaizen inventory system.
   d. vertical vendor system.
   e. co-op inventory system.

26. At the Acme Company, inventory is building at workstation B because workstation A moves its completed material as soon as it is finished, whether workstation B is ready for it or not. Acme is most likely using a _____ production systems.
    a. LIFO
    b. FIFO
    c. push
    d. query
    e. pull

27. The only viable alternative to reduce the economic lot size (Q) is to
    a. reduce demand.
    b. increase carrying cost.
    c. increase the production rate.
    d. increase demand.
    e. reduce setup cost.

28. McDonald's uses a _____ production system.
    a. LIFO
    b. FIFO
    c. push
    d. query
    e. pull

29. The time required to develop a new strategy and complete its implementation refers to the
    a. new strategy development cycle.
    b. new strategic orientation cycle.
    c. new product development cycle.
    d. new task cycle.
    e. new implementation approach cycle.

30. In a push manufacturing system, the effects of equipment problems most often show up in the form of
    a. increased idle time.
    b. decreased idle time.
    c. increased work-in-process.
    d. increased throughput.
    e. decreased quality.

SHORT ANSWER QUESTIONS

1. What is the recommended sequence of steps for the implementation of JIT?

2. List at least three misconceptions about JIT. Explain briefly why each misconception arose and why it is not true.

3. List and describe briefly the three elements of the JIT philosophy.

4. What are the requirements for JIT implementation?

5. List and describe the similarities and differences between a push production system and a pull production systems.

CHAPTER 17
DESIGN AND SCHEDULING OF SERVICE SYSTEMS

INTRODUCTION

THE EVOLUTION OF THE SERVICE SYSTEM
    Service Strategy
    The Service Package
    OPERATIONS MANAGEMENT IN PRACTICE 17.1: SABRE - The Evolution of an Airline
        Demand Management System

STRATEGIC APPROACHES TO SERVICE SYSTEM DESIGN
    Production-Line Approach
    GLOBAL OPERATIONS MANAGEMENT 17.2: McDonald's Invades the World
    Isolating the Technical Core Approach
    Consumer Participation Approach

STRATEGIES FOR MANAGING SERVICE DEMAND
    Price Incentives
    Promoting Off-Peak Demand
    Partitioning Demand
    Inventorying Demand - Reservation Systems
    OPERATIONS MANAGEMENT IN PRACTICE 17.3: On-Line Shopping: Consumers Begin
        to Take a Bite
    Inventorying Demand - Queuing Systems
    Developing Complementary Services

STRATEGIES FOR CONTROLLING SERVICE SUPPLY
    Daily Work Shift Scheduling
    Weekly Work Shift Scheduling
    Part-time Staffing
    Cross-training Employees
    Customer Self-Service
    Adjusting or Sharing Capacity
    OPERATIONS MANAGEMENT IN PRACTICE 17.4: Restaurant Drive-Throughs Improve
        Services

VEHICLE ROUTING
    The Clarke-Wright Savings Heuristic

CHAPTER SUMMARY

1. The operations manager in a service business contends with the same kinds of problems as the operations manager in a manufacturing business: they both make strategic decisions about the market niche they will serve; they both develop a product or service to provide to the consumer; and they both design and put into place systems that will provide the goods or services.

2. The design process begins with a focus on the customer and a determination of an idea for product or service is established.

   a. The marketing department is typically responsible for making the determination of customer needs and wants.

   b. The description of the needed product or service is called the performance specification, and it describes exactly what the product, or service does for the customer.

   c. The performance specifications is next translated into the design specifications by product/service designers, or engineers. The design specifications indicate what type of service system will satisfy the performance specification.

   d. In the final step, the service system is then put into place.

3. There are a number of critical aspects of service organizations that should be emphasized:

   a. Designing and managing a successful service delivery system requires the skillful organization and integration of (1) marketing, (2) human resources, and (3) operations management.

   b. Service operations provides for the delivery of a service product that is consumed as the service occurs.

   c. Many services are provided by geographically dispersed networks connected by a communications system and an overall marketing program.

4. The evolution of a successful service system can be thought of as a three stage process: the service strategy which is what defines the service business, the service package which defines exactly what the customer will get, and the service system which defines how the service is to be created and delivered.

   a. The service strategy defines the service business - what it is and what it will do. Certain important differences between strategy formulation in manufacturing companies and service companies exist:

      (1) Fewer barriers for entering service markets exist because the capital required to enter is usually lower.

      (2) Technology that cannot be copied is harder to acquire for service business.

      (3) Service product uniqueness is harder to achieve.

      (4) It is harder to determine the cost of services, so price competition is more difficult.

      (5) Developing new services through research and development is not easy because of the lack of a tangible product.

      (6) Acquisitions as a growth strategy pose a risk because the key personnel that are the major asset of the service firm can simply leave.

b. There are three major operations strategies that can be used by service organizations:

   (1) Strategically locating the service unit - because a service is an abstract, perishable entity, it needs to be accessible to its customers.

   (2) Establishing economies of scale - centralized purchasing and centralized advertising as an example for multi-site services will create opportunities for establishing economies of scale.

   (3) Developing service differentiation - this refers to the service quality identification and customer loyalty achieved by established service companies. It can be accomplished by past advertising, word of mouth recommendations, previous good service, etc.

c. The service package defines exactly what will be provided, where and how it will be provided, and to whom. The service package can be defined by a bundle of goods consisting of four features:

   (1) Supporting facilities - the physical resources that must be available.

   (2) Facilitating goods - the materials purchased or consumed by the buyer.

   (3) Explicit services - the intrinsic benefits that are readily observable by the senses.

   (4) Implicit services - the extrinsic, or psychological, benefits of the service.

d. The service system defines how the service is to be created and delivered to the customer. Service system design can be approached strategically in several ways, (1) personalized service, (2) production-line approach, (3) isolating the technical core, (4) consumer participation, (5) self-service.

   (1) Production-line approach - Services can achieve success by applying a manufacturing style of thinking to a people-intensive service situation. The entire service system can be viewed as a piece of equipment with the capability of producing a standardized, customer-satisfying output while giving little operating discretion from its employees. Other important features of this approach can include:

      (a) Use of hard technologies - the substitution of machinery or tools for people intensive performance of service work.

      (b) Use of soft technologies - the substitution of organized, preplanned systems for individual service operations.

      (c) Service standardization - the limiting of service options in order to achieve uniformity and predictability.

      (d) Division of labor - the breaking down of the total job into a group of tasks to allow labor skill specialization.

(e) Limited discretion by personnel - the provision of a well defined set of tasks to the service employee so that standardization, uniformity, and quality can be achieved.

(2) Isolating the technical core approach - the extent of customer contact can have a big impact on service system design. Customer contact refers to the physical presence of the customer in the system. Not all service businesses have the same degree of customer contact. Extent of contact refers to the percentage of time the customer is in the service system compared to the total time it takes to perform the service. The low-contact system has the capability of decoupling operations and sealing off the technical core from the environment, while the high-contact system does not. There are several generalizations about the two classes of service systems that can be made.

(a) High contact operations require people with good public relations skills.

(b) The ability to match supply and demand is much better for low-contact systems.

(c) High contact systems will generally suffer from lack of standardization and uncertainty with respect to day-to-day operations.

(d) In high contact systems time pressures are more prevalent because orders cannot be stored to smooth production flows.

(3) Customer participation approach - consumer participation in services can have many forms. The variety will be influenced by whether there is continuous delivery versus discrete delivery service transactions and formal versus informal relationships between customers and the service organization.

(a) In many service systems, the consumer is present during the time the service is occurring. This presents opportunities for involving the consumer in the service process in a way that increases productivity.

(b) The design of service systems involving increased consumer participation is becoming more prevalent as a result of increasing wage levels, which requires the substitution of consumer labor for service provider labor.

5. The major factor in the success of many businesses is the extent to which they are able to utilize their available capacity faced with erratic demand. Some specific strategies used to manage service demand are:

a. Employing price incentives - examples of this strategy are offering discounts during slow periods of demand, (telephone service, movie theaters, restaurants, etc.), seasonal rates at resorts, pricing of airline tickets, etc.

b. Promoting off-peak demand - this refers to the demand strategy in which different sources of demand are sought out in order to fill unused capacity. Promoting off-peak demand can also be used to keep from overtaxing available capacity.

c. Partitioning demand - since service demand usually does not originate from a homogenous source, it can be partitioned into planned arrivals and random arrivals. The planned arrivals can then be controlled using an appointment system, leaving the random arrivals to fill out the remaining capacity.

d. Inventorying demand - reservation systems - many services, particularly those of a personal nature are provided by reservation or appointment systems. Taking reservations presells the service capacity.

e. Inventorying demand - queuing systems - waiting lines are another way in which service firms can inventory demand. Customers can be asked to wait in line for service on a first-come-first served basis.

f. Developing complementary services - many services have discovered the capacity expanding benefits of developing complementary services. By developing complementary services overall demand can be made more uniform.

6. For many services demand cannot be smoothed very easily. So, the service operations manager must also have strategies for controlling service supply.

a. Chase-demand strategy - this involves adjusting work force levels so that output matches service demand over the planning horizon. It is appropriate where demand is volatile and unpredictable and there is an adequate supply of relatively low-skilled labor. It requires more employees, and those employees exhibit a higher rate of turnover.

b. Level-capacity strategy - this involves maintaining a constant work force level over the planning horizon. Service operations managers use the level capacity strategy where more highly skilled people perform jobs for high pay.

c. Other strategies that can be used to control service supply include:

(1) Daily work force scheduling - also called shift scheduling is an important problem for service organizations such as telephone companies, banks, hospitals, etc.

(2) Weekly work shift scheduling - daily work shift scheduling is only a part of the bigger problem of weekly work shift scheduling. Service employees want to be scheduled for five consecutive work days with two consecutive days off. This method tries to assign employees to a specific combination of work days during a week/period. The goal of this method is to identify the two consecutive days off for each employee that minimizes the total slack capacity, while meeting the overall weekly requirement.

(3) Part-time scheduling - in services where the demand pattern exhibits peaks which are pronounced around certain times of the day or days of the week. When this occurs part-time employees can be used to supplement regular employees. This method helps trade off the risks associated with over staffing and under staffing.

246 Chapter 17 - Design and Scheduling of Service Systems

(4) Cross-training employees - cross-training employees so they are multi-skilled is perhaps one of the best strategies for controlling service supply. By cross-training employees to perform several, or all, operations, flexibility and additional service supply is created.

(5) Customer self service - in these operations the consumer provides the demand input at the exact time it is desired.

(6) Adjusting or sharing capacity - many service organizations attempt to physically design their facilities to allow for adjusting capacity. Many service organizations also share their resources i.e. airlines sharing gates, schools and churches used by outside groups, etc. By adjusting or sharing capacity service firms are able to effectively utilize capacity during periods of under utilization.

7. Scheduling customer service and routing service vehicles are key considerations in many service operations. In many service companies the routing of vehicles is a major operational problem that has a profound impact on the quality of service provided. The Clarke-Wright savings heuristic is a procedure that is often used in vehicle routing situations. It is used to determine routes from a central depot or warehouse to N delivery points or customers.

KEY TERMS

a. chase-demand strategy
b. Clarke-Wright savings heuristic
c. core service
d. customer contact
e. design specifications
f. extent of contact
g. level-capacity strategy
h. performance specifications
i. peripheral services
j. service differentiation
k. service package
l. service strategy
m. service system
n. shift scheduling
o. technical core

DEFINITIONS

_____ 1. strategy of adjusting work force levels so that service output matches service demand over the planning horizons.

_____ 2. this defines exactly what will be given to the customer.

_____ 3. this defines the service business - what it is and what it will do.

_____ 4. physical presence of the customer in the system.

_____ 5. the percentage of time the customer is in the service system compared to the total time it takes to perform the service.

_____ 6. this indicates what type of service system will satisfy the performance specification.

_____ 7. the bundle of secondary outputs that surround the primary output of a service.

_____ 8. maintaining a constant work force level over the planning horizon.

_____ 9. how the service is to be created and delivered to the customer.

_____ 10. another term for production processes.

_____ 11. the description of the needed product, or service.

_____ 12. the service quality identification and loyalty achieved by established service companies.

_____ 13. the primary output or purpose of the service.

_____ 14. used to determine routes from a central depot to various delivery points or customers.

MULTIPLE CHOICE QUESTIONS

1. Systems design and implementation is done in a way that makes the system controllable with respect to the following EXCEPT
   a. cost.
   b. quality.
   c. durability.
   d. timeliness.
   e. none of the above.

2. The exact description of what the service does for the customer is called
   a. performance specification.
   b. design specification.
   c. service strategy.
   d. service package.
   e. service system.

3. Design specifications
   a. define how the service is to be created and delivered to the customer.
   b. describe exactly what the service does for the customer.
   c. define exactly what will be given to the customer.
   d. defines what the service business is and what it will do.
   e. indicates what type of service system will satisfy the desired customer requirements.

4. Which of the following is NOT a critical function in designing and managing a successful service delivery system?
   a. marketing
   b. engineering
   c. human resources
   d. operations management
   e. none of the above

5. The three stage process of service system development is
   a. design specifications - service strategy - performance specifications.
   b. service strategy - service package - service system.
   c. service strategy - performance specifications - service system.
   d. service system - service package - service strategy.
   e. performance specifications - design specifications - service strategy.

6. The service strategy
   a. indicates what type of service system will satisfy the desired customer requirements.
   b. defines what the service business is and what it will do.
   c. defines exactly what will be given to the customer.
   d. describes exactly what the service does for the customer.
   e. defines how the service is to be created and delivered to the customer.

7. This defines exactly what will be given to the customer.
   a. performance specifications
   b. design specifications
   c. service strategy
   d. service package
   e. service system

8. The service system
   a. defines how the service is to be created and delivered to the customer.
   b. indicates what type of service system will satisfy the desired customer requirements.
   c. defines what the service business is and what it will do.
   d. defines exactly what will be given to the customer.
   e. describes exactly what the service does for the customer.

9. Which of the following is NOT a major operations strategy used by service organizations?
   a. strategically locating the service unit
   b. the chase - demand strategy
   c. establishing economies of scale
   d. developing service differentiation
   e. none of the above

10. Service differentiation can be achieved by all the following EXCEPT
    a. past advertising.
    b. word of mouth.
    c. previous good service.
    d. first entrant into a market.
    e. none of the above.

11. The service package can be defined by a bundle of goods consisting of
    a. supporting facilities.
    b. facilitating goods.
    c. explicit services.
    d. all of the above.
    e. only b and c.

12. The extrinsic, or psychological benefits of the service are
    a. implicit services.
    b. facilitating goods.
    c. supporting facilities.
    d. explicit services.
    e. none of the above.

13. Which of the following are NOT examples of physical items of the service package?
    a. meals in a restaurant
    b. atmosphere in a restaurant
    c. dishes used in a restaurant
    d. silverware used in a restaurant
    e. uniforms of wait staff in a restaurant

14. Wickham Skinner has asserted that strategy involves matching what the organization is good at, its "distinctive competence" with its
    a. service package.
    b. primary task.
    c. peripheral service.
    d. all of the above.
    e. only b and c.

15. In airline travel, the cleanliness of the plane's interior, the attitude of the flight attendants, the food and drinks are all examples of
    a. core service.
    b. explicit services.
    c. peripheral services.
    d. facilitating goods.
    e. none of the above.

16. The substitution of machinery or tools for people intensive performance of service work is an example of
    a. limited discretion by personnel.
    b. division of labor.
    c. service standardization.
    d. use of soft technologies.
    e. use of hard technologies.

17. The physical presence of the customer in the system refers to
    a. labor intensity.
    b. responsiveness.
    c. customer contact.
    d. customization.
    e. extent of contact.

250   Chapter 17 - Design and Scheduling of Service Systems

18. The percentage of time the customer is in the system compared to the total time it takes to perform the service is the
    a. level of responsiveness.
    b. customer contact.
    c. labor intensity.
    d. extent of contact.
    e. level of customization.

19. Which of the following is an example of a low contact service?
    a. hospital
    b. school
    c. gourmet restaurant
    d. parcel service company
    e. lawyers office

20. Which of the following are strategies for controlling service supply?
    a. chase-demand strategy
    b. weekly workshift scheduling
    c. level-capacity strategy
    d. daily workshift scheduling
    e. all of the above

PROBLEMS

PROBLEM SITUATION #1

The operations manager for B and H Trash Removal has determined the minimal personnel required to drive trash trucks during various days of the week. From the information below develop a work force schedule that covers all requirements while giving two consecutive days off to each worker, there is a preference by all workers to have a Monday through Friday work schedule

DAY	MON	TUES	WED	THR	FRI	SAT	SUN
Minimum Personnel required	6	5	5	4	3	3	2

21. What are the days off for worker number 1?
    a. Saturday and Sunday
    b. Thursday and Friday
    c. Tuesday and Wednesday
    d. Friday and Saturday
    e. Sunday and Monday

22. How many drivers are needed to meet weekly demand?
    a. 4
    b. 5
    c. 6
    d. 7
    e. none of the above

23. How much excess capacity is in this work schedule?
    a. 2
    b. 3
    c. 7
    d. 8
    e. none of the above

PROBLEM SITUATION #2

The manager of public safety at Wrightsville Beach has the task of scheduling life guards for weekly shifts. He has determined the minimal number of lifeguards required to satisfy daily demand. From the information below develop a work force schedule that covers all requirements while giving two consecutive days off each week. the lifeguards have no preference regarding which days they have off.

DAY	MON	TUES	WED	THR	FRI	SAT	SUN
Minimum lifeguards required	6	7	8	8	10	10	9

24. How many lifeguards are required to satisfy daily demand?
    a. 8
    b. 9
    c. 12
    d. 13
    e. none of the above

25. What are the days off assigned to worker 3?
    a. Saturday - Sunday
    b. Sunday - Monday
    c. Thursday - Friday
    d. Wednesday - Thursday
    e. all of the above

26. How much excess capacity is in this work schedule?
    a. 2
    b. 3
    c. 5
    d. 7
    e. 8

PROBLEM SITUATION #3

At the University by the Sea, student workers are used for freshman orientation. The Vice-Chancellor for Academic Affairs has calculated the minimum number of student workers required as shown below. From this information develop a work force schedule that covers all requirements while giving two consecutive days off to each worker, there is no preference by the workers regarding which days they have off.

DAY	MON	TUES	WED	THR	FRI	SAT	SUN
Minimum workers required	5	4	3	4	5	4	3

27. What is the minimum number of workers required to meet demand?
    a. 4
    b. 5
    c. 6
    d. 7
    e. none of the above

28. How much excess capacity is in the final work schedule?
    a. 0
    b. 2
    c. 3
    d. 7
    e. 9

29. What are the days off assigned to worker 1?
    a. Monday - Tuesday
    b. Tuesday - Wednesday
    c. Wednesday - Thursday
    d. Thursday - Friday
    e. Saturday - Sunday

PROBLEM SITUATION #4

A Dry Cleaner has three branch locations, but does all dry cleaning at their central facility. Each day a truck makes a separate trip directly to each branch location and back again. Using the Clark-Wright savings heuristic and the information below answer the questions that follow.

Distance, in miles, from the central facility (node 0) to each branch location, as well as distances between branches are below:

FROM CENTRAL FACILITY	TO BRANCH LOCATIONS	0	1	2	3
0		-	4	5	6
1			-	4	7
2				-	8
3					-

30. How many miles are saved by connecting node 1 and node 3?
    a. 1
    b. 2
    c. 3
    d. 4
    e. 5

31. How many miles are saved by connecting node 2 and node 3?
    a. 2
    b. 3
    c. 4
    d. 5
    e. 6

32. In the final solution, node 3 is always connected to node ____.
    a. 0
    b. 1
    c. 2
    d. more than one of the above
    e. all of the above

APPLICATION QUESTIONS

The owner of Kitchen Town, a Kitchen and Bath wholesaler delivers appliances and cabinets to job sites each morning. Currently, there is a separate trip made to each job site from the warehouse because of limitations on the amount a delivery truck will hold. The owner will invest in a larger truck if he can be shown that there would be a savings with a different distribution system. Using the information below and the Clark-Wright savings heuristic, answer the questions that follow:

Distance, in miles, from the central warehouse (node 0) to each job site, as well as distances between job sites are below:

FROM WAREHOUSE	TO JOB SITE	0	1	2	3	4
0		-	7	10	6	8
1			-	8	8	12
2				-	10	10
3					-	12
4						-

1. What are the savings obtained by connecting node 3 to node 4?

2. What are the savings obtained by connecting node 1 to node 4?

3. What savings could be obtained by connecting node 2 to node 3?

4. Connecting which two nodes provides the greatest savings?

5. What are the savings obtained by connecting node 2 to node 4?

6. What is the optimum route to minimize travel between job sites?

7. What is the total distance traveled if the truck makes a separate trip directly to each location and back again?

8. What is the minimum distance traveled to service all locations?

SHORT ANSWER QUESTIONS

1. Describe the three-stage process of developing a successful service system. What is accomplished at each stage?

2. List and describe the bundle of goods that can define a service package.

3. What options are available to service organizations to manage service demand?

4. What options are available to service organizations to control service supply?

5. What is the Clarke-Wright savings heuristic? What is its major contribution to service efficiency?

CHAPTER 18
PROJECT MANAGEMENT

INTRODUCTION
Work Breakdown Structures (WBS)
Gantt Charts

PERT AND CPM
Construction of a Project Network
Calculating the Completion Time for a Project
OPERATIONS MANAGEMENT IN PRACTICE 18.1: Project Management for Product Launch at Oldsmobile

MANAGING PROJECT RESOURCES
Developing Project Budgets
Monitoring and Controlling Project Costs
Resource Limitations
Time/Cost Tradeoffs in Project Management
OPERATIONS MANAGEMENT IN PRACTICE 18.2: Using Project Management Tools in Building Construction at Michigan State University

PERT NETWORKS AND UNCERTAIN TIME ESTIMATES

GUIDELINES FOR MANAGING PROJECTS
OPERATIONS MANAGEMENT IN PRACTICE 18.3: Platform Teams in the U. S. Auto Industry

CHAPTER SUMMARY

1. Projects are low-volume production products, like ship and aircraft production. Projects are successful if they are completed on time, within budget, and to performance requirements. Today's organizations make more frequent use of cross-functional projects and processes, which require managers to lead diverse teams effectively. This follows in part from flatter organizational structures and empowered employees.

2. Two precursors to network analysis are work breakdown structures and Gantt charts.

   a. Work Breakdown Structures (defined by NASA) "is a family tree subdivision of effort required to achieve an objective (e.g., program, project, contract, etc.). The WBS is developed by starting with the end objective required and successively subdividing it into manageable components in terms of size and complexity, such as program, project, system, subsystems, components, tasks, subtasks, and work elements. It should be product or task oriented and should include all the necessary effort which must be undertaken to achieve the end objective."

   b. Gantt charts give a timeline for each of a project's activities, but do not show the precedence relationships of activities.

3. Neither WBS nor Gantt charts is a complete tool. WBS illustrates precedence but not timing of elements; Gantt charts illustrate timing but not precedence. PERT and CPM evolved to provide project management tools containing both precedence and timing in a single tool. A project network is used to portray graphically the interrelationships among the elements of a project and shows the order in which the activities must be performed.

   a. Networks can be constructed activity-on-arc or activity-on-node. (The textbook uses activity-on-arc). In this form, each node represents an event (the time when all activities leading to that node are completed); each arc represents an activity.

   b. Two rules govern the construction of activity-on-arc networks:

   (1) Each activity must be represented by only one directed arc.

   (2) No two activities may begin and end on the same node.

   c. Since all activities are identified by their beginning and ending node numbers, a "dummy" activity is added to avoid having two activities identically represented. Dummy activities are also used to correctly represent precedence.

4. Minimum completion time for a project is calculated by determining the earliest time an activity can start based on the activities which precede it, and assuming that all activities start as soon as possible and are completed as soon as possible. This process begins at the originating event and continues to the terminal event. From this calculation come the early start and early finish times for each activity, and the minimum completion time for the project.

5. Using the minimum completion time from the step above, and working from the terminal note to the originating node calculates the late finish time and late start time for each activity.

   a. Early start (ES) of an activity is the latest of the early finish times of all its predecessors.

   b. Early finish (EF) of an activity is its early start plus its duration.

   c. Late finish (EF) of an activity is the earliest of the late start times of all successor activities.

   d. Late start (LS) of an activity is its late finish less its duration.

   e. Slack is the amount of time an activity can be delayed without delaying the entire project, assuming its preceding activities are completed as early as possible. Slack can be calculated as LS-ES or LF-EF.

   f. The critical path is that set of activities that have zero slack. Every network has at least one critical path

6. The critical path is that set of all activities that have no slack -- whose early start and late start are the same. Delaying any task on the critical path must delay the project. The critical path can also be identified as the longest of all paths through the network.

7. Projects are not static; they need monitoring and managing after they are underway because activities will diverge from the plan.

   a. Two cash flow budgets can be prepared. One is based on activities beginning as early as possible. In the other, all activities begin as late as possible. In either case, the amount expended by a specific time can be calculated. Actual cash flow at any time period should lie between the two extreme values calculated.

   b. Determining whether a project is "under budget" requires both the expenditures to date and an estimate of the status of activities. Comparing actual costs to planned costs identifies areas of cost overrun.

   c. Activity durations may not be constant; they may vary with the extent of resources devoted to them. This complicates network calculations, and means a trial and error solution rather than an optimizing one. Space or labor limitations may make some activities compete for the same limited resource. As one activity gets more of the resource, its duration shrinks, while the other activity grows longer.

   d. Project crashing shortens the project by assigning more resources to one or more of the critical tasks. The primary inputs are the normal time and cost of an activity, and the "crash" time and cost of the same activity. The crashing heuristic looks first to that activity with the smallest cost increase per unit of time the project is shortened. This continues as long as the critical path is longer than the target completion time.

   e. If one of the activities on the critical path is shortened, a different path may become critical. Crashing procedures must consider the impact of crashing an activity on all paths in the network.

8. PERT techniques are based on the notion that activity durations are probabilistic.

   a. Terminology

      (1) Optimistic time estimate (a) is an estimate of the minimum time an activity will require.

      (2) Most likely time estimate (m) is an estimate of the normal time an activity will require.

      (3) Pessimistic time estimate (b) is an estimate of the maximum time an activity will require.

   b. The mean activity time (t) is estimated as (a+4m+b)/6

   c. The standard deviation for an activity (s) is estimated as (b-a)/6, one sixth of the estimated range.

   d. Three assumptions required are:

(1) The time it takes to complete an activity does not affect the time it takes to complete any other activity.

(2) There are no "near-critical" paths. If another path has an expected completion time near that of the critical path, it is unclear which path is truly critical when the randomness of activity times is considered.

(3) Project completion time has a normal distribution since it is the sum of many independent random variables.

e. The mean completion time for the project is the sum of the expected activity times for activities on the critical path; the variance of the completion time of the project is the sum of the critical path activity variances. When combined with the assumption of normality, the normal areas curve can be used to calculate the probability of project completion for any specific time.

KEY TERMS

a. activity-on-arc
b. activity on node
c. critical activities
d. critical path
e. critical path method (CPM)
f. dummy activity
g. earliest finish time (EF)
h. early start time (ES)
i. Gantt chart
j. latest finish time (LF)
k. latest start time (LS)

l. mean activity time
m. most likely time estimate (m)
n. optimistic time estimate (a)
o. pessimistic time estimate (b)
p. program evaluation and review technique (PERT)
q. project management techniques
r. project crashing
s. project network
t. slack time
u. variance of activity time
v. work breakdown structure (WBS)

DEFINITIONS

Directions: Select from the key terms list, the word or phrase being defined below.

_____ 1. is a family tree subdivision of effort required to achieve an objective.

_____ 2. an activity introduced in the construction of a project network to avoid identical representations of activities.

_____ 3. is used to portray graphically the interrelationships among the elements of a project and shows the order in which the activities must be performed.

_____ 4. of an activity is the latest of the early finish times of all its predecessors.

_____ 5. is the early start of an activity plus its duration.

_____ 6. of an activity is the earliest of the late start times of all successor activities.

_____ 7. of an activity is its late finish less its duration.

_____ 8. is the amount of time an activity can be delayed without delaying the entire project, assuming its preceding activities are completed as early as possible.

_____ 9. is that set of activities in a project network that controls the duration of the entire project.

_____ 10. is shortening the project by assigning more resources to one or more of the critical tasks.

_____ 11. is an estimate of the minimum time an activity will require.

_____ 12. is an estimate of the normal time an activity will require.

_____ 13. is an estimate of the maximum time an activity will require.

_____ 14. is used to portray graphically the interrelationships of the elements of a project.

_____ 15. visual device that shows the duration of tasks in a project.

MULTIPLE CHOICE QUESTIONS

Directions: Indicate your choice of the best answer to each question.

1. Which of the following statements regarding project management is TRUE?
   a. The Work Breakdown Structure is a useful tool in project management.
   b. Project networks give a timeline for each of a project's activities, but do not show the precedence relationships of activities.
   c. The Work Breakdown Structures addresses the timing of individual work elements.
   d. Gantt charts combine the qualities of Work Breakdown Structures and of project networks.
   e. None of the above is true.

2. Which of the following statements regarding project management is FALSE?
   a. Work Breakdown Structures are useful tools in project management.
   b. Gantt charts give a timeline for each of a project's activities, but do not show the precedence relationships of activities.
   c. Work Breakdown Structures do not address the timing of individual work elements.
   d. Gantt charts combine the qualities of Work Breakdown Structures and of project networks.
   e. All of the above are true.

3. Which of the following statements regarding project management is TRUE?
   a. The critical path is the longest of all paths through the network.
   b. The critical path is that set of activities that have zero slack.
   c. Every network has at least one critical path.
   d. All of the above are true.
   e. Only a and b are true.

4. Which of the following statements regarding project management is FALSE?
   a. The critical path is the shortest of all paths through the network.
   b. The critical path is that set of activities that have positive slack.
   c. Every network has exactly one critical path.
   d. All of the above are false.
   e. Only b and c are false.

5. Which of the following statements regarding project management is TRUE?
   a. Project crashing is a PERT technique.
   b. Shortening the project by assigning more resources to one or more of the critical tasks is called "project crashing."
   c. Crashing procedures need not consider the impact of crashing an activity on other paths in the network.
   d. Project crashing is an optimizing technique.
   e. Crash cost depends upon the variance of the activity to be crashed.

6. Which of the following statements regarding project management is TRUE?
   a. Project crashing is a CPM technique.
   b. Shortening the project by reducing resources to one or more of the critical tasks is called "project crashing."
   c. Crashing procedures need not consider the impact of crashing an activity on other paths in the network.
   d. Project crashing is an heuristic technique.
   e. Both a and d are true.

7. A retail construction project being analyzed by PERT has 68 activities, 23 of which are on the critical path. If the estimated time along the critical path is 80 days with a variance of 25 days, the probability that the project will be completed in 90 days or less is _____.
   a. 0.0228
   b. 0.6556
   c. 0.3444
   d. 0.9772
   e. 0.4

8. A project being analyzed by PERT has 45 activities, 19 of which are on the critical path. Analysis of the path reveals that the estimated time for the critical path is 120 days. The sum of all activity variances is 64, while the sum of variances along the critical path is 36. The probability that the project can be completed between days 110 and 120 is _____.
   a. 0.3942
   b. 0.4525
   c. 0.1058
   d. 0.9524
   e. -1.67

9. A project being analyzed by PERT has 36 activities, 21 of which are on the critical path. Analysis shows the estimated time for the critical path to be 108 days with a variance of 64 days. There is a .75 probability that the project will be completed after day _____.
    a. 140
    b. 102.6
    c. 113.6
    d. 110
    e. 112.2

10. Which of the following "projects" would be least likely to involve use of PERT?
    a. building a tract house
    b. installing new transaction processing software system
    c. designing and constructing an airport
    d. planning, constructing a new hospital
    e. preparing for visit of an important world leader

11. Activities that are NOT on a PERT critical path but have little slack need to be monitored closely because
    a. PERT treats all activities as equally important.
    b. there are near-critical paths which could become critical with small delays in these activities.
    c. they are causing the entire project to be delayed.
    d. slack is undesirable and needs to be eliminated.
    e. both b and d are correct.

12. Dummy activities are used in PERT/CPM for which of the following reasons?
    a. to indicate a zero-length activity duration
    b. no two activities can have the same starting and ending nodes
    c. to reflect slack time in the same manner as slack variables in linear programming
    d. all of the above are valid reasons
    e. only a and b are valid reasons

13. If an activity whose normal duration is 14 days can be shortened to 10 days for an added cost of $1500, the crash cost per unit time is ____.
    a. $375
    b. $1500
    c. $6000
    d. $15,000
    e. $21,000

14. Which of the following statements regarding time-cost tradeoffs in CPM networks is FALSE?
    a. Crashing shortens the critical path by assigning more resources to one or more non-critical tasks.
    b. Crashing is not possible unless there are multiple critical paths.
    c. Crashing a project reduces the length of critical activities only.
    d. Project crashing is a CPM technique, not a PERT technique.
    e. Both a and b are false.

15. Two activities are candidates for crashing on a CPM network. Activity details are in the table below. To cut one day from the project's duration, activity _____ should be crashed first, adding _____ to project cost.

Activity	Normal Time	Normal Cost	Crash Duration	Crash Cost
R	7 days	$6,000	6 days	$6,600
V	11 days	$4,000	9 days	$6,000

   a. R; $6,600
   b. R; $600
   c. V; $1,000
   d. V; $2,000
   e. R; $12,600

16. Activity SIGMA on a CPM network has predecessors GAMMA and DELTA, and has successor THETA. SIGMA has duration 6. GAMMA's late finish is 18, while DELTA's is 20. DELTA's early start is 20. THETA's late start is 26. Which of the following is FALSE?
   a. SIGMA is a critical activity.
   b. GAMMA is a critical activity.
   c. DELTA's early finish is 20.
   d. THETA is a critical activity.
   e. None of the above is false.

17. Which of the following statements regarding project management is FALSE?
   a. Project management differs from the management of more traditional activities due to the limited lifetime of projects.
   b. Dummy activities are added to paths to make all paths of equal length, analogous to adding slack variables in linear programming.
   c. A Gantt chart contains no precedence relationships, but may be useful for simple projects.
   d. Heuristic procedure is a "rule-of-thumb" technique that provides a good (and perhaps, optimal) solution.
   e. Slack is the amount of time an activity can be delayed without delaying the entire project, assuming its preceding activities are completed as early as possible.

18. The critical path for the network activities shown below is _____ with duration _____.

Activity	Nodes	Duration
A	1-2	10
B	1-3	8
C	2-4	6
D	2-3	3
E	3-4	2

   a. A-C; 16
   b. A-D-E; 16
   c. A-D-E; 15
   d. A-B-C-D-E; 15
   e. none of the above

19. Which of the following statements regarding CPM networks is TRUE?
    a. The early finish of an activity is the latest early start of all preceding activities.
    b. The late finish of an activity is the earliest late start of all preceding activities.
    c. On a specific project, there can be multiple critical paths, all of which will have exactly the same duration.
    d. There can be multiple critical paths on the same project, all of which may have different durations.
    e. Both b and c are true.

PROBLEMS

PROBLEM SITUATION #1

A local custom cabinet maker operates his shop entirely make-to-order. Each project begins with the construction of CAD drawings for client approval, and ends with installation in the clients home or business. The list of project activities appears below, along with the appropriate CPM diagram.

Activity	Duration	Description	Activity	Duration	Description
A	2	Compose drawings	I	3	Cut cabinet frame parts
B	1	Drawings approved	J	3	Assemble cabinet frames
C	16	Order countertop laminate	K	1	Finish frame fronts
D	7	Order hinges & hardware	L	1	Ship to client location
E	10	Order hardwoods	M	2	Final assembly
F	2	Cut raised panels			
G	2	Assemble doors			
H	2	Finish doors			

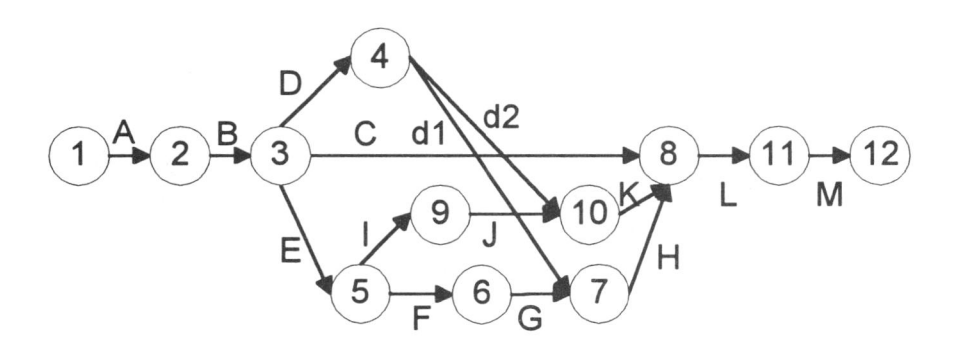

20. Which of the following statements regarding this project network is TRUE?
    a. Activity A is critical and has no slack.
    b. Activity C must be critical because it is the longest activity in the network.
    c. Activity F can be delayed, but any delay must delay the entire project.
    d. Since activity K begins at node 10 and ends at node 8, a precedence condition has been violated.
    e. Both a and c are true.

266 Chapter 18 - Project Management

21. One task that must be on the critical path, regardless of activity durations, is ____.
    a. L
    b. 8
    c. C
    d. J
    e. there is no such activity

22. The duration of path A-B-E-F-G-H-L-M is ____.
    a. 10
    b. 23
    c. 22
    d. 52
    e. none of the above

23. The critical path of this network consists of activities ____.
    a. A-B-D-d2-K-L-M
    b. A-B-E-I-J-K-L-M
    c. 1-2-3-5-9-10-8-11-12
    d. 1-2-3-8-11-12
    e. A-B-C-L-M

24. The length of the critical path is ____.
    a. 14
    b. 23
    c. 52
    d. none of the above
    e. cannot be determined

25. Slack time at activity H is ____.
    a. 1
    b. 2
    c. 7
    d. zero
    e. cannot be determined

26. The Late Start of activity H is ____.
    a. 10
    b. 47
    c. 18
    d. 20
    e. cannot be determined

27. The Early Finish of activity D is ____.
    a. 11
    b. 7
    c. 3
    d. 10
    e. none of the above

28. If activity D were delayed by five time units, the project duration would be ____.
    a. 27
    b. increased
    c. 23
    d. unchanged
    e. both c and d are correct

PROBLEM SITUATION #2

Three activities are candidates for crashing on a CPM network. Activity details appear below.

Activity	Normal Time	Normal Cost	Crash Duration	Crash Cost
R	7 days	$6,000	6 days	$6,600
T	4 days	$1,200	2 days	$3,000
V	11 days	$4,000	9 days	$6,000

29. The crash cost per unit time for activity R is ____.
    a. $6,600
    b. $600
    c. $900
    d. $2,000
    e. $12,600

30. The crash cost per unit time for activity T is ____.
    a. $3,000
    b. $1,200
    c. $4,200
    d. $1,800
    e. $900

31. To cut one day from the project's duration, activity ____ should be crashed first, adding ____ to project cost.
    a. R; $6,600
    b. R; $600
    c. V; $1,000
    d. V; $2,000
    e. T; $900

32. Assuming no other paths become critical, this project can be shortened by a maximum of ____ days at a total added cost of ____.
    a. 5; $4,400
    b. 2; $4,400
    c. 1; $600
    d. 5; $15,600
    e. 2; $15,600

Chapter 18 - Project Management

APPLICATION QUESTIONS

A firm that develops landing spaces for riverboat casinos has formulated the following list of activities necessary to release a contract for the preparation of a new gaming site. Times are given in weeks.

Activity	Description	Preceding	Optimistic	Most Likely	Pessimistic
A	Feasibility study	none	4	8	10
B	Acquire site	A	2	8	24
C	Prepare concept design	A	8	12	16
D	Coast Guard approval	A	4	6	10
E	Geologic/Hydrologic testing	B	1	2	3
F	Legal approvals and permitting	E, C	6	8	20
G	Loan application	E, C	2	3	4
H	Loan approval	F	2	2	2
I	Obtain bids	F	6	6	6
J	Negotiate contract	D, G	4	6	12
K	Release contract	I, J	2	2	3

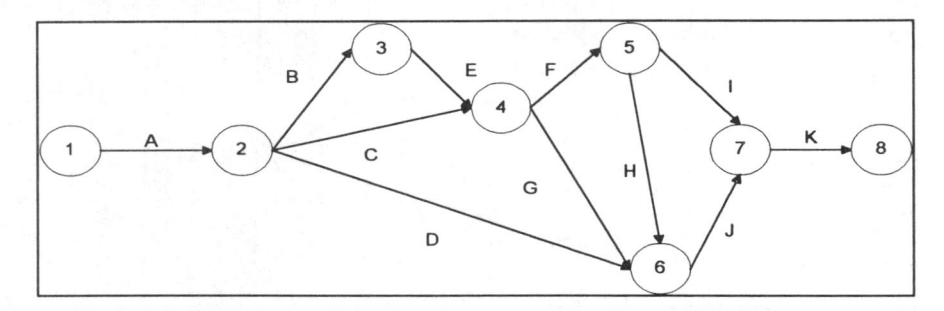

1. What is the total number of paths in this network?

2. What is the expected time for activity C?

3. What is the variance for activity C is?

4. Based on the calculation of estimated times, the critical path is made up of what sequence of activities?

5. What is the estimated duration of the critical path?

6. What is the activity variance along the critical path?

7. What is the probability that the project will be completed before week 36?

8. What is the probability that the project will take more than 50 weeks to complete?

SHORT ANSWER QUESTIONS

1. What is a Work Breakdown Structure? How does it compare with a Gantt chart? What are the limitations of each of these tools?

2. Figure 18.1 suggests that project management requires some major tradeoffs. Briefly describe these tradeoffs, and explain why they are necessary.

3. PERT and CPM are two network approaches to analyzing projects. Discuss their origins, similarities, and differences.

4. What is project "crashing?" Describe the process of crashing a CPM project. Explain what crashing analysis attempts to accomplish.

5. PERT calculations typically include the duration variance of each activity. How is the activity variance useful in project analysis? What information can be obtained using variance measures that would be impossible otherwise?

CHAPTER 19
QUALITY ANALYSIS, MEASUREMENT, AND IMPROVEMENT

INTRODUCTION

TOTAL QUALITY MANAGEMENT IMPLEMENTATION PROCESS

PROCESS ANALYSIS FOR CONTINUOUS IMPROVEMENT
Process Improvement Model
Benchmarking
OPERATIONS MANAGEMENT IN PRACTICE 19.1: Aerospace and Defense Contractors
    Use Strategic Benchmarking for Improvement
Data Collection, Analysis, and Presentation
    Brainstorming
    Process Mapping
    Run Diagrams
    Check Sheets
    Pareto Charts
    Cause-and-Effect Diagrams

STATISTICAL TOOLS FOR PROCESS IMPROVEMENT
Statistical Sampling and Control
Sampling and the Central Limit Theorem
Using Statistics to Test Inferences about Quality Control
Process Control Charts
    Control Charts for Variable Data
    Control Charts for Attribute Data
Control Limits Versus Specification Limits
Acceptance Sampling

CHAPTER SUMMARY

1. This chapter focuses on the analysis, measurement, and improvement of quality. The two major sections are continuous improvement and statistical process control.

2. Continuous improvement is the term used to describe the organizational culture in support of quality efforts that are prevention-oriented rather than detection-oriented.

3. The TQM implementation process is reviewed (see Chapter 7).

4. The eight step process improvement model can be effectively applied in all organizations regardless of the type of organization or the type of process to be improved.

    a. Define the problem in the context of the process. Improvement teams are better than a single responsible person. Such teams better represent vested interests internal and external, and provide user involvement which leads to user acceptance, or "buy-in." Customer needs and expectations are identified in these teams.

b. Identify, analyze, and document the process. This is necessary to an understanding of how the pieces of the current system interrelate.

c. Measure current performance. Two reasons for this are:

(1) Assess the strengths and weaknesses of the current process. Communication with customers is very important so that the critical factors are properly identified.

(2) Obtain actual performance data to provide a benchmark for alternative solutions.

d. Understand why the process is performing as it is. This step is an attempt to uncover causes of problems indicated by performance measures.

e. Develop alternative solutions and select the best one.

f. Develop strategy and implement the chosen alternative. Small-scale installation is recommended. If that is not possible, contingency plans should be made to cover the unexpected at overall implementation.

g. Evaluate the results of the new process. Use the same performance measures of Step 3. Don't rush, especially regarding customers' expectations.

h. Commit to continuous improvement of the process. Even with favorable assessment, improvement activity continues. The organization should never be satisfied with current performance, but should continue to assess process performance and maintain customer contact.

5. Tools and activities of the process improvement model include:

a. Benchmarking is the search for industry "best practices" that lead to superior business performance. A firm identifies processes that are important to its competitive position, and attempts to identify other firms (in the same or in a different industry) (or areas within the same firm) that are known for superior performance in this process.

b. Data collection, analysis, and presentation tools support several steps in the eight-step process. They underlie measuring current performance, evaluating alternatives, and assessing implementation outcomes.

(1) Brainstorming is a group technique used to generate ideas in an environment free of criticism and intimidation.

(2) A process map is a graphic representation of the interrelationships between several activities accomplished in the completion of a total process. Five activity types are: operation, transportation, inspection, delay, or storage. Process map is synonymous with process flow chart.

(3) Run diagrams are useful for displaying trends in process performance measures. An example would be graphing the value of a variable over time.

(4) Check sheets are used to collect data about a process. It is designed after the team knows what data are needed. Often designed for ease of response.

(5) Pareto charts use a bar chart to indicate the frequency of different sources of non-conformities in a product or service, in order to indicate which potential improvement will have the greatest effect on the overall quality of the item. Pareto charts attempt to separate the "vital few" sources of non-conformities from the "trivial many."

(6) A cause-and-effect diagram, (or fishbone diagram, or Ishikawa diagram) is a tool for clarifying the causes of a quality problem. This device coordinates the selection of an approach to correcting the problem.

6. Statistical tools for process improvement

   a. Sampling from a population subject to natural variation can result in samples not very representative of the population. Statistical hypothesis testing methodologies cover this situation. The Type I and Type II errors of hypothesis testing are now referred to as producer's risk and consumer's risk. Design of statistical problems, including selection of sample size, affects the sizes of these errors.

   (1) Producer's risk (α) is the probability of a Type I error or the risk that a good production lot would be incorrectly rejected.

   (2) Consumer's risk (β) is the probability of a Type II error or the risk that a bad production lot would be incorrectly accepted.

   b. The two types of data encountered are variable and attribute.

   (1) Variable data is associated with anything measured.

   (2) Attribute data is associated with anything counted.

7. Process control charts are used during manufacture to determine whether a process is in control or whether the process is out of control and needs to be changed. Process control charts for both types of data (variable and attribute) are useful.

   a. Five types of process control charts are listed below, with a reminder of the type of data associated with the chart and the type of parameter being studied.

   (1) x-bar chart (variable; averages)

   (2) R-chart (variable; ranges)

   (3) p-chart (attribute; proportions)

   (4) np-chart (attribute; number)

   (5) c-chart (attribute; number)

b. The logic behind all process control charts is to react to "significant" events without being misled by natural variation in processes. As with all forms of statistical hypothesis testing, this involves balancing the Type I and Type II errors. This is most commonly done by constructing ranges around the central value of the chart. If such ranges vary by ±2s from the central value, the risk of Type I error is about 5 percent. If the ranges vary by ±3s, the Type I risk is about one-quarter of one percent.

c. In practice, control chart construction uses the range to estimate the standard deviation. This leads to standard statistical tables (in the Appendix to the textbook) that calculate upper and lower control limits without directly measuring the standard deviation.

d. R-charts and X-bar charts complement one another. A process is in control for a variable when samples are within the control limits of both the R-chart and the x-bar chart and no non-random pattern is apparent in either chart.

e. The p-chart is based on the binomial distribution, and tracks the proportion of samples that are non-conforming. The np-chart has the same theoretical basis, but tracks the number defective, not the proportion.

f. The c-chart counts the number of countable defects in a sample (for example, flaws per yard of fabric). It is based on the Poisson distribution.

8. Control limits versus specification limits. Processes have natural variation, stemming from limits to raw material evenness, to tool precision or to human skill. This natural variation may or may not be adequate to the specifications of customers or designers. The process capability index C_P determines the adequacy of a process to meet specifications. A modified version, C_{PK}, allows for the process mean to be uncentered between the process limits (implying that the process average is not equal to the design target).

9. Acceptance sampling draws random samples from a population of items, tests the sample, and draws conclusions about the quality of the population based on the quality of the sample. The name of this tool implies its use: that the entire population will be accepted if the sample is good enough, and that the entire population will be rejected if the sample is poor enough. Acceptance sampling is at odds with prevention-oriented quality philosophies; it does not improve manufacturing, and is a costly operation.

a. The sampling plan contains information about the sample size to be drawn and the accept/reject numbers for that sample size. The simplest is single sampling, for which testers need to know what sample size n is to be taken from a population N, and the maximum number of defects c that will be tolerated.

b. Each combination of n, N, and c has an operating characteristic (OC) curve showing the likelihood of accepting a population of a particular quality. That is, an OC curve plots the consumer's risk against population quality.

KEY TERMS

a. acceptance sampling
b. assignable variation
c. benchmarking
d. common cause variation
e. consumer's risk
f. natural variation
g. operating characteristics curve
h. process capability
i. process control charts
j. producer's risk
k. sampling plan
l. special cause variation
m. specification limits

DEFINITIONS

Directions: Select from the key terms list, the word or phrase being defined below.

_____ 1. indicate acceptable variation in a process from the view of the product designer or customer.

_____ 2. is the search for industry "best practices" that lead to superior business performance.

_____ 3. process variation that is not expected to occur and is usually caused by some outside factor.

_____ 4. process variation that is inherent to the process.

_____ 5. is the risk that a buyer would incorrectly reject a lot that is actually good.

_____ 6. is the probability that a lot or population that is actually out of control is accepted as "good."

_____ 7. draws random samples from a population of items, tests the sample, and accepts the entire population if the sample is good enough, and rejects it if the sample is poor enough.

_____ 8. contains information about the sample size to be drawn and the accept/reject numbers for that sample size.

_____ 9. shows the likelihood of accepting a population of a particular quality, and plots the consumer's risk against population quality.

_____ 10. determines the adequacy of a process to meet specifications.

_____ 11. detects shifts the mean value of a process so that assignable causes can be found and corrective action can be taken.

MULTIPLE CHOICE QUESTIONS

Directions: Indicate your choice of the best answer to each question.

1. Sampling plans typically specify
    a. lot size.
    b. sample size.
    c. acceptance/rejection criteria.
    d. all of the above.
    e. only a and b above.

2. Type I error occurs when
    a. a good lot is rejected.
    b. a bad lot is accepted.
    c. the number of defectives is very large.
    d. the proportion defectives is very small.
    e. none of the above.

3. Type II error occurs when
    a. a good lot is rejected.
    b. a bad lot is accepted.
    c. the number of defectives is very large.
    d. the proportion defectives is very small.
    e. none of the above.

4. An acceptance sampling plan's ability to discriminate between low quality lots and high quality lots is described by
    a. a Gantt chart.
    b. an Operating Characteristics curve.
    c. the Central Limit Theorem.
    d. a process control chart.
    e. a range chart.

5. Acceptance sampling's primary purpose is to
    a. estimate process quality.
    b. estimate lot quality.
    c. detect and eliminate defectives.
    d. decide if a lot meets predetermined standards.
    e. determine whether defective items found in sampling should be replaced.

6. Which of the following statements regarding continuous improvement is TRUE?
    a. Consumer's risk is the risk that a buyer would incorrectly reject a lot that is actually good.
    b. Producer's risk is the probability that a lot or population that is actually out of control is accepted as "good."
    c. The term Type I error can be properly used to refer to producer's risk and to consumer's risk.
    d. Both a and b are true.
    e. None of the above are true.

7. Which of the following statements on continuous improvement is TRUE?
   a. Brainstorming is a group technique used to generate ideas in an environment free of criticism and intimidation.
   b. Benchmarking is the search for industry "best practices" that lead to superior business performance.
   c. A process map is a graphic representation of the interrelationships between several activities accomplished in the completion of a total process.
   d. Pareto charts attempt to separate the "vital few" sources of non-conformities from the "trivial many."
   e. All of the above are true.

8. Which of the following statements on acceptance sampling is TRUE?
   a. Acceptance sampling draws random samples from a population of items, tests the sample, and accepts the entire population if the sample is good enough, and rejects it if the sample is poor enough.
   b. The sampling plan contains information about the sample size to be drawn and the accept/reject numbers for that sample size.
   c. As an operating characteristic curve is flatter, it is more able to discriminate between good and bad lots.
   d. Acceptance sampling is used to test lots from an ongoing process to determine whether output meets specifications.
   e. Both a and b are true.

9. An operating characteristics curve shows
   a. product quality under different manufacturing conditions.
   b. how the probability of accepting a lot varies with the population percent defective.
   c. when product specifications don't match process control limits.
   d. how operations affects certain characteristics of a product.
   e. upper and lower product specifications.

10. Using a micrometer to measure the diameter of steel rods is an example of
    a. non-random sampling.
    b. sampling by attributes.
    c. sampling by variables.
    d. sampling by characteristics.
    e. none of the above.

11. The normal application of a p-chart is in
    a. process sampling by variables.
    b. acceptance sampling by variables.
    c. process sampling by attributes.
    d. acceptance sampling by attributes.
    e. none of the above.

12. In the process improvement model, the tool ordinarily used to aid understanding of a process is
    a. a process control chart.
    b. a Pareto chart.
    c. a check sheet.
    d. a process map (process flow chart).
    e. brainstorming.

13. The process improvement technique that sorts the "vital few" from the "trivial many" is
    a. Pareto analysis.
    b. benchmarking.
    c. brainstorming.
    d. acceptance sampling.
    e. a check sheet.

14. Which of the following statements concerning statistical tools for quality improvement is TRUE?
    a. Process control involves monitoring both before and after production.
    b. Acceptance sampling involves monitoring before and/or after production.
    c. Monitoring output during production is known as acceptance sampling.
    d. Monitoring output during production is known as process control.
    e. Both b and d are true.

15. Which of the following statements concerning statistical tools for quality improvement is FALSE?
    a. Process control involves monitoring during production.
    b. Acceptance sampling involves monitoring before and/or after production.
    c. Monitoring output during production is known as acceptance sampling.
    d. Monitoring output during production is known as process control.
    e. Both a and c are false.

16. If x-bar = 23 ounces, s = 0.5 ounces, and n = 16, the ±3s control limits will be _____.
    a. 21.5 to 24.5 ounces
    b. 3 ounces
    c. 22.56 to 23.37 ounces
    d. 22.906 to 23.094 ounces
    e. none of the above

17. A wood carver has been making small seasonal miniatures. Among the last 100 blanks -- seasoned chunks of wood waiting to be carved -- inspected, the defect rate has been 0.03. The upper and lower control limits for this supply process for 99.7% confidence are _____.
    a. 0.03 ± 0.0003
    b. 0.0291 to 0.0309
    c. zero to 0.0813
    d. zero to 0.0642
    e. none of the above

18. Repeated sampling of a certain production process reveals the average of all sample means = 40 cm, the average of all sample ranges = 0.5 cm. These values are based on a constant sample size of n = 6. The control limits for an R chart are _____.
   a. zero to 2.504
   b. zero to 1.002
   c. 37.996 to 42.004
   d. -1.504 to 2.504
   e. none of the above

PROBLEMS
PROBLEM SITUATION #1

A small spice and condiment company uses process control charts for the packaging processes within its operations. One of the products is a Cajun grill seasoning, Tony's Hot-Hot-Hot! When this packaging process is in control, package weight is normally distributed with mean 6.25 ounces, standard deviation .10 ounces. Each hour, a sample of four packages is taken to collect data about the process. The results for Thursday's work are presented below:

	Observations					
Sample	1	2	3	4	X-BAR	R
8 am	6.350	6.400	6.200	6.200	6.288	0.200
9 am	6.150	6.300	6.400	6.250	6.275	0.250
10 am	5.900	6.300	6.150	6.250	6.150	0.400
11 am	6.200	6.250	6.150	6.400	6.250	0.250
noon	6.400	6.350	6.050	6.250	6.263	0.350
1 pm	6.350	6.300	6.250	6.050	6.238	0.300
2 pm	6.300	6.000	6.350	6.250	6.225	0.350
3 pm	5.950	6.200	6.350	6.150	6.163	0.400
					6.2312	0.312

19. What is the mean weight for the noon sample?
   a. 0.312
   b. 6.2312
   c. 0.350
   d. 6.263
   e. none of the above

20. What is the mean of the sampling distribution, if the process is under control?
   a. 6.25
   b. 6.2312
   c. 0.10
   d. 0.60
   e. none of the above

280   Chapter 19 - Quality Analysis, Measurement, and Improvement

21. What is the mean of all sample means for Thursday?
   a. 6.25
   b. 6.2312
   c. 0.312
   d. cannot be determined from the data provided
   e. none of the above

22. What are the ±3s LCL and UCL for the mean?
   a. 6.004 to 6.459
   b. 5.521 to 6.979
   c. 5.538 to 6.962
   d. cannot be determined from the data provided
   e. none of the above

PROBLEM SITUATION #2

A pipe manufacturer sampled lots of 200 parts for defectives. The last 10 lots had 6, 7, 3, 4, 10, 7, 6, 2, 5, and 4 defective parts in each respective lot.

23. What is the average proportion of defectives in these lots?
   a. 0.054
   b. 0.027
   c. 5.4
   d. 2.7
   e. 54

24. What is the 3σ upper control limit for this process?
   a. 0.0615
   b. 0.076
   c. 0.081
   d. 0.513
   e. zero

25. What number of defectives in a sample would represent an out-of-control situation?
   a. 2.7
   b. 3
   c. 5
   d. 10
   e. 12

PROBLEM SITUATION #3

A local artisan -- a woodworker and toy maker -- is concerned about the quality of the finished appearance of his work. In sampling units of a historic reproduction wooden hobby horse, he has found the following number of finish defects (voids, sags, pits, dust specks, etc.) in ten units sampled: 0, 0, 3, 0, 1, 0, 1, 0, 0, 2.

26. The average number of defects per wooden hobby horse is _____.
    a. 7
    b. 0.7
    c. 70
    d. cannot be determined from the data provided
    e. none of the above

27. If ±3s control limits are used, what are the lower control limit, centerline, and upper control limit of this problem?
    a. -1.8, 0, and 3.2
    b. 0, 0.7, and 3.2
    c. 1.8, 0.7, and 3.2
    d. 0, 0.7, and 2.4
    e. 0, 7, and 8.5

28. This problem is a typical illustration of the _____, which is based on the _____ distribution.
    a. c-chart, normal
    b. np-chart, binomial
    c. c-chart, binomial
    d. c-chart, Poisson
    e. x-bar, normal

PROBLEM SITUATION #4

A valve manufacturer makes a part to a diameter specification of 0.20 ± 0.01 inches. The process has a standard deviation of 0.003 inches.

29. What is the process capability of this process?
    a. 0.56
    b. 1.11
    c. 1.50
    d. 0.67
    e. none of the above

30. If a process improvement reduced the standard deviation to 0.002 inches, what would be the process capability?
    a. 1.00
    b. 1.11
    c. 1.33
    d. 1.67
    e. none of the above

31. If the process average of parts was 0.205 inches, what would be the process capability (standard deviation = 0.002 inches)?
    a. 0.83
    b. 1.25
    c. 1.00
    d. 1.67
    e. none of the above

APPLICATION QUESTIONS

Data below show the results of taking 10 samples of size 7 from an ongoing process.

Sample	\multicolumn{7}{c}{Observations}	X-BAR	R
	1	2	3	4	5	6	7	X-BAR	R
A	1.100	1.350	1.200	1.100	1.050	0.900	1.150	1.121	0.450
B	1.200	1.100	1.400	1.300	1.250	1.150	1.350	1.250	0.300
C	1.150	1.200	1.350	1.050	0.950	0.950	1.100	1.107	0.400
D	1.300	1.100	1.250	1.150	1.000	1.050	1.300	1.164	0.300
E	1.200	1.100	1.050	1.250	1.300	1.150	1.200	1.179	0.250
F	0.950	1.050	1.300	1.200	1.150	1.050	1.200	1.129	0.350
G	1.150	1.200	1.350	1.400	1.200	1.100	1.150	1.221	0.300
H	1.200	0.900	1.100	1.150	1.000	1.300	1.250	1.129	0.400
I	1.300	1.250	1.300	1.150	1.050	1.100	1.200	1.193	0.250
J	1.100	1.200	1.350	1.250	1.200	1.150	1.150	1.200	0.250

1. What is the sample mean for sample G?

2. What is the sample range for sample C?

3. What is the average of all sample means?

4. What is the average range?

5. Using the standard table for control chart factors, what would be the UCL for the x-bar chart?

6. Using the standard table for control chart factors, what would be the UCL for the range chart?

SHORT ANSWER QUESTIONS

1. Suppose customers in the restaurant you own and manage are constantly complaining about it taking too long for them to get in and out. You are going to lead a process improvement team to address the problem. List the eight steps of the process improvement model and describe what you are going to do in your situation at each step.

2. Why is the step in the problem solving process where you measure current performance (Step 3) so important?

3. What is benchmarking? What are some ways one might identify potential benchmarking partners?

4. What is the "central limit theorem" and why is it important to statistical process control?

5. What is the difference between attribute data and variable data? Provide examples of each. What types of control charts are used with attribute data and variable data?

CHAPTER 20
BUILDING COMPETITIVE ADVANTAGE THROUGH WORLD CLASS MANUFACTURING: ALLEN-BRADLEY'S WORLD CONTACTOR FACILITY

INTRODUCTION

ALLEN-BRADLEY'S WORLD CONTACTORS
　　The World Contactor Facility

IDENTIFYING STRATEGIC THREATS AND OPPORTUNITIES

THE COMPETITIVE CHALLENGE
　　Defining Competitive Advantage
　　　　Cost
　　　　Quality
　　　　Flexibility and Lead Times
　　The Foundation for Success
　　　　Operations Strategic Planning
　　　　Benchmarking the Competition

BUILDING COMPETITIVE ADVANTAGE: TOWARD WORLD CLASS MANUFACTURING
　　Cost
　　Quality
　　Flexibility and Lead Times

MANUFACTURING APPROACHES, METHODS, AND TECHNOLOGIES
　　Concurrent Engineering and the Team Approach
　　Computer Integrated Manufacturing and the Productivity Pyramid
　　Bar Coding
　　Total Quality Management
　　Just-in-Time Manufacturing
　　Human Resource Management

WORLD CLASS MANUFACTURING AT ALLEN-BRADLEY: OUTCOMES AND BENEFITS

WORLD CLASS MANUFACTURING: A SYNOPSIS

CHAPTER SUMMARY

1. This final chapter of the text focuses on the competitive advantage that Allen-Bradley has achieved in the global marketplace for its World Contactor products. The definition of competitive advantage as applied to Allen-Bradley describes both the state of advantage; increases in market share and the profitability performance associated with it, and how it can be gained; relative superiority in skills and resources.

　　a. Allen-Bradley's World Contactor Assembly facility manufactures both contractors and control relays for the global market. Prior to the mid-1980's both of these products were designed primarily for the North American market in accordance with National Electrical Manufacturers Association

(NEMA) standards. The output from their World Contactor facility is designed to meet International Electrotechnical Commission (IEC) standards. NEMA products are durable and are designed to be repaired with comparable ease. In contrast IEC products are designed to be replaced rather than repaired.

b. The World Contactor automated assembly is best described as a Computer-Integrated Manufacturing (CIM) "factory within a factory". The operation is capable of producing four varieties of contactors and three styles of relays, with more than 1,000 different customer specifications, in lot sizes as small as one, with world class quality, zero direct labor and a lead time of twenty-four hours. The operation is controlled primarily by Allen-Bradley products and serves as a showcase for a number of the company's control and communication products. As a CIM showcase, it not only demonstrates the capabilities of the company's control and communication products, but also proves that quality products can be produced at competitive prices using advanced manufacturing technologies.

2. Prior to the mid-1980s Allen-Bradley contactors and relays were built primarily for the North American market in accordance with NEMA standards. However, not only was the global market for IEC standard products rapidly expanding, but overseas manufacturers were bringing their IEC-type products into the United States. The importation of the IEC standard product by overseas manufacturers was a serious threat to Allen-Bradley. At the same time, the rapidly expanding global market for IEC type products posed an attractive opportunity for the firm. The company at that time had a limited line of international products and wanted to become a global manufacturer. Allen-Bradley viewed the contactor product as an opportunity for penetrating the global marketplace and as a way to expand its distributor and selling networks world wide.

3. For Allen-Bradley to position its new IEC-type contactors and relays to have clear advantage over the competition, they had to accomplish the following: (1) differentiate the product from competitors' products, and (2) provide a lower-cost product than competitors to beat the competitors' prices in the market place. Allen-Bradley's plan focused on unsurpassed quality, product flexibility, rapid manufacturing in lot sizes as small as one and one day delivery lead times in a cost efficient manner.

a. Allen-Bradley's strategic objectives encompassed several of the manufacturing competitive priorities introduced throughout this textbook, i.e., design quality, quality of conformance, product reliability, product flexibility, production lead time, delivery speed, low manufacturing cost, and new product introduction.

b. Cost was a key competitive priority for Allen-Bradley. They realized their products had to be cost competitive in all markets and that international competition was stiff. The bottom line was that they would have to reduce their manufacturing costs by approximately 25% to 30% to be competitive on a global basis.

c. Allen-Bradley knew that the quality of its contactors and relays would have to be better than the competition in order to gain world market share. The achievement of unsurpassed quality was thus a key competitive requirement for the World Contactors and acted as a key driver in the definition of both the product and the manufacturing process.

d. The ability to build to order a wide variety of products in lot sizes as small as one with minimal lead times was also critical. It was also something that had never been done before - not even by the Japanese.

4. Contributing to Allen-Bradley's foundation for success, the manufacturing functional area had initiated two parallel activities prior to the start of the World Contactor project that greatly contributed to the success of this endeavor. One of these was the development of a strategic plan for manufacturing operations, the other was a global examination of alternative manufacturing systems and methods. Essentially, they had been expending a good bit of time and effort into "benchmarking the competition".

    a. Allen-Bradley was one of the first companies to realize the critical role of manufacturing in achieving competitive advantage. Recognizing the important contributions that manufacturing can make to the competitiveness of a firm, the management incorporated manufacturing strategic planning into their well-established business strategic planning process in the early 1980s.

    b. As Allen-Bradley started operations strategic planning, it also began to comprehensively study and evaluate alternative manufacturing methods. As a result of this benchmarking expedition, Allen-Bradley managers developed various manufacturing theories and strategies, and in particular, a series of programs associated with "stockless production".

5. Once the competitive challenge was clearly defined, Allen-Bradley managers examined various ways to meet it. In particular they investigated the advantages and disadvantages of offshore manufacturing, joint ventures, making the products under license and manufacturing the products in-house in the U.S. Allen-Bradley decided to manufacture its World Contactors in the U.S. because of two major reasons; (1) availability of skilled labor and (2) lower overall shipping costs. Their next major hurdle was how to make the products cost competitive.

    a. To be competitive on a global basis, Allen-Bradley had to reduce its cost by 25 to 30%. To achieve cost savings of this magnitude, it was obvious that an automated manufacturing system was needed. It was clear to Allen-Bradley that they had to do more than just cut direct labor costs, it would also be necessary to substantially reduce material and overhead costs. Allen-Bradley dispensed with traditional, short-term return on investment methods to evaluate the CIM investment because these would preclude approval of the project.

    b. To attain market share in the world market, Allen-Bradley's World Contactors had to be better than the competition's. Allen-Bradley's total quality management system was integrated into the manufacturing system. The concern for quality extended to the firm's suppliers as well. The manufacturing system itself was designed to encompass 3,500 automated data collection points and 350 automated assembly test points to check each component and the final product.

    c. To attain the objective of a delivery lead time of one day (inclusive of manufacturing time) Allen-Bradley developed a just-in-time manufacturing system with its associated low inventories and high flexibility. This allowed the production to customer demand in lot sizes as small as one. The ability to manufacture in lot sizes of one required the ability to identify each product being assembled so the line would not have to be stopped to assemble a different end-item. Allen-Bradley made use of bar code technology to automatically identify different contactors and relays coming down the line. The use of the bar code technology in the computer integrated manufacturing system allowed Allen-Bradley to manufacture over 1,000 different styles of IEC products at an average capacity of 600 units per hour.

6. Various manufacturing technologies and methods have greatly contributed to the success of the world contactor facility.

a. Allen-Bradley Management concluded that the product and manufacturing process should be designed simultaneously (i.e., concurrent engineering). Several task forces or teams were formed and charged with the responsibility of jointly designing the product and manufacturing process.

b. To accomplish their goals Allen-Bradley developed a world class computer-integrated manufacturing system. As defined by Allen-Bradley, "Computer Integrated Manufacturing (CIM) integrates the "factors of production" to organize every event that occurs in a manufacturing business from receipt of a customer's order to delivery of the product. The ultimate goal is to integrate the production process, the material, sales, marketing, purchasing, administration and engineering information flows into a single, closed-loop controlled system. Allen-Bradley's approach to CIM is embodied in its Productivity Pyramid. The Productivity Pyramid is a step-by-step approach to automation. It represents a systems approach to automated manufacturing in which each control level builds on the technology provided by the level beneath it.

c. As noted, bar coding was essential in enabling the automated line to produce lot sizes of one according to customer demand at mass production speeds. At the start of the manufacturing process, individual parts are labeled with a bar code to direct them to the correct machines. At the end of the process, a laser-marking machine inscribes catalog numbers and other electrical information on the fully assembled product; which is then packaged and bar coded again.

d. Product quality has always been at the cornerstone of Allen-Bradley's business philosophy. Prior to the start of the World Contactor project, Allen-Bradley had succeeded in implementing a comprehensive Total Quality Management System (TQMS). TQM and its associated techniques was the foundation for the unsurpassed quality achieved by the World Contactor facility. Allen-Bradley's World Contactor suppliers were also required to adhere to the TQMS doctrine. The automated manufacturing process was specifically designed with quality management in mind.

e. Allen-Bradley's management desired a just-in-time manufacturing system with its associated low inventories and high flexibility. The World Contactor's flexible, automated line has led to the elimination of most inventories, parts, work-in-process and finished goods. A local supplier delivers springs on a just-in-time basis. Work-in-process inventories are practically nonexistent, and the finished product is immediately shipped, so there are no end item inventories.

f. Allen-Bradley management viewed people as key to the success of the manufacturing facility. Employee satisfaction was increased by giving employees a lot of freedom. They gave workers considerable responsibility and allowed machine operators to set their own objectives. Job rotation has also contributed to the human resource success of the facility.

7. Allen-Bradley has realized its goal of becoming a world-class manufacturer. A world-class manufacturer is a superior competitor. It is better than its major competitors in at least one aspect of manufacturing performance that is important in the marketplace. It is able to achieve and sustain a competitive advantage. Key attributes of world-class manufacturers include:

a. just-in-time manufacturing and the application of JIT principles throughout the company's supply chain

b. a customer orientation that is reflected in the vision and values of top management and in a clearly defined customer-focused manufacturing strategy

c. an unrelenting emphasis on continuous improvement

d. an understanding that people are a company's most important asset

e. the ability to rapidly respond to changes in products and markets

f. the close integration of product design with process design, including the development of engineering expertise relative to manufacturing processes and technologies

KEY TERMS

a. bar codes
b. benchmarking the competition
c. competitive advantage
d. computer integrated manufacturing (CIM)
e. concurrent engineering
f. flexible automation
g. global manufacturing strategy
h. just-in-time manufacturing

i. job rotation
j. productivity pyramid
k. stockless production
l. statistical process control
m. team approach
n. total quality management
o. world-class manufacturer
p. zero inventory

DEFINITIONS

Directions: Select from the key terms list, the word or phrase being defined below.

_____ 1. relative superiority in skills and resources.

_____ 2. the integration of "the factors of production" to organize every event that occurs in a manufacturing business.

_____ 3. comparing and documenting the way competitors operate in comparison to your own operation.

_____ 4. the reduction or removal of raw materials and component parts in the production process.

_____ 5. a quality program that involves all aspects and employees of the organization.

_____ 6. a manufacturing system characterized by low inventories and high flexibility.

_____ 7. a tag that contains data concerning the product that can be used to automatically identify a product and its attributes.

_____ 8. product and manufacturing process designed simultaneously.

_____ 9. the grouping of employees with various backgrounds into a decision making body.

_____ 10. a step-by-step approach to automation.

_____ 11. the ability to changeover the production facility automatically to accommodate demand for lot sizes as small as one.

_____ 12. the concept of removal of all inventories.

_____ 13. the cross training and reassignment of workers to different tasks throughout the facility.

_____ 14. a manufacturer that can gain world market share for their product.

MULTIPLE CHOICE QUESTIONS

1. Distinctive competence is often used interchangeably with
   a. House of Quality.
   b. competitive advantage.
   c. total quality management.
   d. service differentiation.
   e. none of the above.

2. Which of the following statements is TRUE of world-class manufacturers?
   a. A world-class manufacturer is an average competitor.
   b. Just-in-time manufacturing is key to the success of world-class manufacturers.
   c. A world-class manufacturer is inflexible.
   d. Short-term focus is crucial to world-class manufacturers.
   e. None of the above.

3. Bulletin 100 contactors are
   a. switches for heavy-duty high amperage power circuits.
   b. switches for low amperage power circuits.
   c. IEC type products.
   d. NEMA type products.
   e. all of the above.

4. Which of the following are markets for Allen-Bradley IEC products?
   a. machine tool industry
   b. petrochemical industry
   c. automotive industry
   d. mining industry
   e. all of the above

5. Allen-Bradley's World Contactor facility is best described as
   a. factory within a factory.
   b. cellular manufacturing.
   c. batch processing.
   d. all of the above.
   e. none of the above.

6. Which of the following are key areas of the World Contactor facility?
   a. the automated assembly line
   b. a contact fabrication cell
   c. a plastic molding cell
   d. all of the above
   e. only a and b

7. Which of the following are NOT examples of purchased components used in Allen-Bradley's World Contactor facility?
   a. brass
   b. silver
   c. steel
   d. molding powder
   e. none of the above

8. Allen-Bradley's plan for achieving differentiation focused on which of the following?
   a. exceptional quality
   b. product flexibility
   c. one-day delivery lead times
   d. cost efficiency
   e. all of the above

9. Delivery speed, low manufacturing cost, and new product introduction are all examples of
   a. dimensions of quality.
   b. manufacturing competitive priorities.
   c. technical core.
   d. universal product attributes.
   e. all of the above.

10. To be competitive on a global basis, Allen-Bradley had to reduce its manufacturing costs by approximately _____.
    a. 10% to 15%
    b. 20% to 25%
    c. 25% to 30%
    d. 40% to 45%
    e. greater than 45%

11. Prior to the start of the World Contactor project, Allen-Bradley had initiated which of the following activities that greatly contributed to the success of this endeavor?
    a. development of a strategic plan for manufacturing operations
    b. design of flexible manufacturing systems
    c. global examination of alternative manufacturing systems
    d. only a and b
    e. only a and c

12. Which of the following are key success factors for the Allen-Bradley operations group?
    a. cost
    b. quality
    c. new product introduction
    d. competitive delivery
    e. all of the above

13. Which of the following was NOT an approach investigated by Allen-Bradley to meet the competitive challenge?
    a. offshore manufacturing
    b. joint ventures
    c. subcontracting
    d. making the products under license
    e. manufacturing in-house

14. To attain their quality objectives, the IEC products at Allen-Bradley were developed in an inter-functional effort involving all of the following EXCEPT
    a. manufacturing.
    b. marketing.
    c. development.
    d. quality control.
    e. none of the above.

15. The original conceptualization by Allen-Bradley for the automated system was assembly in batch mode to accommodate production to customer demand in lot sizes as small as one required a
    a. process layout.
    b. just-in-time system.
    c. cellular manufacturing system.
    d. fixed position layout.
    e. none of the above.

16. A system that integrates the "factors of production" to organize every event that occurs in a manufacturing business, is called
    a. flexible manufacturing system.
    b. world-class manufacturer.
    c. computer-integrated manufacturing.
    d. concurrent engineering.
    e. MRP II system.

17. Which of the following is NOT a level in the productivity pyramid?
    a. machine level
    b. station level
    c. group level
    d. center level
    e. plant level

18. Total quality management as implemented at Allen-Bradley involved all the following EXCEPT
    a. outside suppliers.
    b. manufacturing.
    c. marketing.
    d. management.
    e. none of the above.

19. Which of the following are views Allen-Bradley had for the contactor product?
    a. opportunity for penetrating the global market place
    b. a means to expand its distributor network
    c. a way to expand its worldwide selling network
    d. all of the above
    e. only a and c

20. At the _____ level in Allen-Bradley's productivity pyramid, each machine is electrically controlled by an Allen-Bradley PLC - 2/30.
    a. plant
    b. center
    c. cell
    d. station
    e. machine

SHORT ANSWER QUESTIONS

1. What were the three strategic objectives set by Allen-Bradley as it introduced its new line of contactors and relays?

2. What were the make-up and mission of the various teams Allen-Bradley formed to assist in its concurrent engineering efforts?

3. Describe the productivity pyramid that Allen-Bradley uses to illustrate its approach to computer-integrated-manufacturing. Could the productivity pyramid be used as effectively by other manufacturers?

4. Describe the characteristics of a world-class manufacturer. Do you think that Allen-Bradley has achieved world-class status in its manufacture of contactors and relays?

5. What role did the operations function play in Allen-Bradley's success? What was the contribution made by operations strategic planning?

STUDY GUIDE SOLUTIONS

CHAPTER 1

DEFINITIONS

1. q	7. u	13. t
2. v	8. cc	14. x
3. h, i	9. r	15. k
4. n	10. aa	16. m
5. o	11 c	
6. a	12. z	

MULTIPLE CHOICE QUESTIONS

1. d	7. d	13. a	19. b	25. a
2. a	8. d	14. b	20. c	26. e
3. e	9. c	15. b	21. a	27. a
4. c	10. c	16. c	22. e	28. c
5. d	11. b	17. e	23. e	29. d
6. b	12. e	18. b	24. b	30. c

SHORT ANSWER QUESTIONS

Question #	1	2	3	4	5
Text Page Reference	10	15	17-18	18-19	29-30

CHAPTER 2

DEFINITIONS

1. o	6. m	11. n
2. b	7. t	12. l
3. w	8. q	13. k
4. u	9. r	14. e
5. v	10. p	

MULTIPLE CHOICE QUESTIONS

1. a	7. a	13. d	19. a	25. b
2. b	8. a	14. d	20. d	26. e
3. e	9. e	15. a	21. c	27. a
4. d	10. a	16 b	22. d	28. c
5. b	11. c	17. b	23. d	29. a
6. d	12. d	18. e	24. e	30. e

SHORT ANSWER QUESTIONS

Question #	1	2	3	4	5
Text Page Reference	55	55-57	47-49	49-55	57-58

CHAPTER 3

DEFINITIONS

1. a	6. b	11. g
2. f	7. u	
3. s	8. c	
4. d	9. k	
5. e	10. t	

MULTIPLE CHOICE QUESTIONS

1. d	7. d	13. a	19. a	25. d
2. c	8. d	14. c	20. c	26. b
3. c	9. e	15. d	21. e	27. d
4. c	10. a	16. d	22. a	28. a
5. c	11. b	17. d	23. d	29. c
6. d	12. b	18. b	24. a	30. b

SHORT ANSWER QUESTIONS

Question #	1	2	3	4	5
Text Page Reference	81-84	85	90-91	99-102	88

CHAPTER 4

DEFINITIONS

1.	dd	7.	zz	13.	t
2.	o	8.	xx	14.	d
3.	ww	9.	a	15.	h
4.	v	10.	oo	16.	aa
5.	u	11	rr	17.	qq
6.	nn	12.	aaa	18.	yy

MULTIPLE CHOICE QUESTIONS

1.	e	9.	d	17.	b	25.	d	33.	d
2.	b	10.	e	18.	c	26.	b	34.	c
3.	e	11.	b	19.	d	27.	c	35.	b
4.	c	12.	c	20.	d	28.	d	36.	b
5.	e	13.	b	21.	b	29.	d	37.	b
6.	e	14.	a	22.	e	30.	b		
7.	b	15.	c	23.	b	31.	a		
8.	a	16.	d	24.	b	32.	b		

APPLICATION QUESTIONS

Question #	ANSWER
1	298 units
2	292.6 units
3	299.5 units
4	299.8 units
5	298.2 units
6	The exponential smoothing model with the 0.1 smoothing constant (299.8)
7	The exponential smoothing model with the 0.1 smoothing constant
8	The exponential smoothing model with the 0.9 smoothing constant
9	Since forecasts lag behind actual by one period, a continued increasing or decreasing trend in the data could be problematic. The forecast will continue lagging the actual and the amount of error will get greater and greater unless some action is taken. Using a model that is very responsive to current period changes can help lessen the error.

SHORT ANSWER QUESTIONS

Question #	1	2	3	4	5
Text Page Reference	118-119	119-120	131-132, 145-146	154-156	157-159

CHAPTER 5

DEFINITIONS

1. a	7. b	13. r
2. p	8. n	14. e
3. w	9. m	15. t
4. d	10. u	16. h
5. x	11 g	17. q
6. s	12. j	

MULTIPLE CHOICE QUESTIONS

1. e	7. d	13. b	19. a	25. a
2. d	8. c	14. a	20. d	26. d
3. c	9. e	15. b	21. e	27. a
4. a	10. e	16. d	22. c	28. c
5. c	11. e	17. b	23. c	29. c
6. b	12. e	18. b	24. a	30. b

SHORT ANSWER QUESTIONS

Question #	1	2	3	4	5
Text Page Reference	177	179	179-183	190-196	199

CHAPTER 6

DEFINITIONS

1. f	6. o	11. dd
2. a	7. r	12. ff
3. d	8. s	13. i
4. g	9. u	14. l
5. m	10. cc	15. e

MULTIPLE CHOICE QUESTIONS

1. b	9. c	17. c	25. a	33. c
2. e	10. e	18. e	26. b	34. e
3. e	11. d	19. b	27. d	35. a
4. a	12. b	20. b	28. b	36. d
5. a	13. a	21. b	29. a	37. c
6. c	14. d	22. b	30. b	
7. d	15. b	23. a	31. d	
8. b	16. b	24. d	32. d	

APPLICATION QUESTIONS

Question #	ANSWER
1	750
2	680
3	710
4	Location A is preferred since it has the highest weighted score.
5	If location A's score for climate had been a 5, then its weighted score would also have been 710, just the same as location C.
6	If location A's labor supply was equal to 6, then its weighted score would have been 710.
7	If these errors were corrected in location B's scores, then location B would also have a weighted score of 710. At these values, she would be indifferent between all three locations.

SHORT ANSWER QUESTIONS

Question #	1	2	3	4	5
Text Page Reference	212-213	216	216-217	225	229-231

CHAPTER 7

DEFINITIONS

1. a	8. n	15. x
2. s	9. e	16. j
3. v	10. r	17. cc
4. i	11. h	18. q
5. k	12. f	19. m
6. o	13. y	20. c
7. p	14. w	

MULTIPLE CHOICE QUESTIONS

1. d	7. b	13. d	19. d	25. c
2. b	8. d	14. b	20. d	26. d
3. c	9. a	15. d	21. c	27. e
4. b	10. c	16. b	22. b	28. b
5. d	11. b	17. c	23. e	29. c
6. d	12. d	18. c	24. d	30. b

SHORT ANSWER QUESTIONS

Question #	1	2	3	4	5
Text Page Reference	273-275	276-277	280-282	284-286	291-292

CHAPTER 8

DEFINITIONS

1.	cc	6.	r	11.	w
2.	bb	7.	j	12.	ff
3.	dd	8.	q	13.	n
4.	e	9.	a	14.	i
5.	p	10.	o	15.	h

MULTIPLE CHOICE QUESTIONS

1.	e	7.	b	13.	b	19.	d	25.	b
2.	b	8.	a	14.	b	20.	c	26.	c
3.	e	9.	b	15.	d	21.	c	27.	e
4.	e	10.	d	16.	b	22.	c	28.	a
5.	d	11.	b	17.	e	23.	c	29.	d
6.	c	12.	a	18.	b	24.	c	30.	c

SHORT ANSWER QUESTIONS

Question #	1	2	3	4	5
Text Page Reference	323	325-327	318	320	325

CHAPTER 9

DEFINITIONS

1.	r	6.	n	11.	d
2.	a	7.	s	12.	t
3.	c	8.	h	13.	w
4.	x	9.	f	14.	v
5.	l	10.	j	15.	u

MULTIPLE CHOICE QUESTIONS

1.	e	10.	b	19.	b	28.	a	37.	b
2.	c	11.	a	20.	c	29.	b	38.	d
3.	d	12.	e	21.	d	30.	a	39.	c
4.	e	13.	e	22.	a	31.	b	40.	d
5.	e	14.	c	23.	b	32.	c	41.	a
6.	e	15.	e	24.	d	33.	d		
7.	b	16.	e	25.	d	34.	d		
8.	e	17.	a	26.	b	35.	c		
9.	d	18.	b	27.	a	36.	d		

APPLICATION QUESTIONS

Question #	ANSWER
1	The observed time was 4.14 minutes.
2	If the observed worker was working 15 percent slower than average, the normal time would be 3.52 minutes.
3	If the observed worker was working 30 percent faster than average, the normal time would be 5.38 minutes.
4	If the observed worker was working 30 percent faster, and with an allowance factor of 10 percent, the standard time would be 5.92 minutes.
5	The manager should make 41 observations to get the desired 95 percent confidence.

SHORT ANSWER QUESTIONS

Question #	1	2	3	4	5
Text Page Reference	345-346	350	352	360-365	366-369

CHAPTER 10

DEFINITIONS

1. b	6. d	11. j
2. f	7. h	
3. e	8. i	
4. g	9. l	
5. k	10. c	

MULTIPLE CHOICE QUESTIONS

1. c	7. c	13. d	19. c	25. b
2. d	8. d	14. d	20. a	26. c
3. d	9. b	15. e	21. a	27. d
4. d	10. b	16. c	22. b	28. b
5. a	11. d	17. c	23. c	29. a
6. d	12. b	18. c	24. a	30. d

APPLICATION QUESTIONS

Question #	ANSWER
1	The total cost to buy the paddles next year will be $18,000.
2	The total cost to make the paddles next year in-house will be $16,500.
3	The company should MAKE the paddles next year and SAVE $1,500.
4	At a demand of 2,000 units, the company would be indifferent between making and buying.
5	At a demand of 3,000 units, the company would be better off by $1,500 if it made the units in-house versus buying them outside.

SHORT ANSWER QUESTIONS

Question #	1	2	3	4	5
Text Page Reference	384	386-387	394-395	396-397	403-406

CHAPTER 11

DEFINITIONS

1. a	6. c	11. u
2. i	7. g	12. h
3. bb	8. o	13. b
4. r	9. z	14. k
5. f	10. j	15. e

MULTIPLE CHOICE QUESTIONS

1. d	7. e	13. c	19. c	25. d
2. d	8. e	14. a	20. b	26. a
3. c	9. e	15. e	21. a	27. a
4. b	10. e	16. e	22. b	28. b
5. a	11. c	17. b	23. d	29. b
6. b	12. b	18. e	24. a	30. b

APPLICATION QUESTIONS

Question #	ANSWER
1	The company will need to produce 100 units on overtime in June.
2	The company will need to subcontract 40 units over the eight-month period.
3	The inventory at the end of September will be 60 units.
4	In May, a total of 170 units will be produced from all sources.
5	Overtime will account for 160 units over the eight-month period.
6	The only backorder will occur in July.
7	The maximum inventory of 60 units will occur in September.
8	The cost of the optimum solution will be $308,000.

SHORT ANSWER QUESTIONS

Question #	1	2	3	4	5
Text Page Reference	415-416	421	425	448	426

CHAPTER 12

DEFINITIONS

1. u	6. y, bb, t	11. e, r, mm
2. l	7. qq	12. jj, ll
3. h	8. b	13. d
4. gg	9. z	14. p, ff
5. i	10. hh	15. o, aa

MULTIPLE CHOICE QUESTIONS

1. e	12. e	23. c	34. a	45. d
2. e	13. b	24. c	35. d	46. a
3. a	14. b	25. d	36. b	47. c
4. a	15. d	26. c	37. a	48. d
5. b	16. e	27. d	38. b	49. c
6. b	17. e	28. a	39. d	50. a
7. d	18. c	29. d	40. c	51. b
8. a	19. e	30. c	41. b	52. d
9. b	20. e	31. b	42. d	53. b
10. b	21. a	32. c	43. b	54. b
11. e	22. c	33. c	44. c	55. a

APPLICATION QUESTIONS

Question #	ANSWER
1	Batch sizes of 338 units will minimize relevant inventory costs.
2	The company will need to place 27 orders per year at that optimal quantity.
3	The average inventory would be 169 units.
4	The minimum total cost would be $2,701.
5	The new batch size, allowing shortages, would be 378 units.
6	The maximum shortage level would be 76 units.
7	There will be about 3 days when shortages will occur.

SHORT ANSWER QUESTIONS

Question #	1	2	3	4	5
Text Page Reference	465-466	468-469	471-472	489-490	501-502

CHAPTER 13

DEFINITIONS

1. b	8. v	15. bb
2. n	9. y	16. k
3. m	10. l	17. p
4. f	11. z	18. t
5. o	12. j	19. g
6. a	13. r	
7. i	14. d	

MULTIPLE CHOICE QUESTIONS

1. e	9. a	17. c	25. a	33. a
2. a	10. c	18. b	26. e	34. a
3. c	11. e	19. b	27. a	35. c
4. a	12. c	20. e	28. c	36. b
5. b	13. e	21. b	29. a	37. e
6. e	14. b	22. c	30. a	
7. e	15. c	23. d	31. d	
8. e	16. c	24. b	32. a	

APPLICATION QUESTIONS

Question #	ANSWER
1	The Gross Requirements for base (B) will be 100 in week 4 and 150 in week 7.
2	There will need to be a Planned Order Release for base (B) in week 6 only.
3	The Available Balance of base (B) in week 5 is 20 units.
4	The Gross Requirements for fastener (F) will be 260 in week 6.
5	There will need to be a Planned Order Release for 400 units of fasteners (F) in week 5 in order to meet MPS requirements.
6	The available balance of fastener (F) in week 9 is 140 units.
7	There will need to be a Planned Order Release for casting (C) of 50 units in week 1 and 150 units in week 4 in order to meet MPS requirements.

SHORT ANSWER QUESTIONS

Question #	1	2	3	4	5
Text Page Reference	514-519	520	525-531	535	538

CHAPTER 14

DEFINITIONS

1. e	4. d	7. g
2. c	5. f	8. a
3. b	6. h	

MULTIPLE CHOICE QUESTIONS

1. a	9. e	17. d	25. a	33. b
2. b	10. c	18. a	26. c	34. c
3. c	11. b	19. d	27. d	35. a
4. b	12. e	20. b	28. b	36. c
5. c	13. b	21. a	29. d	37. a
6. d	14. d	22. b	30. c	38. c
7. c	15. d	23. b	31. a	
8. e	16. b	24. a	32. b	

APPLICATION QUESTIONS

Question #	ANSWER
1	It takes 2.4 hours to process one unit of Curio A through all operations.
2	Using the Capacity Bill technique, 15 hours of Molding work would be required in week 4.
3	Using the Capacity Bill technique, 11 hours of Assembly work would be required in week 3.
4	The MPS requirement of 15 units of Curio A in week 6 creates 6 hours of Assembly work in week 5.
5	Using the Resource Profile technique, 11 hours of Molding work would be required in week 4.
6	Using the Resource Profile technique, an MPS requirement in week 8 would create requirements in week 7 for Packing and in week 4 for Molding.
7	The Molding work center is the first to experience low-level loss of visibility and its horizon is only 5 of the 8 weeks.

SHORT ANSWER QUESTIONS

Question #	1	2	3	4	5
Text Page Reference	561	562-564	583	576-577	581

CHAPTER 15

DEFINITIONS

1. e	6. k	11. o
2. q	7. l	12. b
3. p	8. d, g	13. h
4. j	9. c	14. f
5. n, m	10. a	

MULTIPLE CHOICE QUESTIONS

1. c	8. c	15. c	22. b	29. c
2. a	9. b	16. a	23. c	30. c
3. c	10. d	17. c	24. a	31. d
4. d	11. a	18. b	25. b	32. b
5. d	12. e	19. e	26. b	33. a
6. a	13. c	20. a	27. e	34. a
7. c	14. a	21. a	28. a	35. b

APPLICATION QUESTIONS

Question #	ANSWER
1	Critical ratio would generate the job sequence: D-A-B-C.
2	Shortest processing time would generate the job sequence: D-C-B-A.
3	Earliest due date would generate the job sequence: D-B-A-C.
4	Slack time remaining would generate two job sequences: D-A-B-C and D-B-A-C.
5	The total flowtime with shortest processing time would be 26 days.
6	The average flowtime with critical ration would be 7.5 days.
7	The average number of jobs in the system with first come, first served would be 3.
8	Under the earliest due date, there would be no late jobs.
9	Under shortest processing time, the latest job will be 2 days late.
10	Shortest processing time yields the minimum flowtime, that is 13 days.

SHORT ANSWER QUESTIONS

Question #	1	2	3	4	5
Text Page Reference	597	601-602	604-605	609-610	617-619

CHAPTER 16

DEFINITIONS

1. b	6. i	11. h
2. b	7. d	12. g
3. j	8. e	
4. k	9. f	
5. c	10. a	

MULTIPLE CHOICE QUESTIONS

1. d	7. c	13. e	19. c	25. b
2. c	8. e	14. d	20. e	26. c
3. d	9. d	15. c	21. a	27. e
4. d	10. c	16. b	22. a	28. e
5. e	11. e	17. a	23. d	29. a
6. e	12. d	18. c	24. a	30. c

SHORT ANSWER QUESTIONS

Question #	1	2	3	4	5
Text Page Reference	646-647	632	631	638	642-643

CHAPTER 17

DEFINITIONS

1. a	6. e	11. h
2. k	7. i	12. j
3. l	8. g	13. c
4. d	9. m	14. b
5. f	10. o	

MULTIPLE CHOICE QUESTIONS

1. c	8. a	15. c	22. c	29. c
2. a	9. b	16. e	23. a	30. c
3. e	10. e	17. c	24. c	31. b
4. b	11. d	18. d	25. d	32. d
5. b	12. a	19. d	26. a	
6. b	13. b	20. e	27. c	
7. d	14. b	21. a	28. b	

APPLICATION QUESTIONS

Question #	ANSWER
1	Connecting node 3 to node 4 would save 2 miles.
2	Connecting node 1 to node 4 would save 3 miles.
3	Connecting node 2 to node 3 would save 6 miles.
4	Connecting node 1 to node 2 yields the greatest savings, 9 miles.
5	Connecting node 2 to node 4 would save 8 miles.
6	The routes that minimizes travel between job sites are: 0-3-1-2-4-0 or 0-4-2-1-3-0.
7	The total distance traveled would be 62 miles.
8	The optimum route covers 40 miles.

SHORT ANSWER QUESTIONS

Question #	1	2	3	4	5
Text Page Reference	658	661-664	672-676	676-683	685

CHAPTER 18

DEFINITIONS

1. v	6. j	11. n
2. f	7. k	12. m
3. s	8. t	13. o
4. h	9. d	14. s
5. g	10. r	15. i

MULTIPLE CHOICE QUESTIONS

1. a	8. b	15. b	22. c	29. b
2. d	9. b	16. b	23. b	30. e
3. d	10. a	17. b	24. b	31. b
4. d	11. b	18. a	25. a	32. a
5. b	12. e	19. c	26. c	
6. e	13. a	20. a	27. d	
7. d	14. e	21. a	28. e	

APPLICATION QUESTIONS

Question #	ANSWER
1	The total number of paths in the network is 7.
2	The expected time for activity C is 12 weeks.
3	The variance for activity C is 1.778.
4	The critical path is made up of activities: A-C-F-H-J-K
5	The estimated duration of the critical path is 40.17 weeks.
6	The activity variance along the critical path is 10.03.
7	There is a 0.0934 probability that the project will be completed before week 36.
8	There is a near zero probability that the project will take more than 50 weeks to complete.

SHORT ANSWER QUESTIONS

Question #	1	2	3	4	5
Text Page Reference	701-702	699-700	703	715-719	719-723

CHAPTER 19

DEFINITIONS

1. m	5. j	9. g
2. c	6. e	10. h
3. b, l	7. a	11. i
4. d, f	8. k	

MULTIPLE CHOICE QUESTIONS

1. d	8. e	15. c	22. a	29. b
2. a	9. b	16. c	23. b	30. d
3. b	10. c	17. c	24. a	31. a
4. b	11. c	18. b	25. e	
5. d	12. d	19. d	26. b	
6. b	13. a	20. a	27. b	
7. e	14. e	21. b	28. d	

APPLICATION QUESTIONS

Question #	ANSWER
1	The mean of sample G is 1.221.
2	The range of sample C is 0.400.
3	The average of all sample means is 1.169.
4	The average range is 0.325.
5	The UCL for the x-bar chart is 1.305.
6	The UCL for the range chart is 0.6253.

SHORT ANSWER QUESTIONS

Question #	1	2	3	4	5
Text Page Reference	743-746	744	746-748	757-758	760-766

CHAPTER 20

DEFINITIONS

1. c	6. h	11. f
2. d	7. a	12. p
3. b	8. e	13. i
4. k	9. m	14. o
5. n	10. j	

MULTIPLE CHOICE QUESTIONS

1. b	6. d	11. e	16. c
2. b	7. e	12. e	17. c
3. a	8. e	13. c	18. e
4. e	9. b	14. e	19. d
5. a	10. c	15. b	20. d

SHORT ANSWER QUESTIONS

Question #	1	2	3	4	5
Text Page Reference	785	788-789	790-791	794-796	785-786